Political Entrepreneurship

Political Entrepreneurship

Regional Growth and Entrepreneurial Diversity in Sweden

Edited by

Charlie Karlsson

Professor Emeritus of the Economics of Technological Change, Jönköping International Business School and Professor of Industrial Economics, Blekinge Institute of Technology, Sweden

Charlotte Silander

Senior Lecturer in Political Science, Department of Education, Linnaeus University, Sweden

Daniel Silander

Associate Professor, Department of Political Science, Linnaeus University, Sweden

 Edward Elgar
PUBLISHING

Cheltenham, UK • Northampton, MA, USA

Published by
Edward Elgar Publishing Limited
The Lypiatts
15 Lansdown Road
Cheltenham
Glos GL50 2JA
UK

Edward Elgar Publishing, Inc.
William Pratt House
9 Dewey Court
Northampton
Massachusetts 01060
USA

A catalogue record for this book
is available from the British Library

Library of Congress Control Number: 2016942174

This book is available electronically in the **Elgar**online
Social and Political Science subject collection
DOI 10.4337/9781785363504

ISBN 978 1 78536 349 8 (cased)
ISBN 978 1 78536 350 4 (eBook)

Typeset by Columns Design XML Ltd, Reading
Printed and bound in Great Britain by TJ International Ltd, Padstow

Contents

Contributors

Åke E. Andersson is Professor of Economics at Jönköping International Business School, Sweden. His research interests are oriented towards programming models of regional and industrial models. He has also focused on theories and models of regional and industrial economic growth and the role of infrastructure in the regional and urban economies.

David E. Andersson is Assistant Professor of Economics in the School of Entrepreneurship and Management at Shanghai Tech University, China. His research profile is economics of IPR, markets for technology, innovation and technological change and patents and inventive activity.

Staffan Andersson is Associate Professor of Political Science at Linnaeus University, Sweden. His research mainly concerns the functioning of democracy, how power is organized, why institutions work well or badly and the integrity of public administration.

Per Assmo is Associate Professor of Human & Economic Geography at University West, Sweden. His research interests include regional geography, rural development, local economic development and political ecology with a focus on both Sweden and Africa.

Caroline Berggren is Associate Professor of Education at Gothenburg University, Sweden. Her general research interest is social division based on class and gender with specific focus on the structure of education and the labour market in Sweden.

Marie-Louise von Bergmann-Winberg is Professor of Political Science at Mid Sweden University. She has conducted research on social and political entrepreneurship, multilevel governance, regionalization and regional reforms in Sweden and plural economy and socioeconomic regulation.

Tobias Bromander is lecturer in Political Science at Linnaeus University. Sweden. His research interests include higher education and entrepreneurship, media, Swedish politics and the European Union and politics and gender perspectives on media and political scandals.

Yvonne von Friedrichs is Professor of Business Administration at Mid Sweden University. Her research includes societal entrepreneurship, community entrepreneurship, local and regional development and women's entrepreneurship.

Charlie Karlsson is Professor Emeritus of the Economics of Technological Change at Jönköping International Business School and Professor of Industrial Economics at Blekinge Institute of Technology, Sweden. In his research, Charlie Karlsson has focused on infrastructure economics, urban economics, the economics of technological change, regional economics, spatial industrial dynamics, entrepreneurship and small business economics, and the economics of R&D and higher education.

Martin Nilsson is Senior Lecturer of Political Science at Linnaeus University, Sweden. His research focuses on politics and higher education, European politics, the European Union and prerequisites to democracy, including political elite theories on democratic change.

Charlotte Silander is Senior Lecturer of Political Science at Linnaeus University, Sweden. She works at the Center for Educational Development in Higher Education at Linnaeus University. Her research focuses on European Union educational policy, gender equality in higher education, systems of higher education and university research policies.

Daniel Silander is Associate Professor of Political Science at Linnaeus University, Sweden. His main areas of interests are political entrepreneurship on a domestic and international level, international politics, democracy and state and human security.

Per Strömblad is Associate Professor of Political Science at Linnaeus University, Sweden. He has conducted research on citizenship, integration and political participation with focus on immigrants' democratic influence in Swedish society.

Elin Wihlborg is Professor of Political Science and Public Administration at Linköping University, Sweden. Her research interests focus on theoretical and empirical analysis of regional and local public policy issues and public administration, especially regarding policies in the information society and sustainable development issues.

PART I

Political entrepreneurship and
entrepreneurship

1. Introduction: the political entrepreneur for regional growth and entrepreneurial diversity

Daniel Silander and Charlotte Silander

Using social science and economics perspectives, the goal of this study is to complement the dominant business administration research on entrepreneurship by increasing our knowledge of the economic-political context in which entrepreneurship and private enterprise are conducted. This book explores the role of political entrepreneurs for regional growth and entrepreneurial diversity in Sweden. We define a political entrepreneur as a politician/bureaucrat/officer/department within the publicly funded sector who with innovative approaches encourages entrepreneurship/business and where the goals are growth, employment and the common good. The approach of this book is to enrich the established research on entrepreneurship with in-depth knowledge of the conditions for entrepreneurship in Sweden. The main focus of study is the role the political entrepreneur might play in promoting entrepreneurship, enterprise and entrepreneurial diversity in the Swedish economy.

This study problematizes political entrepreneurship by analysing the circumstances under which political entrepreneurs operate, and by examining the interaction between political entrepreneurs and private sector entrepreneurs. It is assumed that the political entrepreneur and political entrepreneurship can influence the conditions for entrepreneurship and businesses, but previous research on entrepreneurs and entrepreneurship has to a large extent failed to recognize this political dimension. Research on the political entrepreneur in Sweden is limited, despite the fact that Swedish public debate has often expressed expectations of the political entrepreneur to promote regional growth, employment and welfare. It is also despite the fact that Swedish governments have promoted a vision of entrepreneurial diversity that sees a heterogeneous group of citizens as being entrepreneurial, integrated and equal in Swedish society. Nevertheless, this study on the political entrepreneur and political entrepreneurship is not restricted to an outcome-related definition. It is not just necessary that the political entrepreneur creates growth, employment and welfare, but by challenging existing norms and values in Swedish society, they should also seek to promote entrepreneurship in a new, innovative way that favours entrepreneurship and entrepreneurial diversity.

The aim of the study is two-fold: (1) to explore how political entrepreneurs may act to promote formal and informal institutions favourable to regional growth and welfare and (2) to investigate how political entrepreneurs may act to promote entrepreneurial diversity that promotes entrepreneurship and private enterprise among traditionally less entrepreneurial societal groups in Sweden. The study can be seen in relation to the research areas of entrepreneurship for growth and employment and entrepreneurship for social equality and integration. Overall, Swedish economy and social welfare would benefit from improved entrepreneurship and entrepreneurial diversity. Political entrepreneurs have the potential to be innovative and to promote entrepreneurship and entrepreneurial diversity by fundamentally challenging the prevailing formal and informal institutions for entrepreneurship in Swedish society. This is an important area of inquiry, particularly in times of economic recession and structural change for states and rural areas, when political leadership is crucial for private sector entrepreneurship, growth and welfare and when entrepreneurial ambitions, to lower the unemployment rate, are mostly welcomed from all societal groups and especially from those that have been less focused on by political entrepreneurs. The authors expect the analysis and discussions to be of great interest to politicians, public servants and political entrepreneurs in the public sector as well as entrepreneurs, business owners and investors in the economic sector, in addition to students of political science and economics.

An essential part of this study focuses on political entrepreneurship and regional growth, but another part is devoted to political entrepreneurship and entrepreneurial diversity with a focus on women, immigrants and young educated adults in Sweden. Throughout the study, the main focus is on how the complex networks of politicians and civil servants have a coordinating role to play, one that encourages cooperation, goal formulation and creative networking aimed at promoting entrepreneurship, private enterprise and regional growth.

There are three thematic areas covered throughout the book: 'Part I: Political entrepreneurship and entrepreneurship'; 'Part II: Political entrepreneurship and regional growth'; and 'Part III: Political entrepreneurship and entrepreneurial diversity'. Part I introduces a discussion on the political entrepreneur and political entrepreneurship. It is argued that, in times of economic stress, political entrepreneurship is essential to finding new ways of promoting growth, employment and welfare. The political entrepreneur is discussed from an actor-oriented perspective, focusing on how to promote favourable political, judicial and/or financial conditions by challenging traditional norms, values and regulations for entrepreneurship. This part of the book concludes with a discussion on the rule of law and the democratic boundaries to political entrepreneurs and political entrepreneurship. The political entrepreneur and political entrepreneurship are discussed in terms of legitimate and legal boundaries. To be a political entrepreneur is about challenging traditional patterns of behaviour to find new grounds for innovative methods to promote entrepreneurship. However, pushing for new norms and values in entrepreneurial policies may at times teeter on the edge of illegitimacy or even illegal activities. It is of great importance for the political entrepreneur to act within the legal and legitimate framework of entrepreneurial policies, while seeking new grounds for innovative ideas and methods to promote entrepreneurship.

Part II of the book discusses how the political entrepreneur and political entrepreneurship may provide for favourable institutional structures and policies for entrepreneurship and regional growth in Sweden. This may include pushing for entrepreneurial development among established entrepreneurs and businesses and/or to attracting individuals and companies with entrepreneurial aspirations to the region. It is argued that how formal and informal institutions are developed will have an impact on the entrepreneurial possibilities and problems in the region. Research on how to promote regional growth and welfare has, however, been overwhelmingly theoretical in nature. There are multiple models and theories on how policies could be developed and implemented and how the institutional framework for entrepreneurship should look, but there is a scarcity of empirical studies on how such models and theories may actually say something on regional entrepreneurship, business enterprises, growth and welfare. The remaining questions are, therefore, what types of interventions are needed to support entrepreneurship and business and what should the political entrepreneur actually do to develop a dynamic, successful policy for regional entrepreneurship and growth? The goal is to increase our understanding of what tools the political entrepreneur uses to promote favourable political entrepreneurship for a successful business policy. What are the policies to be developed and the institutional frameworks to be established to promote entrepreneurship and business that result in regional growth and welfare in the Swedish economy? It is obvious that there is a great need for both economic and political science research into how political entrepreneurs should primarily seek to actively work for a functioning business policy and how such empirical studies should be designed in collaboration between economists and political scientists.

Part III focuses on the role of political entrepreneurs and political entrepreneurship to promote entrepreneurial diversity. In its efforts to increase economic growth and employment, the Swedish government has been interested in widening entrepreneurship to different social groups. While business and entrepreneurship have traditionally been viewed as a male phenomenon, Swedish politicians have often emphasized how the Swedish economy needs all groups of society to be part of approaching the economic recession with new innovations and businesses and so on. The Swedish government has associated future economic growth with entrepreneurial diversity, but also with social equality and integration. When Swedish officials have spoken out on entrepreneurial diversity as a way of pushing for gender equality and growth, improved diversity has also been stressed as a tool for growth and integration of immigrants and young adults. It has been shown that women, immigrants and young adults are positioned outside the white, middle-aged male norm of entrepreneurship in Swedish society. Despite decades of Swedish political discussions on the importance of entrepreneurial diversity, women, immigrant and young adults are still less established in important social networks for political and economic entrepreneurship. The presence of homosocial networks therefore risks disadvantaging their participation and influence, with negative results for economic growth, employment and welfare.

This book concludes in Part IV by summarizing the study on political entrepreneurship for regional growth and entrepreneurial diversity. This concluding chapter sheds light on who the political entrepreneur may be and what formal and informal institutions may be challenged and changed by political entrepreneurs to favour entrepreneurship and businesses. The political entrepreneur is particularly important in times where normal work routines and everyday work do not necessarily solve societal challenges. Sometimes society faces major challenges, not necessarily a global economic crisis, that require extraordinary means to secure economic and social development. In times of profound economic crisis it is particularly important to have political entrepreneurs who dare to challenge traditional norms and values about promoting entrepreneurship by trying to introduce new ideas that later can become the prevailing norms and values for dynamic entrepreneurship. The study of political entrepreneurs is thus to examine the alternative methods that politicians, bureaucrats, officials and institutions may use to create better conditions for entrepreneurship and entrepreneurial diversity.

2. The political entrepreneur

Daniel Silander

Entrepreneurship and entrepreneurs are vital aspects of a growing and dynamic economy. Entrepreneurs are expected to, through entrepreneurship, provide innovations and know-how that promote a society of growth, employment and welfare. While research on entrepreneurs and entrepreneurship has mostly taken place within economics, there are very limited studies on entrepreneurial activities in the public sector. This chapter on the political entrepreneur is a theoretical discussion on what constitutes a political entrepreneur and how the political entrepreneur in the public sector may play an important role for entrepreneurs and entrepreneurship in the business sector. As stated in Chapter 1, a political entrepreneur is a 'politician/bureaucrat/officer/department within the publicly funded sector who with innovative approaches encourages entrepreneurship/business and where the goals are growth, employment and the common good'.

The political entrepreneur is to be found in the public sector. However, the public entrepreneur acts not only in relation to other public actors, but also in relation to the business sector with entrepreneurs. To discuss and understand who is the political entrepreneur is to explore the relationships and networks between the public sector and the business sector and the entrepreneurs involved and how the political entrepreneur must act to promote favourable conditions for entrepreneurs. In times of global economic competition, economic recession and transformation of the urban and rural economic landscapes, it is important from local and regional perspectives to have political entrepreneurs who seek new opportunities for growth. This is done by changing traditional norms and values of who the entrepreneur might be and how entrepreneurship is to be conducted. It is about identifying windows of opportunity and exploring new formal and informal favourable conditions for existing and potential entrepreneurs.

This chapter starts with a discussion on the traditional perspectives on the entrepreneur and entrepreneurship and is followed by a discussion on entrepreneurs in the public sector. Thereafter, a discussion on what constitutes a political entrepreneur is followed by a final discussion on the role of the political entrepreneur as innovative and promoter of new norms and values that could better provide for entrepreneurship and, in the long run, growth and welfare.

ENTREPRENEURS IN THE PUBLIC SECTOR?

In academia, the concept of entrepreneurship has its roots in technology and business (Schumpeter, 1943). Here, to be entrepreneurial has been defined as being driven. Such persons are seen as role models. An entrepreneur is economically enterprising, a 'go-getter' (Bjerke, 2005; Von Bergmann-Winberg and Wihlborg, 2011). It was not until the second half of the twentieth century that new perspectives on the entrepreneur and entrepreneurship were developed. Slowly, the new academic perspectives led to a growing multidisciplinary approach to entrepreneurship with new insights from behavioural science, sociology and anthropology. The multidisciplinary approach resulted in new questions being asked on what entrepreneurship is all about, on who may become entrepreneurial and how to promote successful entrepreneurship. Two main aspects of entrepreneurship were scrutinized: first, research developed on what characteristics an entrepreneur may have and what entrepreneurial behaviour is, and second, how entrepreneurs should act in relation to other actors within networks and organizations to become successful. There were also a growing number of studies on how to market and teach entrepreneurship to become successful (Grant, 1998; Landström, 2005).

In the 1990s, research on entrepreneurship had become a solid multidisciplinary research area. It included theories, concepts and methods on how to understand and explain entrepreneurship, with growing empirical insights into the role of entrepreneurs in a vital, booming economy. Research on entrepreneurship was conducted on different analytical levels: from the individual level focusing on entrepreneurial behaviour to a societal level exploring different types of entrepreneurship for a healthy economy. However, interest in the concept of entrepreneurship was not limited exclusively to business administration. In the 1990s, multidisciplinary approaches to the entrepreneur and entrepreneurship had also widened the discussion to include new types of entrepreneurs and entrepreneurial activities in society. Instead of only focusing on entrepreneurship as an economic activity within the business sector, new research with a social science perspective began to focus beyond the profit-seeking economic entrepreneur. The widened definition on entrepreneurship focused on societal and social entrepreneurs (Westlund, 2010) such as entrepreneurs and entrepreneurial activities in cooperative associations, interest organizations, aid workers and rights and liberties movements and so on. It was argued that the entrepreneur and entrepreneurial activities existed in the public sphere and not only in the business sector and how the entrepreneur could work for the common good rather than just for economic interests (Brickerhoff, 2000; Borzaga et al., 2008; Gawell et al., 2009). Based on the traditional notion of an entrepreneur, the societal and social entrepreneur was also defined as goal-oriented, a go-getter and successful actor, but with the objective to work for some normative good that was not necessarily economic in nature. The objectives could be to promote improved welfare for the young and the elderly, cooperative day care centres, rural infrastructure, socioeconomic equality, integration, human rights, sustainable development, fair trade, animal protection, ecological production, sports and leisure and so forth (Borzaga et al., 2008; Gawell et al., 2009; Von Bergmann-Winberg and Wihlborg, 2011).

Social science research has elucidated the importance of political entrepreneurs and entrepreneurial politicians (political leaders) (Scheingate, 2003). Studies on the political entrepreneur have, however, been limited in number. Political entrepreneurs are said to be elected politicians and public servants in the political system, from the local level to the national, but also actors within societal engines of growth, committees and councils and so on (Scheingate, 2003).

Political scientist Robert Dahl introduced the concept of the political entrepreneur, who defined the latter as a resourceful and masterful leader in the political sphere. Dahl stressed how the entrepreneur was 'the epitome of the self-made man' (1974, p. 25). He argued how citizens were influenced by politics and how they could use their different resources to influence the political outcome. Some citizens, *homo civicus*, were citizens that had their occupations beyond politics, but as citizens decided to now and then influence politicians to provide favourable policies. Other citizens, however, *homo politicus*, decided to stay politically active to shape politics (Dahl, 1974, pp. 223–7, 282).

In this study, we use the concept of political entrepreneur as an overarching concept for all of those actors in the political arena (the public sector) who work to create the conditions for other entrepreneurs and for the common good (i.e., the good of society) (Silander and Silander, 2015). This includes politicians and civil servants in government departments, public authorities, departments of public works, and engines of economic growth. In social science, the conditions encompass both formal and informal institutions (North, 1990).

The Political Entrepreneur

The political entrepreneur operates beyond traditional and routinized procedures and is innovative and creative in using formal and informal institutions and networks to improve the public sector's activities towards entrepreneurs and entrepreneurship by developing and promoting new norms that have not been embedded in traditional day-to-day public activities (Silander and Silander, 2015).

In the Swedish political and economic debate, as within the European Union (EU) and in academia at large, the idea of the political entrepreneur and political entrepreneurship has received growing interest. In academia, the political entrepreneur's objective has been to push for entrepreneurship by questioning traditional norms and values and by seeking new paths. Although it has been argued that entrepreneurial activities are very much due to individual willingness, skills and capacity, it has been argued that entrepreneurs may face more favourable or less favourable entrepreneurial conditions and how entrepreneurship may be more or less driven from the political/public domain. In other words, although individual characteristics are always interesting and important to take into consideration when focusing on entrepreneurship, the political entrepreneur may have to play a crucial role in assisting entrepreneurs in their interests and activities to become successful (Henrekson and Stenkula, 2007, pp. 90–91). It is the political entrepreneur's main objective to seek new grounds for improved conditions for entrepreneurship by shaping and reshaping formal and informal institutions. This requires having good insights into the existing entrepreneurial conditions in a society and what formal and informal institutional changes need to be undertaken for existing and potential entrepreneurs to become successful. When the political entrepreneur is successful in the public sector, this promotes successful entrepreneurship in the business sector, with positive long-term outcomes for society in terms of growth, employment and improved welfare.

One obvious potential political entrepreneur is the active elected politician. However, there is also substantial research on the impact on politics by public servants. Based on this bulk of studies, it is reasonable to believe that both politicians and public servants could be potential political entrepreneurs. For some time, political science research has stated how public servants have enjoyed growing power in politics. Instead of only implementing political decisions within a hierarchical structure of politicians deciding on issues and public servants implementing those decisions (Weber, 1947), research has pointed to the role of public servants in all political phases – from initiating a political issue to deciding on it and eventually implementing the decision in society. As backbones of public services, these public servants, it has been argued, have a strengthened position in the overall decision-making process: to influence political agenda setting, by defining problems and potential solutions, to advise on where to find resources and how to prioritize problems and scarce resources, to interpret political decisions to become implemented in the society and to implement decisions and assess their outcome (Aberbach et al., 1981; Aberbach and Rockman, 1994; Mintrom and Norman, 2009).

Although we need more research on the role of public servants in politics and especially on when and how public servants and politicians can become political entrepreneurs, research has pointed to an intensified and influential role of public servants in politics. This is very much due to the growing linkages between politics and public services and the intensified collaboration between elected politicians and public servants (Rhodes, 1997). Here are several examples of public servants influencing politics (see Hysing and Olsson, 2012, pp. 20–22; see also Hall and Löfgren, 2006) and who could be seen as political entrepreneurs:

● Public servants may be influential in politics by initiating a political process. Being in daily contact with political issues in the public sector, public servants often pursue expertise in certain areas and how political issues are to be solved and with what resources. Public servants may therefore initiate a political discussion and become agenda setters for politicians.

● Public servants may also be influential by setting priorities for politicians on the relevance of different political issues to be discussed. Public servants have a broader view and knowledge of the public sector than most politicians. They are informed about what challenges exist, the need for reforms and what resources are available. It is therefore possible for public servants to report to politicians with their own ideas of what should be done immediately and what political decisions could be postponed.

● Public servants may also have an impact on shaping the political decision. Besides providing politicians with information about political issues, public servants may also provide politicians with advice on how best to address the political issue; in other words how to shape the political decision appropriately.

● Public servants may also be influential in the implementation phase of a decision. This includes public servants' reading and evaluation of politicians' decisions, how they interpret the content of the decisions and how they should be implemented in society at large.

- Public servants may also be influential through the assessment of previous implementation of a political decision. It is the duty of public servants not only to implement decisions, but also to follow up on decisions and assess their impacts and consequences. First, this addresses whether the implementation has had the intended consequences, but also to see if there is more to be done and/or if the implementation has caused new problems to be addressed. It is often public servants who develop criteria and methods for such assessment and are therefore influential in choosing what tools to be used when evaluating and understanding if previous decisions have attained the goals or not. The outcome of such evaluation may shape future political agendas.

The above-mentioned examples of the possible impact of public servants on politics and political decision-making indicate that both politicians and public servants may be political entrepreneurs. At stated earlier, there is only limited research on the political entrepreneur. There is also very limited research on how politicians and public servants should act as political entrepreneurs. Although research on entrepreneurship has discussed favourable and unfavourable conditions for entrepreneurs and entrepreneurship, there seems to be no clear-cut policy on how to become politically entrepreneurial.

In addition, what political entrepreneurs should or should not do more specifically to promote better conditions for entrepreneurs and entrepreneurship is to some extent a 'black box' that needs further empirical research. Research does, however, point to different potential favourable factors for entrepreneurial activities and growth: on the one hand, internal factors that are embedded in the entrepreneurial activity or the specific business, and on the other, external factors focusing on the societal conditions that entrepreneurs and entrepreneurial activities develop from (Unionen, 2009, p. 6).

Overall, empirical research on Swedish political entrepreneurs is limited. There is also very limited empirical research on what conditions are more or less favourable for Swedish entrepreneurship. Further, Sweden, like most states, has different entrepreneurial settings due to local and regional contexts. A universal recipe for the public sector on how to promote entrepreneurship is therefore impossible to find; rather, it is the main duty of the political entrepreneur themselves to identify and understand the local and regional context and to see how the given setting can best be used and how to become innovative in such a setting by providing new entrepreneurial paths for existing and potential entrepreneurs (Myndigheten för tillväxtpolitiska utvärderingar och analyser,

2011, pp. 3, 8). There does seem, however, to be some kind of scholarly consensus that political entrepreneurship should be about approaching entrepreneurs and entrepreneurship in the business sector with a wide range of public tools: to provide for enduring, stable and precise institutional conditions in different political areas such as energy supply, education, infrastructure, rule of law, bureaucracy and taxation.

First, it has been argued that one favourable condition for entrepreneurship is solid and endurable tax regulations that make tax levels on investments and capital transparent, long-lasting and predictable. It has been argued that politicians must make sure that small businesses and entrepreneurs have secured capital flows to develop and that the tax level must be favourable for entrepreneurship and business growth and so on. It is also stated in the research that all entrepreneurial activities are costly and that political entrepreneurs should find ways to accommodate the costs and risks taken by business owners and entrepreneurs. Second, research also points out the importance of infrastructure, both material and non-material. Entrepreneurship is based on physical and virtual infrastructure, with well-developed systems and networks of transportation (roads, railways, airports and harbours etc.) as well as virtual networks and know-how (universities and technology etc.), encouraging entrepreneurs and businesses to seek investments, clients, markets, distributors and partners. Infrastructure also facilitates input of know-how in terms of educated staff and new ideas and trends. Third, research has also pointed to the importance of a cost-efficient and stable energy supply. Without a secured and predictable energy supply system, entrepreneurs and businesses face insecurity and increased costs due to the challenges of planning and investing in new ideas, products and services. Fourth and finally, it has also been stated how the rule of law and a stable and transparent bureaucracy is essential for entrepreneurs and entrepreneurship. Economic activities need a political and judicial framework that is predictable and stable over time. Too many political and judicial changes or biased political and judicial decisions will cause insecurity and prevent entrepreneurship. It is important to know what political and legislative platform exists and to be able to foresee future political and judicial decisions when planning new economic activities (see Svenskt näringsliv, 2007; Unionen, 2009).

THE POLITICAL ENTREPRENEUR FOR NORM CHANGE

The discussion above has identified different important political areas for improved conditions for entrepreneurship. Much more research is needed to provide a better empirical idea of what political entrepreneurs should do in their day-to-day activities to favour entrepreneurs and entrepreneurial activities in the Swedish economy. However, political entrepreneurship is about seeking new windows of opportunity within the above-mentioned political areas to promote entrepreneurship in the business sector. Seeking windows of opportunity is to question established norms on entrepreneurship and to be innovative in finding new ways of being entrepreneurial.

A norm consists of expected and accepted standards of behaviour in society (Finnemore and Sikkink, 1998, p. 891). On an aggregated, societal level, institutions create norms. While formal institutions constitute laws, regulations, rules, policies and finances, informal institutions are about collective ideas, perceptions, images and values that become structures for social interaction. Norms in formal and informal institutions symbolize what is normal in social interactions: what we expect others to do and what others expect us to do in our societal meetings. What makes a politician or public servant a political entrepreneur is when existing norms are challenged by the initiation of new ideas on how formal and informal institutions should be shaped to better serve – for example, the interests of entrepreneurial activities. The political entrepreneur not only questions existing formal and informal institutions, but is also willing and innovative enough to challenge their existence in order to initiate and promote new norms within the public and business sectors (ibid., pp. 893–6).

The role and actions of the political entrepreneur need further empirical research, but could be theoretically understood in terms of innovative actions for norm emergence, norm cascade and norm internalization:

1.   The first phase of norm emergence embeds the innovative questioning and challenge from the political entrepreneur of established and traditional institutional conditions for entrepreneurial activities in a society. The political entrepreneur challenges formal and informal institutions on standards of behaviour on entrepreneurship and takes on the mission to become a go-getter by initiating the ideas of new norms to better serve entrepreneurship. Again, such questioning may be to challenge existing formal institutions in laws, rules, regulations and existing policies or to change informal institutions in their established ideas and values on how the public sector approaches entrepreneurs and entrepreneurial activities in the business sector. As argued, 'Norms do not appear out of thin air; they are actively built by agents having strong notions about appropriate or desirable behaviour' (ibid., p. 896).

2.   The second phase – the norm cascade – includes the spread of the new initiated norms to larger groups of politicians and public servants in the public sector. The initiated norms are expanded to the activities of the public sector by reorganizing formal activities through new rules and regulations and policies and/or by rethinking how to approach and value entrepreneurial activities and existing and potential entrepreneurs based on new ideas, images and values. If the political entrepreneur is successful in the norm cascade, this will provide new formal and informal frameworks for public sector activities towards the business sector.

3.   The third phase – norm internalization – consists of the consolidation of new norms in the public sector in its relation to entrepreneurship in the business sector. Norm internalization has occurred when the old traditional formal and informal institutions have changed to reflect the initiated ideas from the political entrepreneur. The new norms are now accepted and have become 'the new game in town' on how entrepreneurs and entrepreneurial activities are approached by the public sector. The consolidation of the norms means that politicians and public servants are guided by these norms of formal and informal institutions in their day-to-day activities, until the day when a new political entrepreneur initiates new norms.

Based on research on organizational and cultural conditions for the public sector to influence economic activities, it is likely that these conditions also influence the role of political entrepreneurs in entrepreneurial activities. The organizational aspect of political entrepreneurship is, as mentioned above, to shape favourable formal institutions. It is about setting up formal rules, regulations and policies on entrepreneurship to improve its conditions as far as possible. However, political entrepreneurs may have different sets of formal institutions that might be more favourable or less favourable for entrepreneurship. There might be differences in political steering, leadership, responsibilities and positions, strategies and policies, rules and regulations and the amount and distribution of financial and other resources for entrepreneurial activities. These are founding institutional components for public sector activities and have been scrutinized in research on Swedish public activities (Rothstein, 1994, 1997).

In addition, the cultural aspect of political entrepreneurship concerns the informal conditions for entrepreneurship in public sectors' cultural approaches towards the entrepreneur and entrepreneurial activities. These cultural approaches embed existing and prevailing ideas, attitudes, values and images that shape the day-to-day activities and perceptions in the public sector on entrepreneurship and the entrepreneur (Morgan, 1986; North, 1990; Hofstede, 1991). As in the case of formal institutions, it is likely that different public actors and political entrepreneurs may approach entrepreneurs and entrepreneurial activities in different ways based on different ideas, images and values of how best to promote entrepreneurship and among what groups of society. There might therefore exist similar and different sets of informal conditions for entrepreneurship depending on what political entrepreneurs we are studying. There is research showing that politicians and public servants have different attitudes towards who is entrepreneurial and what groups of citizens entrepreneurial activities are expected to derive from (see Chapters 7–10).

Scholars have argued that both organizational and cultural conditions for political entrepreneurship are important to further explore the role of political entrepreneurs for entrepreneurial activities in the business sector. Although the organizational conditions set the framework for politicians and public servants, culture is crucial to understanding why politicians and public servants sometimes act the way they do. One important research finding is the role of social capital in all societal relations. It has been argued that societal cooperation and efficiency is based on social trust. Social trust may be embedded in societal relations between citizens and consists of shared norms and values and exchange of information (Putnam, 1993; Lin et al., 2001). Social trust is developed in the interaction between formal and informal institutions and between organizations and cultures. Good political entrepreneurship must be based on social trust between politicians and public servants, but also between the public and business sector actors. It is important to explore what formal and informal conditions structure political entrepreneurs in their activities and what similarities and differences exist between them, but it is also very important to study the nature of social trust between the public and business sector actors to seek greater insight into how politicians and public servants in general and political entrepreneurs specifically may act to improve the conditions for entrepreneurs and entrepreneurial activities in society at large.

To become a successful political entrepreneur is therefore about contributing to social trust between politicians and public servants and entrepreneurs. It is about working favourably for entrepreneurship by identifying and understanding challenges that exist for entrepreneurs and their activities and how to overcome them by setting up new windows of opportunity where both new potential formal and informal institutions are explored. The public and business sectors are tied together today in a way never seen before (Hedlund and Montin, 2009). Politicians and public servants in, for example, Swedish regions and municipalities, are working in close relation with entrepreneurs and business owners. They have a common goal to provide for entrepreneurship and growth and are active in networks. Research on entrepreneurship has acknowledged these changes and identified how politics and economics and the public and business sector actors are tied together in a network society. The network society (see Castells, 1998), has from a political entrepreneurial perspective, led to a greater interest in social trust. It has been argued that existing networks are crucial to understanding what political entrepreneurs may do or not do to promote entrepreneurial activities in Swedish society. It is within existing networks that ideas, cooperation, resources and initiatives may be identified that could lead to improved conditions for entrepreneurship (Dennis, 2000). It is also likely that through these networks new alliances are born. An important role for the political entrepreneur is to identify and develop constructive and inclusive relations between different types of entrepreneurs. It requires being creative, user-friendly, strategic and innovative to promote favourable networks for existing and potential entrepreneurs.

There are, however, identified challenges for the political entrepreneur to overcome. First, there is a legal framework for all political activities to follow. This framework is further discussed elsewhere in this book (see Chapter 3). Second, research has also identified tension, competition and exclusion strategies within existing networks. In other words, networks may be fruitful and essential for some entrepreneurs, but may also hinder and marginalize others. Some entrepreneurs may have better contact with politicians and public servants than others. Some entrepreneurs may also be engaged in entrepreneurial activities that are more favoured than others by these politicians and public servants. Some entrepreneurs may also have better resources than others or be provided with better opportunities by the public sector. In other words, existing networks may consist of equal and collaborating partners or of unequal and competing ones and they may both promote and obstruct different types of entrepreneurial activities and entrepreneurs.

CONCLUSIONS

Social science research of the last two decades has identified new types of entrepreneurship in the public sector. Based on a tradition of research on entrepreneurship in economics, a multidisciplinary approach to entrepreneurship within academia has led to greater insight into what could favour entrepreneurs and entrepreneurship in society. It has been argued that politicians and public servants may play a crucial role for regional growth, employment and welfare by acting favourably to entrepreneurship. Although there exists limited empirical research on what politicians and public servants could and should do to promote entrepreneurship, a broad approach to societal reforms has been discussed.

This chapter has conceptualized the political entrepreneur. A political entrepreneur has been defined as a 'politician/bureaucrat/officer/ department within the publicly funded sector who with innovative approaches encourages entrepreneurship/business and where the goals are growth, employment and the common good'. Public sector actors may become political entrepreneurs by acting innovatively as go-getters and goal-oriented by challenging existing norms to open up windows of opportunity in new sets of formal and informal institutions. More research on the political entrepreneur is needed. It might provide us with important insights into how politicians and public servants could act to provide for regional growth, employment and sustainable welfare in times of global competition, structural transformations and recession.

REFERENCES

Aberbach, J.D. and B.A. Rockman (1994), 'Civil servants and policymakers: neutral or responsive competence?' *Governance*, **7**(4), 461–9.
Aberbach, J.D., R.D. Outnam and B.A. Rockham (1981), *Bureaucrats and Politicians in Western Democracies*, Cambridge, MA: Harvard University Press.
Bjerke, B. (2005), *Förklara eller förstå entreprenörskap?* [Explain or Understand Entrepreneurship?], Lund: Studentlitteratur.
Borzaga, C., G. Galera and R. Nogales (eds) (2008), *Social Enterprise: A New Model for Poverty Reduction and Employment Generation*, New York: EMES/ UNDP.
Brickerhoff, P.C. (2000), *Social Entrepreneurship – The Art of Mission-Based Venture Development*, New York: John Wiley and Sons.
Castells, M. (1998), *Nätverkssamhällets framväxt* [Network-based Society], Göteborg: Daidalos.
Dahl, R. (1974), *Who Governs? Democracy and Power in an American City*, New Haven, CT and London: Yale University Press.
Dennis, C. (2000), 'Networking for marketing advantage', *Management Decision*, **38**(4), 287–92.
Finnemore, M. and K. Sikkink (1998), 'International norm dynamics and political change', *International Organizations*, **52**(4), 887–917.
Gawell, M., B. Johannisson and M. Lundqvist (2009), *Samhällets entreprenörer – En forskarantologi om samhällsentreprenörskap* [Social Entrepreneurs – A Research Anthology on Social Entrepreneurship], Stockholm: KK-stiftelsen.

Grant, A. (1998), 'Entrepreneurship – the major academic discipline for the business education curriculum for the 21st century', in M.G. Scott, P. Rosa and H. Klandt (eds), *Educating Entrepreneurs for Wealth Creation*, Burlington, VT: Ashgate.

Hall, P. and K. Löfgren (2006), *Politisk styrning i praktiken* [Political Governance in Practice], Malmö: Liber.

Hedlund, G. and S. Montin (eds) (2009), *Governance på svenska* [Swedish Governance], Stockholm: Santérus Academic Press.

Henrekson, M. and M. Stenkula (2007), *Entreprenörskap* [Entrepreneurship], Stockholm: SNS förlag.

Hofstede, G. (1991), *Organisationer och kulturer – om interkulturell förståelse* [Organizations and Cultures – Intercultural Understanding], Lund: Studentlitteratur.

Hysing, E. and J. Olsson (2012), *Tjänstemän i politiken* [Officials in Politics], Lund: Studentlitteratur.

Landström, H. (2005), *Entreprenörskapets rötter* [Entrepreneurship Roots], Malmö: Liber.

Lin, N., K. Cook and R.S. Burth (eds) (2001), *Social Capital: Theory and Research*, New Brunswick, NJ and London: Aldine Transaction.

Mintrom, M. and P. Norman (2009), 'Policy entrepreneurship and policy change', *The Policies Studies Journal*, **37**(4), 649–67.

Morgan, G. (1986), *Images of Organizations*, Los Angeles, CA: Sage Publications.

Myndigheten för tillväxtpolitiska utvärderingar och analyser [Agency for Growth Policy Analysis] (2011), 'Tillväxtanalys: Regional och lokal tillväxtpolitik – Vad kan och bör offentliga aktörer göra?' [Growth analysis: regional and local growth policy – what can and should the public sector do?], *Working Paper No. 28*, Östersund: Myndigheten för tillväxtpolitiska utvärderingar och analyser.

North, D.C. (1990), *Institutions, Institutional Change and Economic Performance*, Cambridge, UK: Cambridge University Press.

Putnam, R. (1993), *Making Democracy Work – Civic Traditions in Modern Italy*, Princeton, NJ: Princeton University Press.

Rhodes, R.A.W. (1997), *Understanding Governance. Policy Networks, Governance, Reflexivity and Accountability*, Maidenhead, UK: Open University Press.

Rothstein, B. (1994), *Vad bör staten göra? – Om välfärdsstatens moraliska och politiska logik* [What Should the State Do? The Welfare State's Moral and Political Logic], Stockholm: SNS Förlag.

Rothstein, B. (ed.) (1997), *Politik som organisation – förvaltningspolitikens grundproblem* [Politics as Organization – Fundamental Challenges to Public Policies], Stockholm: SNS Förlag.

Scheingate, A.D. (2003), 'Political entrepreneurship, institutional change and American political development', *Studies in American Political Development*, **17**(2), 185–203.

Schumpeter, J.A. (1943), *Capitalism, Socialism and Democracy*, London: Unwin.

Silander, D. and C. Silander (2015), *Politiskt entreprenörskap – Den offentliga sektorns sätt att skapa bättre förutsättningar för entreprenörskap lokalt, regionalt och nationellt* [Political Entrepreneurship – Public Sector Ways to Create Better Conditions for Entrepreneurship Locally, Regionally and Nationally], Stockholm: Santérus förlag.

Svenskt näringsliv [Swedish Business] (2007), *Globaliseringens utmaningar och möjligheter – företagare som växer lokalt med global strategi för sina affärer* [Globalization Challenges and Opportunities – Entrepreneurs that Grow Locally with a Global Strategy for their Business], Stockholm: Svenskt näringsliv.

Unionen (2009), *En politik för innovation, entreprenörskap och tillväxt* [A Policy of Innovation, Entrepreneurship and Growth], Stockholm: Blomquist and Co.

Von Bergmann-Winberg, M.L. and E. Wihlborg (eds) (2011), *Politikens entreprenörskap – kreativ problemlösning och förändring* [Political Entrepreneurship – Creative Problem Solving and Change], Malmö: Liber.

Weber, M. (1947), *The Theory of Social and Economic Organization*, New York: Free Press.

Westlund, H. (2010), 'Multidimensional entrepreneurship: theoretical considerations and Swedish empirics', paper presented at the 50th Anniversary Congress of the European Regional Science Association, Jönköping, Sweden, 19–23 August.

3. Legitimate and legal boundaries for political entrepreneurship

Staffan Andersson and Tobias Bromander

Does entrepreneurship always contribute positively to society? It is tempting to unequivocally answer yes, given the positive effects of entrepreneurship on development and growth. Indeed, research often focuses on entrepreneurship as something inherently good, with positive effects (Foss et al., 2007, p. 1897). However, as pointed out by William Baumol (1990), entrepreneurship could be used for different purposes and its contribution may therefore vary greatly depending on how the activities of entrepreneurs are divided between productive activities (such as innovations) and unproductive activities (such as rent-seeking[1] or organized crime). So we can think of entrepreneurship as having negative consequences for society (Hansson, 2011, p. 194). In an extreme case, such 'negative entrepreneurship' can be illustrated by entrepreneurial activities in organized crime, but such unethical activities are sometimes not included in research at all (Nählinder, 2011, p. 107). Our initial point thus is that we cannot always assume that entrepreneurship only has positive social effects – the effects may vary.

This chapter will specifically highlight negative political entre-preneurship that can occur in close collaborations between entrepreneurs from the private sector and political entrepreneurs (see Chapter 2). We problematize negative entrepreneurship and its societal impact by linking it with the effects of conflicts of interest and corruption. The discussion is particularly focused on political entrepreneurship in a context where public services are operated and organized in forms where both public and private actors are involved in the execution of operations or funding, which raises questions of governance and political accountability. We also illustrate this problem through a case study of an arena project in the municipality of Solna (a new football stadium for the Swedish Football Association) where conflicts of interest and corruption were revealed in the intersection of private sector entrepreneurs and political entre-preneurs. Finally, we discuss how public administration, where both private and public actors are involved, can mean big opportunities for political entrepreneurship but also risks in terms of negative political entrepreneurship.

POLITICAL ENTREPRENEURSHIP AND PUBLIC ADMINISTRATION UNDER CHANGE: OPPORTUNITIES AND RISKS

Changes in society in the last 30 years have meant that boundaries between the private sector and the public sector have become less clear. Public administration is run in a variety of mixed forms in terms of how activities are financed and carried out (Christensen et al., 2005). Private organizations operate in the public sector and vice versa. These hybrid forms of business together with network governance may also lead to unclear lines of accountability. The governance of the public sector, which has traditionally been seen as a task for the politically responsible agencies, is nowadays commonly viewed as an interaction between actors both from the public sector and the private (Pollit and Bouckaert, 2004, pp. 135–6). In many areas, the rules for governance are not as clear as in the traditional forms of organization and in some cases the legislation is complex, resulting in grey areas and scope for interpretation of what rules apply. In these alternative forms of public service and organization, there is room for entrepreneurs to act and to think anew (Tillmar, 2011, pp. 177–9). In particular, we are interested in political entrepreneurship, characterized by the stretching of existing legal boundaries or the creation of new forms of public administration and decision-making and so on.[2] In particular, we focus on questions about room for and the impact of negative political entrepreneurship on society and democratic values and we do so where political entrepreneurship meets organizational change – at the intersection of the private and public sectors.

Private and public actors thus cooperate in various ways on issues of importance for the development of the national economy and democracy. This takes place in the form of networks rather than traditional political hierarchies. For public sector operations, the changes involve the introduction of market-like mechanisms, for example by using profit centres in public administration, responsible for generating their own revenues, or how users of elderly care can choose between various municipal and private providers of publicly funded care. International companies running tax-funded health care in Sweden is a very clear example of change in this area. Another example is when municipal or state agencies procure activities where a private company then carries out the work, such as construction of roads or provision of transport or care. Procurement has become an important and vital mechanism in public administration in general in industrialized countries, and not least in Sweden. Estimates indicate that public procurement today accounts for between 15 and 20 per cent of Swedish gross domestic product (e.g., Bergman, 2008, p. 4).

We can hence conclude that in the interface between the public and the private sectors, the forms of financing, execution and governance vary significantly (Christensen et al., 2005). Norms governing these activities also vary, both formal (laws and written rules) and informal norms (culture, morality and ethics) (Andvig, 2002, Chapter 2, pp. 2–6; Lawton et al., 2013, pp. 42–4). How actors in different activities act, and goals of activities, are expected to be dependent upon the forms under which activities are operated. In very simplified terms, we usually expect private companies typically to have profit as their main goal (although of course other criteria such as social responsibility, environment, etc. have become more and more important) and their activities are primarily a means to this end, while the reverse is often held to be true for public administration operated in the traditional agency form: economic resources are a means to achieve their business objectives. The legal regulation of the activities is also dependent on how activities are run. As an example of this, we use the Swedish legislation on publicity.

The Freedom of the Press Act (Tryckfrihetsförordning, 1949, Chapter 2, Article 1) entitles all Swedish citizens to have free access to official documents. Also, employees who give information to the media have constitutional protection from being disclosed as the source and the employers are banned from inquiring who gave the information in public activities carried out in the traditional form of management of that sector (ibid., Chapter 1, Article 1; Chapter 3, Article 4). In cases where a public authority outsources operations to be carried out by a private firm, this constitutional protection does not apply. Instead, public access to official records has to be secured through agreements between a municipality and the company that performs the service (Kommunallag, 1991, Chapter 3, Section 19a). Briefly, the principle of publicity becomes weaker as businesses are moved out of the authority's own execution.

Against this background, this area is highly interesting for democracy research in general and especially concerning issues of governance and political accountability and how the public can exercise control and ensure that citizens' preferences are heard in this new landscape of public sector activities. Previous research shows that some of the aspects that are of crucial importance for the functioning of democracy, legitimacy and economic efficiency, conflict of interest and corruption, are influenced by and behave differently depending on how operations are conducted and regulated (Andersson and Erlingsson, 2012). With this in mind, we do not argue that the risks necessarily increase, rather that they change and therefore can require different management, regulation and control.

In the remainder of this chapter, we will study and discuss issues relating specifically to entrepreneurship and democracy in the sphere where public and private actors come together in different activities. The focus is political entrepreneurship in activities where public and private actors are jointly involved in operations in different ways and where a variety of interests may be in conflict. Our overarching issues relate to how private operators in activities for which public sector organizations are responsible affect structures and decision-making and especially when it results in negative entrepreneurship. We approach this issue by focusing in particular on what kinds of conflicts of interest arise in contexts where entrepreneurs from the private sector engage with political entrepreneurs. We can therefore throw light on our understanding of corruptive conflict of interest in areas undergoing rapid change and where political entrepreneurship influences the rules of the game for these activities.

Below, we first discuss more thoroughly what we mean by negative political entrepreneurship and conflicts of interest. We define the concepts and discuss approaches to enable us to understand and identify new types of conflicts of interest in the context of marked change in the public sector where collaboration and private elements nowadays are normal elements. Based on this discussion, we then employ a case study of the project to construct a new football stadium for the Swedish Football Association in Solna municipality (a city in the greater Stockholm area) where corruption and conflict of interest was revealed in 2011. The consequences in this case of the chosen policy strategies for the public authority and its confidence were thus very negative. The case also represents a situation where municipal organizations are a leading actor, which is a deliberate choice as the local government sector largely manages the public activities that are the subject of public–private cooperation and partnership and furthermore according to previous studies is particularly associated with risks of conflicts of interest and corruption (Andersson, 1999; Erlingsson, 2006; Erlingsson et al., 2008; Bergh et al., 2013).

NEGATIVE POLITICAL ENTREPRENEURSHIP – CONFLICT OF INTEREST AND CORRUPTION

In general, entrepreneurship is about processes to find new and unique ways to combine resources (Sobel et al., 2010, p. 270). Entrepreneurs shape new solutions within existing boundaries or may entirely change these and existing conditions. Looking at political entrepreneurship, focus is not only on the actor, but also on the system, structure and institutions that the entrepreneur can change (see Chapter 2; cf. Sheingate, 2003, pp. 185, 190). We particularly direct the light towards actors who participate in public administration where public and private organizations meet. Political entrepreneurs, through their knowledge of political structures and through their anchoring in networks of contacts that have been built up over a long time, pursue issues and enable structures to be stretched in the context of their work (Wihlborg, 2011b, pp. 118–19, 128).

How can we understand the effects of political entrepreneurship? Baumol (1990, p. 6), building on Schumpeter's starting points for entrepreneurship and its preconditions, starts from a rational assumption of entrepreneurs as being resourceful and creative people in their path to increase wealth, status, or power, thus it is not expected that all are concerned whether these goals lead to improved outcomes for society at large. The ways entrepreneurs behave are consequently dependent on how the rules of the game are designed in society. Different environments/communities have different rules and thus the pay-offs of various activities differ: entrepreneurs are then expected to be affected in their choice between productive, unproductive or destructive activities. The usefulness of entrepreneurship for society, as well as risks for adverse entrepreneurship, will thus vary depending on what these structures look like. It cannot be taken for granted that all entrepreneurship is done for purposes that are good for society in general. Our main point here is that rules and structures facing political entrepreneurs are important to consider if we are to understand why actors act as they do and the consequences of political entrepreneurship.[3]

Negative entrepreneurship, that is, entrepreneurial strategies that have negative consequences for individuals or society (Hansson, 2011, p. 194), is held together as actors operate in structures that influence them to act in a certain direction. Decision-makers can use legislation to create certain structures for how actors should act. Actors affected can either act in line with these structures, or challenge them by trying to change them. Some entrepreneurial strategies will challenge existing structures (ibid., pp. 196–7, 209). Negative entrepreneurship directs the light to the importance of not letting the ends justify the means especially in light of what Wihlborg (2011b, p. 128) has noted: the perception of entrepreneurship as inherently good for the economy spills over into the political arena where it sometimes tends to lead to greater acceptance even for incorrect action by political entrepreneurs.

Entrepreneurship leading to conflicts of interest and corruption is a type of such potential adverse effects, with a big impact on the economic rationality, the integrity of and citizens' trust in public administration. The politicians, public officers and companies that operate at the intersection of the public and private sectors collaborate in both formal and informal settings and professional and private relationships are intertwined (Sjöstrand, 2008, 2010). The higher the influx of entrepreneurs into public administration, the more pressing the questions of accountability become as it becomes less clear who is responsible for what (Wihlborg, 2011a, p. 214). Political entrepreneurs then also act under greater uncertainty. Procurement and alternative forms of operation create space for political entrepreneurs. The increased diversity of activities and actors means that public administration is becoming more complex and accountability unclear. When responsibility is unclear, political actors act in situations that are indeterminate (ibid., p. 213). In operations conducted in mixed governance form, contracts and commissions are seen as an effective alternative to traditional forms of governance and a way to meet the shortcomings of the legal regulation for organizations that want to interact flexibly in networks or partnerships. In such governance structures, where the network form is not consistent with the traditional hierarchical responsibility, operations are often conducted as projects. As projects in public organizations, they obviously need to be characterized by efficiency, legality, transparency and democracy (ibid., pp. 221–2).

Such networks have an important role in development and growth. Potentially, however, conflicts of interest can also arise in those forms of governance with frequent contact between political and other entrepreneurs; between the public and private spheres (e.g., Sjöstrand, 2005). We define conflicts of interest as situations where an official has some form of external interest that could affect how he or she exercises his or her mission and that are different from those interests (the duties of office) that ought to influence how the task is handled (cf. Getman and Karlan, 2008, p. 56). The Organisation for Economic Co-operation and Development (OECD, 2005, p. 13) similarly defines a conflict of interest as 'a conflict between the public duty and the private interest of a public official, in which the official's private-capacity interest could improperly influence the performance of their official duties and responsibilities'. A conflict of interest may, for example, mean preferential treatment for an entrepreneurship project of lower standard than a better competing project. Such a decision will then have a direct negative impact on economic development and the legitimacy of decision-making agencies.

This traditional conflict of interest concept is, however, insufficient to describe and regulate the complex linkages between the creation of public policy and profit-driven entrepreneurs. The increased ambiguity of boundaries between the public and private sectors with a growing share of public service performed by private providers (OECD, 2009, pp. 7, 12), privatization and corporatization, affect what we define as conflicts of interest, how they manifest and how they are managed (or should be managed) (Andersson and Anechiarico, 2015). In light of this development, the traditional perspective in understanding conflicts of interest with a focus on the role of the individual official is not enough, because in some cases it is the system itself that creates conflicts of interest and affects how they manifest. Therefore, a broader input is needed to understand conflicts of interest and corruption that not only focuses on the individual (and the distinction between the private interests of the official and the interests to adhere to according to the duty of the position which are the basis for legal regulation of conflicts of interest), but also include institutional factors focusing on how routines and structures influence and determine the condition of various actions. In the extreme, it may be the legal framework and its operating conditions that favour specific private interests and build in conflicts of interest in the institutional structures (O'Brien, 2003) whereby a focus on individual morality and behaviour is insufficient in identifying and preventing conflict of interest.

Conflicts are of great importance in relation to entrepreneurship as they are also linked to risks of corruption. With a broad social science definition, corruption is seen as situations where officers abuse power or trust for improper gain. Corruption and conflicts of interest are thus closely linked. A conflict of interest does not need to be equivalent with corruption, but an improperly managed conflict of interest risks leading to corruption (e.g., Kjellberg, 1995, p. 341). The reverse is also true: corruption creates conflicts of interest (Anechiarico and Jacobs, 1996, p. 46). For example, the very purpose of a bribe is to get the receiver to follow the interests of the bribe-giver rather than the interests the bribe-taker is supposed to follow given office rules. Even if an individual actor gains advantages through corruption, the impact on society overall is devastating: financially it has negative impact on resource allocation and growth (e.g., Mauro, 1995), while for democracy it means that decisions are made on false grounds, resulting in less confidence in the democratic system itself (Rothstein and Uslaner, 2005; Rothstein, 2011; Linde and Erlingsson, 2012; Charron et al., 2013). Moreover, even at low levels, corruption can have very negative consequences and once corruption has established itself, it is difficult to eliminate (Andvig and Moene, 1990; Tirole, 1996). Thus corruption is always important to fight even in environments with relatively small problems.

Above we have described the need for a broader understanding of conflicts of interest and this also applies to our take on corruption. We need to pay attention to the effects on democracy, which will not be covered if we stick to a legal definition that basically (in Sweden) focuses on bribes. If we are to capture the effects on transparency and opportunities for accountable public administration, this requires a broader understanding of what corruption is that takes institutional conditions into consideration (Thompson, 1995; Lessig, 2013). In this context, Heywood's (1997, p. 423) view of corruption as a 'betrayal of the democratic transcript' is relevant. He takes democracy as the basis for the definition of corruption, where the possibilities of accountability of those in power is central and how democracy is corrupted if the rulers deliberately try to prevent citizens from accountability. This type of corruption occurs when members of the political class actively act to ensure that citizens do not receive the relevant information in a way to hinder or circumvent the opportunities for accountability. Heywood regards this as a very serious form of corruption as decisions might be made that would have been infeasible if information and accountability had been transparent and facilitated respectively. As some situations of this kind are not always clearly unlawful it also shows that a definition of corruption based entirely on the law may miss important aspects of the influence of corruption on democracy.

What does this discussion mean in a Swedish context? Sweden is often cited as a country with relatively minor corruption problems in comparison with other countries. At the same time, we know that these comparisons are affected by many measurement problems (Andvig, 2005; Heywood and Rose, 2014). Moreover, they are focused on one form of corruption, bribery, while in a highly developed economy and long-established democracy such as Sweden it is other forms of corruption that are expected to be relatively common. Michael Johnston (2005) has described the corruption syndrome that characterizes countries like Sweden as 'influence markets'. In those cases corruption is focused around actors dealing in access to and influencing within strong state institutions, making the discussion about conflicts of interest particularly important. In addition, previous research shows that the regulation of conflicts of interest in Sweden and sanctioning of them are relatively weak (Falk, 2015), in particular the possibilities for penal sanctioning of officials who are influenced by conflicts of interest in procurement and when recruiting public officials.

THE ARENA PROJECT IN SOLNA MUNICIPALITY

In 2005, the Swedish Football Association (SFA) decided to build a new national football stadium. The former national stadium, Råsunda, also in Solna, was in need of renovation and there was a wish for a new stadium both on behalf of the SFA and Solna municipality. The then Chairman of the Executive Committee in Solna municipality initiated the political debate on building a new arena. Solna municipality also had a strong interest in cooperating with the SFA on the issue. First, the municipality had had good relations with the SFA for many years and to many local councillors it was of high priority that the city continued to be the host of the stadium. Second, the current stadium Råsunda was also hosting the local football team AIK, which thus was also in need of either a new stadium or a renovation of the current one. It was politically out of the question to build two stadiums. Third, an arena project that included housing and the 'Mall of Scandinavia' had the prospect of a positive impact on Solna municipality for the foreseeable future.

In spring 2006, the Chairman of the Executive Committee, who had initiated the project, died. The political work was inherited by his successor. Overnight the new Chairman of the Executive Committee hence became the highest political actor of the arena project. In December 2007, Solna municipality decided to become a partner in the three companies Arenabolaget i Solna, Swedish Arena Management and Råsta Holding.[4] All three companies were formed to build and promote the new arena project. The decision was controversial and critical voices were raised against the project. As late as two months before the city council was to decide on the project, the Vice Chairman of the Executive Committee (representing the opposition parties) expressed in the Swedish broadsheet daily *Dagens Nyheter* that: 'I get cold sweats when I think about it. It is a huge project and we cannot play venture capitalist with taxpayers' money. Although we really want the national stadium to be located in Solna we must make sure that the investment is safe' (Cato, 2007).

Solna municipality would build the stadium together with the construction company Peab and the SFA. Råsta Holding AB and Arenabolaget were established to implement the project. Earlier in 2007, four key individuals in the project had met during the Swedish Open tennis tournament in Båstad. Afterwards, this meeting was described as critical for all those present despite commencing two years before building the stadium in 2009 (Karlsson, 2012). At the meeting, Peab was represented by its Managing Director and Vice Managing Director responsible for business and project development. The Chairman of the Executive Committee and the Municipal Chief Executive represented Solna municipality. The meeting was informal and had only one item on the agenda. During the planning and projection phase of the arena project the Municipal Chief Executive had simultaneously served as consultant for Råsta Holding AB. The question that came to be discussed was whether the Municipal Chief Executive could continue as a consultant for Råsta Holding AB at the same time as he was salaried by the municipality and involved in the project in his role as Municipal Chief Executive. Thus, the Municipal Chief Executive had a foot in both camps. The weekly paper *Dagens Samhälle* reported that the Municipal Chief Executive had invoiced Råsta Holding from his own consulting company SEK 900 000 in total (ibid.).

A large part of the trial that followed concerned the revelation of the possible sideline occupation of the Municipal Chief Executive. The crucial question was whether he had charged for services that were part of his duties as Municipal Chief Executive of Solna municipality. In total, six persons were prosecuted for bribery when the case was tried by the district court in June 2010. In addition to the four people who had participated in the Båstad meeting in 2007, the Managing Director and the Former Managing Director of Råsta Holding were charged. During the trial, both the Chair of the Executive Committee and the Municipal Chief Executive took time out from their posts. All individuals prosecuted bar the Municipal Chief Executive, who was found guilty of gross bribe-taking, were acquitted. He was given a conditional sentence and 140 day-fines (Kayhan et al., 2012). Except for the verdict of acquittal against Peab's Vice Managing Director the prosecutor appealed all verdicts. In 2013 the Court of Appeal affirmed all judgements. However, the Court of Appeal did not try the verdict against the Municipal Chief Executive of gross bribery as he had died before the verdict. The court though affirmed that the Municipal Chief Executive had improperly received approximately SEK 900 000 in compensation for consulting assignments that he ought to have carried out within the scope of his regular duties. His estate was sentenced to pay the SEK 900 000 to the state (Johansson, 2013).

From the perspective of political entrepreneurship, the arena project case illustrates several democratic problems that may arise as an effect of negative entrepreneurship. There are mainly three problems that can occur when public entities such as municipalities have close cooperation with private entrepreneurs. First, conflicts of interest may arise when public actors and political entrepreneurs have strong ties with private entrepreneurs. A political entrepreneur, who has strong links with other interests in a project, risks unduly favouring these interests in the political decision-making process. Second, the Public Procurement Act might be sidelined if self-interest in the project is decisive. In the case of the arena project, the construction of the stadium was not tendered. As the municipality was only a minority partner in the company responsible for the project, tender was not necessary according to the Public Procurement Act (Svensk författningssamling, 2007). Third, when the municipality (or another public owner) is a minority partner in the company operating the project, transparency and possibilities for access to public records might diminish. Such reduced transparency might be viewed favourably by parties involved for operating a project, but simultaneously impede political accountability. All these three aspects are present in the case of the arena project. Below we discuss each of these three problems.

Conflicts of Interest

The case of the arena project in Solna is just one example of where conflicts of interest may arise in connection with key actors having a foot in several camps simultaneously. The Municipal Chief Executive, the highest officer in the municipality administration and also a political entrepreneur, came to be one of the project's key persons. Without the competence and experience of the Municipal Chief Executive it would have been difficult to execute the project with Solna municipality as one of the partners. We will therefore shed light on the role of this key officer who will exemplify the role of the political entrepreneur.

After the death in 2006 of the previous Chair of the Executive Committee there was a vacuum in the project. In this situation, the political entrepreneur evolves as the expert with a knowledge advantage in relation to the politicians who are deciding. Also, the political entrepreneur had a strong self-interest due to his own economic interests in the project (see more below). The self-interest of the political entrepreneur leads to a clear risk of overshadowing the public interest for which he was supposed to serve. One of the many roles of the Municipal Chief Executive was to serve as a bridge between private interests and public interests in the arena project. To prepare the stadium project for political decisions was one of the most important tasks for which he was responsible.

Public Procurement

The other potentially problematic aspect with respect to effects on democratic processes concerned the structure of the set-up of the arena consortium and its effect on public procurement requirements. A key factor here is the role of Solna municipality as a minority partner in the joint company that was formed. In general, public procurement is required when state administration, local or regional government administration contracts have great economic value.[5] However, when the public party is only a minority shareholder there is no requirement to use the public procurement process for a building contract. In this case there was no interest on behalf of the parties involved to put the contract out for tender to explore available alternatives. This affected the opportunity for control of the economic rationality of the project.

The Public Procurement Act includes so-called threshold values that stipulate when procurement is required. The value of the construction contracts that Peab carried out within the framework of the arena project widely exceeded the EU threshold and should therefore have been awarded via the public procurement process had not the municipality in this case been a minority shareholder in the common project company. It was the entrepreneurial structure that allowed the project company to enter an agreement with Peab without tender. The company had four owners where Solna municipality held 16.7 per cent of the shares. The company set-up, with a public minority owner and private majority ownership, is not unique; there are several other examples with the same company structure.[6] In the case of the arena project the political entrepreneur, the Municipal Chief Executive, was a key figure in efforts to anchor contracts and the company set-up with the municipal executive committee. As the highest officer in the municipal administration, the Municipal Chief Executive had a powerful position and there was strong interest in favour of Peab building the arena (Östlund, 2011).

Public Insight and Control

The third democratic deficit in the arena project refers to the effects on transparency of the company structure used. Transparency is important in democracy and the Freedom of the Press Act regulates the right of public access official records. However, those rules do not apply in cases where the operation has been contracted out to companies where the public sector entity is a minority shareholder. The company set-up in the arena project not only secured Peab's role as building contractor but also protected the project from insight. The non-applicability of the principle of public access to official records in this case had two negative consequences for democracy. First, elected politicians on the council had less access to information and insight in the operations of the project, which reduces the potential for informed decisions. When the economic undertakings are huge, as in this case, there is a greater need for transparency but few had insight into the operations of the project. According to one prominent member of the municipal executive committee, both the assembly and the executive committee were lacking insight into the operations of the project (Bergman, 2010). Second, the lack of transparency and insight hampers the ability of citizens to hold individuals accountable. In the case of the arena project, it was nearly impossible for citizens to get access to information. This also impedes the possibility of debate and discussion. The lack of transparency meant that citizens had difficulties in obtaining information independently from the actors involved in the project. In this respect, the political entrepreneur, the Municipal Chief Executive, again was a key actor. The lack of transparency was a precondition that made it possible for the Municipal Chief Executive to act both as the highest administrative officer of the municipality and via his private consultancy company simultaneously do work for Råsta Holding AB. The conflict of interest present meant that there was a strong vested interest from the Municipal Chief Executive in minimizing transparency and insight into the project. The democratic problem with the lack of transparency is also illustrated by the critical debate that followed upon the revelation of the interest conflict of the Municipal Chief Executive. In the event that the transparency and insight was deliberately hampered it would be close to the problems of corruption that Heywood (1997) is pointing to (above).

CONCLUSIONS

Does entrepreneurship always contribute positively to society? This chapter has demonstrated the relevance of raising this question. Our general conclusion is that changes to the way public administration operates create opportunities for political entrepreneurship, but may also entail risks in terms of negative political entrepreneurship. We discuss negative political entrepreneurship by linking it with research on conflict of interest and corruption and thereby we focus the discussion on aspects that research shows has a particularly negative impact on society.

These risks for negative entrepreneurship are clearly illustrated in the case study of the arena project in Solna municipality. The company set-up in the project where both private and municipal actors participated was an entrepreneurial solution that enabled new structures, solutions that moved boundaries and use of resources while lines of municipal accountability were blurred. Regulations applying to public administration were not applicable, including the principle of public access to official records. The project promised positive economic effects with 3000 new homes in the arena city and 15 000 new jobs. However, concerning the financial side of the project there were early warnings about the stadium's financial viability (*Tidningarnas Telegrambyrå*, 2007). We have established that the absence of a procurement process, the lack of transparency and the existence of conflicts of interest contributed to democratic values vital for public activities being neglected. Negative entrepreneurship is here illustrated in an extreme form: through corrupt acts that were directly illegal. The case study also illustrates a major risk with project set-ups that reduce insight and access to information that is vital for the ability of the local community to assess operations and accountability. Would the project have been possible in another form, where those barriers had not existed? It is of course impossible to answer this question, but what we can say is that one of the most important requirements that should be put on these types of projects is not to deliberately impede access to information and possibilities for upholding accountability. Instead, to safeguard these aspects of vital importance for democratic control and to avoid the corruption of decision-making processes should be high priorities.

We can thus conclude that political entrepreneurship is not always only positive and it is therefore important that research also takes into account questions about negative entrepreneurship. Finally, although entrepreneurship is characterized by its ability to stretch boundaries and create new resources, it should also go hand in hand with the democratic demands of society in order to avoid negative entrepreneurship as much as possible, not least in terms of conflict of interest and corruption.

NOTES

1. Actors seek revenue by influencing the economic and legal conditions for an activity, such as getting politicians to introduce restrictive rules (e.g., various trade barriers) on competition, rather than by creating value through production or trade.
2. Economic crises in Sweden and abroad from 1970 and onwards led to the public sector often being described as in need of change and more efficient operation (Gustafsson and Svensson, 1999; SOU, 2001).
3. By identifying and describing current rules affecting the distribution of entrepreneurial activities and modifying and improving these rules, society can influence how entrepreneurship is distributed (Baumol, 1990, pp. 3–4).

4. Other partners in the arena project were Peab, Fabege, the SFA and the landowner Jernhusen.
5. Public procurement is defined by the Swedish Competition Authority (Konkurrensverket, 2011) as measures taken by a contracting authority with the aim of awarding a contract or concluding a framework agreement regarding products, services or public works.
6. Other examples of high-profile cases can be found in the municipality of Falun (Kärrman, 2015), Borlänge (Konkurrenskommissionen, 2014) and Södertälje (Östlund, 2011).

REFERENCES

Andersson, S. (1999), *Hederlighetens pris. En ESO-rapport om corruption* [Price of Honesty. An ESP Report on Corruption] (Ds 1999:62), Stockholm: Finansdepartementet.

Andersson, S. and F. Anechiarico (2015), 'The political economy of conflicts of interest in an era of public private governance', in P.M. Heywood (ed.), *The Routledge Handbook of Political Corruption*, Abingdon, UK: Routledge.

Andersson, S. and G.Ó. Erlingsson (2012), 'New public management and risks of corruption', in D. Tänzler, K. Maras and A. Giannakopoulos (eds), *The Social Construction of Corruption in Europe*, Farnham, UK: Ashgate.

Andvig, J.C. (2002), 'Globalisation, global and international corruption – any links?', *The Globalisation Project, Report No. 6*, Oslo: The Norwegian Ministry of Foreign Affairs.

Andvig, J.C. (2005), '"A house of straw, sticks or bricks"? Some notes on corruption', *NUPI Working Paper No. 678*, accessed 15 May 2016 at http:// www.isn.ethz.ch/Digital-Library/Publications/Detail/?id=27335&lng=en.

Andvig, J.C. and K.O. Moene (1990), *How Corruption May Corrupt*, Oslo: University of Oslo, Department of Economics, reprint series.

Anechiarico, F. and J.B. Jacobs (1996), *The Pursuit of Absolute Integrity: How Corruption Control Makes Government Ineffective*, Chicago, IL: The University of Chicago Press.

Baumol, W.J. (1990), 'Entrepreneurship: productive, unproductive, and destructive', *Journal of Business Venturing*, **98**(5), 641–55.

Bergh, A., G. Erlingsson, M. Sjölin and R. Öhrvall (2013), *Allmän nytta eller egen vinning? – en ESO-rapport om korruption på svenska* [Public Benefit or Advantage? An ESO Report on Swedish Corruption], Stockholm: Regeringskansliet.

Bergman, L. (2010), 'Fuskbygget' [Jerry-building], *Fokus*, No. 40.

Bergman, M. (2008), *Offentlig upphandling och offentliga inköp: omfattning och sammansättning* [Public Procurement and Public Purchase: Scope and Composition], report. Stockholm: Konkurrensverket.

Cato, C. (2007), 'Jättearena blir nav i Solnas nya stadsdel' [Giant arena is the hub of Solna's new neighbourhood], *Dagens Nyheter*, 8 October.

Charron, N., V. Lapuente and B. Rothstein (2013), *Quality of Government and Corruption from a European Perspective: A Comparative Study of Good Government in EU Regions*, Cheltenham, UK and Northampton, MA, USA: Edward Elgar Publishing.

Christensen, T., P. Laegreid, P.G. Roness and K.A. Røvik (2005), *Organisation-steori för offentlig sector* [Organization Theory for the Public Sector], Malmö: Liber.

Erlingsson, G.Ó. (2006), 'Organisationsförändringar och ökad kommunal korruption' [Organizational changes and increased municipal corruption], *Kommunal ekonomi och politik*, **3**(1), 7–36.

Erlingsson, G.Ó., A. Bergh and M. Sjölin (2008), 'Public corruption in Swedish municipalities: trouble looming on the horizon?', *Local Government Studies*, **34**(5), 595–608.

Falk, A.-M. (2015), 'Offentligt maktmissbruk: problematik, regelverk, prevention' [Public abuse of power: problems, regulations, prevention], Master's dissertation, Örebro University.

Foss, K., N.J. Foss and P.G. Klein (2007), 'Original and derived judgment: an entrepreneurial theory of economic organization', *Organization Studies*, **28**(12), 1893–912.

Getman, K. and P.S. Karlan (2008), 'Pluralists and republicans, rules and standards', in C. Trost and A.L. Gash (eds), *Conflicts of Interest and Public Life: Cross-national Perspectives*, Cambridge, UK: Cambridge University Press.

Gustafsson, L. and A. Svensson (1999), *Public Sector Reform in Sweden*, Malmö: Liber Ekonomi.

Hansson, L. (2011), 'Negativt entreprenörskap – fallet upphandling' [Negative entrepreneurship – the case of procurement], in M. von Bergmann-Winberg and E. Wihlborg (eds), *Politikens entreprenörskap – kreativ problemlösning och förändring*, Malmö: Liber.

Heywood, P. (1997), 'Political corruption: problems and perspectives', *Political Studies*, **45**(3), 417–35.

Heywood, P.M. and J. Rose (2014), '"Close but no cigar": the measurement of corruption', *Journal of Public Policy*, **34**(3), 507–29.

Johansson, P. (2013), 'Solna stadsdirektör tog mutor vid arenabygget' [Solna mayor took bribes in the arena construction], *Sveriges Radio*, 29 October.

Johnston, M. (2005), *Syndromes of Corruption: Wealth, Power, and Democracy*, Cambridge, UK: Cambridge University Press.

Karlsson, K. (2012), 'Muthärvan började med ett handslag på tennisveckan i Båstad' [Bribes started with a handshake at a tennis tournament in Båstad], *Expressen*, 26 October.

Kärrman, J. (2015). 'Bröt mot lagen vid VMbygge i Falun' [Broke the law at the World Championship-Construction in Falun], *Dagens Nyheter*, 19 January.

Kayhan, B., M. Randberg and M. Persbo (2012), 'Utgår ifrån att Reinhold vill ha det prövat' [Assume that Reinhold wants it tested], *Sveriges Radio*, 11 May.

Kjellberg, F. (1995), 'Conflict of interest, corruption or (simply) scandals? The Oslo case 1989–91', *Crime, Law and Social Change*, **22**(4), 339–60.

Kommunallag [The Swedish Local Government Act] (1991:900).

Konkurrenskommissionen [Competition Commission] (2014: 14-002), *PM 2, slutlig bedömning* [The Final Evaluation], 6 March.

Konkurrensverket [Swedish Competition Authority] (2011), *Swedish Public Procurement Act*, accessed 10 September 2015 at http://www.konkurrensverket.se/globalassets/english/publications-and-decisions/swedish-public-procurement-act.pdf

Lawton, A., J. Rayner and K. Lasthuizen (2013), *Ethics and Management in the Public Sector*, London: Routledge.

Lessig, L. (2013), 'Institutional corruptions', *Edmund J Safra Working Papers No. 1*, accessed 14 May 2016 at http://ssrn.com/abstract=2233582.

Linde, J. and G.Ó. Erlingsson (2012), 'The eroding effect of corruption on system support in Sweden', *Governance*, **26**(4), 585–603.

Mauro, P. (1995), 'Corruption and growth', *Quarterly Journal of Economics*, **110**(3), 681–712.

Nählinder, J. (2011), 'Entreprenörskap – mer än bara "bara" entreprenören' [Entrepreneurship – more than 'just' the entrepreneur], in M. von Bergmann-Winberg and E. Wihlborg (eds), *Politikens entreprenörskap – kreativ problemlösning och förändring*, Malmö: Liber.

O'Brien, J. (2003), 'Conflicts of interest on Wall Street: corrupted actors or system?', paper presented at the 11th IACC, Seoul, 25–28 May.

Organisation for Economic Co-operation and Development (OECD) (2005), *Managing Conflict of Interest in the Public Sector: A Toolkit*, Paris: OECD.

Organisation for Economic Co-operation and Development (OECD) (2009), *Government at a Glance*, Paris: OECD.

Östlund, A. (2011), 'Peabs fulknep slår ut konkurrensen' [Peab's wrong-doing knocks out competition], *Svenska Dagbladet*, 20 March.

Pollit, C. and G. Bouckaert (2004), *Public Management Reform: A Comparative Analysis*, Oxford: Oxford University Press.

Rothstein, B. (2011), *The Quality of Government: Corruption, Social Trust and Inequality in International Perspective*, Chicago, IL: University of Chicago Press.

Rothstein, B. and E. Uslaner (2005), 'All for all: equality, corruption, and social trust', *World Politics*, **58**(1), 41–73.

Sheingate, A.D. (2003),'Political entrepreneurship, institutional change, and American political development', *Studies in American Political Development*, **17**(2), 185–203.

Sjöstrand, G. (ed.) (2005), *Fiffelsverige: sociologiska perspektiv på skandaler och fusk* [Tamper-Sweden: Sociological Perspectives on Scandals and Cheating], Malmö: Liber.

Sjöstrand, G. (2008), 'Gåvan i Gnosjö: företagares relationer i ett industriellt distrikt' [The gift in Gnosjö: entepreneurs' relationships in an industrial district], doctoral thesis, Göteborg: Göteborgs University.

Sjöstrand, G. (2010), 'Entreprenörskap: om informell kontroll i lokalt näringsliv' [Entrepreneurship – informal control in local business], in B. Larsson and O. Engdahl (eds), *Social kontroll – övervakning, disciplinering och självreglering*, Malmö: Liber.

Sobel, R.S., N. Dutta and S. Roy (2010), 'Does cultural diversity increase the rate of entrepreneurship?', *The Review of Austrian Economics*, **23**(3), 269–86.

Statens offentliga utredningar (SOU) [Swedish Government Official Reports] (2001), *God ekonomisk hushållning i kommuner och landsting* [Good Financial Management in Municipalities and Counties], Report No. 2001:76, Stockholm: Finansdepartementet.

Svensk författningssamling (SFS) [Swedish Code of Statutes] (2007), *Lagen om Offentlig Upphandling* [Public Procurement Act], 2007:1091, Stockholm: Justitiedepartementet.

Thompson, D.F. (1995), *Ethics in Congress: From Individual to Institutional Corruption*, Washington, DC: Brookings Institution.

Tidningarnas Telegrambyrå (2007), 'Kritik mot nya nationalarenan' [Criticism of the new national stadium], 14 December.

Tillmar, M. (2011), 'Företag, offentliga marknader och det politiska entreprenörskapet' [Businesses, public markets and political entrepreneurship], in M. von Bergmann-Winberg and E. Wihlborg (eds), *Politikens entreprenörskap – kreativ problemlösning och förändring*, Malmö: Liber.

Tirole, J. (1996), 'A theory of collective reputations (with applications to the persistence of corruption and to firm quality)', *Review of Economic Studies*, **63**(1), 1–22.

Tryckfrihetsförordning [The Freedom of the Press Act] (1949:105).

Wihlborg, E. (2011a), 'Ansvariga entreprenörer? Ansvarsutkrävande i governancesammanhang' [Responsible entrepreneurs? The accountability of governance context], in M. von Bergmann-Winberg and E. Wihlborg (eds), *Politikens entreprenörskap – kreativ problemlösning och förändring*, Malmö: Liber.

Wihlborg, E. (2011b), 'Entreprenörer på plats i policy och politik' [Entrepreneur on stage in policy and politics], in M. von Bergmann-Winberg and E. Wihlborg (eds), *Politikens entreprenörskap – kreativ problemlösning och förändring*, Malmö: Liber.

PART II

Political entrepreneurship and regional growth

4. Political entrepreneurship, industrial policy and regional growth

Charlie Karlsson

In recent years and not least after the latest financial and economic crisis, we have seen a strongly renewed interest in industrial policy to help developed economies to grow again. Politicians and their experts and advisers have been hunting desperately for new approaches to industrial policy and have increasingly started to act as political entrepreneurs. With regard to political entrepreneurs, we understand them here as politicians/bureaucrats/civil servants/authorities within publicly financed activities who with different methods try to stimulate entrepreneurship and self-employment with the overall goal to increase employment and economic growth. The renewed interest in industrial policy and the increased importance of political entrepreneurs motivate us to ask some fundamental questions once again: What should be the proper focus, measures and extent of industrial policy? Should industrial policy be vertical and focus on specific industries and even specific companies or should it be horizontal and focus on improving the general conditions for all industries and firms? However, there is a related and partly more controversial question, namely, what is the proper spatial scale for policy interventions by political entrepreneurs? Should industrial policy focus on certain places and possibly focus on existing and/or emerging industrial clusters or should it be spatially neutral and not try to discriminate between different regions and places?

The purpose of this chapter is to throw some light on the above questions but with some extra focus on the questions concerning spatial aspects. The above questions are by no means new, but there are very good reasons to throw new light on them, not least against the background of the European Union's (EU) new industrial and regional policy that aims at achieving 'smart specialization'. The next section is devoted to a theoretical discussion of horizontal and vertical industrial policy, but from a spatial perspective. The subsections are devoted to two waves of

cluster policy. The third section discusses the EU's new 'smart specialization policy'. In the fourth section we present some reflections concerning spatial industrial policies and the fifth section concludes.

HORIZONTAL AND VERTICAL INDUSTRIAL POLICY FROM A SPATIAL PERSPECTIVE

There are a number of different factors behind the renewed interest in
industrial policy, such as globalization and its effects (Karlsson et al.,
2010), the climate threat, the need for new infrastructures, new energy
sources and new products to counter environmental problems, the current
economic crisis in the wake of the global financial crisis and a more
general search for new growth mechanisms. However, we must also
acknowledge that there has been a re-evaluation of the results achieved
with earlier experiments with industrial policies (Aghion, 2012). In
addition, political entrepreneurs want to show the citizen/tax payer that
they actually do something concrete to deal with current issues and
problems and this is particularly important for politicians in power in
governments at different levels who are always striving to be re-elected.

With regard to the broader debate, which also includes spatial aspects,
it is obvious that the increased interest in industrial policy has been
driven by an increased interest in clusters (Karlsson et al., 2006;
Karlsson, 2008a) and for place-specific industrial policy that reflects a
mixture of global and country-specific factors (Karlsson et al., 2012b). In
particular, in many countries we can observe an increased interest in the
role of cities and urban regions and in the importance of agglomeration
economies (Glaeser, 2011). This increased interest has been driven partly
by rapid urbanization in many countries and partly by increased aware-
ness that cities and urban regions are central engines in economic
development and growth in countries where the service sector is the
dominating sector in the economy. Today there are numerous examples of
industrial cities that in the 1970s and 1980s were hit by deindustrializa-
tion, but that in recent decades have been able to restructure and renew
their economies and return to a growth path.

A main point in this chapter is the very large interest in industrial
policy in the form of cluster policy among political entrepreneurs. This
interest involves two paradoxes. First, it is certainly true that there are
good theoretical foundations and extensive empirical support for the
theory that co-location, that is, clustering and agglomeration, plays an
important role when it comes to understanding the economic outcome for
companies and cities (Karlsson, Kobayashi and Stough, 2014). However,

to go from these general observations to specific concrete policy recommendations that industrial policy should take the form of cluster policy is to rely on theoretical frameworks that are very vague in terms of both providing analytical instruments and of developing specific policy recommendations (Karlsson, 2008b). Of course, this would mean nothing if there was a broad and deep empirical basis that showed which cluster policy interventions are efficient for different types of clusters, but there is no such empirical basis. This leads to the second paradox, namely that industrial policy in the form of cluster policy generally seems to exhibit severe problems, to be inefficient and to never have been accepted in the academic regional science literature. Despite this, it is obvious that cluster policy is very popular among political entrepreneurs.

The second paradox is easy to understand per se, namely that 'cluster' is a very strong brand name even if cluster thinking often leads to an inefficient industrial policy (Martin and Sunley, 2003). The regional science literature contains an extensive discussion and critique of cluster policy as industrial policy, but despite this, new waves of ideas about cluster and cluster policy have emerged over time both in the research literature and among consultants and policy-makers with the introduction of new creative concepts. Certainly, each new wave introduces new concepts, but the analyses are as untrustworthy as in earlier waves. However, this does not imply that one should disregard spatial aspects and regional dimensions in industrial policy. It only implies that industrial policy should focus on other spatial factors as well as clusters. Political entrepreneurs must devote much more attention to the question of the suitable spatial scale for horizontal industrial policy. What can the political entrepreneurs do to make cities and urban regions function better in a way that makes it easier to start new companies and for existing companies to grow? In other words, how can industrial policy make agglomerations function better? Horizontal industrial policy can partly achieve its goals more efficiently by not only focusing on specific cities and urban regions, but also by allowing important parts of industrial policy to be implemented by political entrepreneurs at lower administrative levels.

The theoretical debate about the proper focus for industrial policy has traditionally moved in circles around the question of whether it should be vertical or horizontal. A vertical industrial policy implies that political entrepreneurs try to stimulate and/or direct resources to specific sectors or even companies that the political entrepreneurs believe are important for economic growth. The ambition is to find 'the winners' despite the fact that historically, political entrepreneurs generally have not been successful in their hunt for winners (Owen, 2012). In contrast, does the horizontal approach to industrial policy stress how important it is that political entrepreneurs should be 'neutral', that is, that they should focus on industrial policy interventions that promote all (many) industries and all (many) companies, such as investments in higher education, R&D and infrastructure?

A problem with the horizontal definition of industrial policy is that it risks becoming very wide and including everything from macroeconomic policy to infrastructure policy, education policy, R&D policy, policy to reduce the administrative burden of companies, and so on. To be able to discuss the spatial aspects of industrial policy we limit the discussion here to policy interventions that have as a direct objective to increase productivity and/or employment, such as, for example, innovation policy, and policy whose aim is to support entrepreneurship and self-employment.

Endogenous growth theory, whose development started in the 1980s, gives economists the fundamental conceptual basis needed to structure theoretical thinking around industrial policy that aims at stimulating innovations, productivity and/or employment (Johansson et al., 2001). In addition, theories about national and regional innovation systems and Schumpeterian entrepreneurship models contribute to the conceptual basis for discussing industrial policy (Weiss, 2011; Karlsson et al., 2013). General theories around innovation and productivity and employment growth provide a good general foundation for discussing industrial policy and guidelines for political entrepreneurs. However, in this chapter we focus mainly on theories that can structure the thinking around the spatial aspects of industrial policy.

Theories in urban economics provide central models for how to think about and analyse the spatial structure of an economy as well as how this structure evolves over time (Overman and Leunig, 2008; Klaesson et al., 2013). According to these theories, the spatial concentration of economic activities generates agglomeration economies that help both employees and companies to become more productive. These agglomeration economies generate location advantages in the form of a critical mass of companies, employees and infrastructures as well as dense networks of suppliers, cooperation partners and customers. Larger cities and urban regions also facilitate the generation and flow of ideas, information and knowledge so that employees and companies can learn from each other (Karlsson et al., 2012b). Naturally, some of these advantages are balanced by higher land prices, rents and wages as well as increased congestion and environmental degradation when the economic activities are concentrated spatially. However, it seems obvious that the agglomeration benefits more than balance the agglomeration costs since cities and urban regions continue to grow. If the agglomeration costs were larger than the agglomeration benefits then companies and households would not choose to locate to cities and urban regions. It is of course possible in principle that when cities and urban regions grow that the agglomeration costs will become higher than the agglomeration benefits and that households and companies would choose to move to other locations. Since the agglomeration benefits and the agglomeration costs vary for different kinds of companies, economic activities and households it is natural that we get a structure with cities and urban regions of varying sizes. Another very important factor is those political regulations that control the use of land in different cities and urban regions. Unfortunately, many political entrepreneurs do not understand the negative effects of many of the current land use controls (Cheshire et al., 2014).

The central role of agglomeration economies has generated an extensive regional science literature that tries to understand their basic character, mechanisms and effects. A central question concerns whether these economies emerge through a concentration of similar or dissimilar economic activities. In the first case, we talk about location economies that stimulate co-location, that is, clustering, of similar activities and thus a specialization of the actual cities. In the second case the literature uses the concept of urbanization economies that relate to the advantages that emerge from a concentration of diversified economic activities and thus from diversified cities. Of course, in reality the economies do appear in all types of cities but to a varying degree.

The above discussion is mainly static with regard to conclusions concerning the relative size and the structural composition of different cities and urban regions at different points in time. From an industrial policy point of view it is fundamental to understand the underlying dynamic processes, that is, which factors can explain the growth (and decline) and structural changes of the economies of cities and urban regions.

The theoretical research in the field of urban economics concerning the dynamics behind the growth (and decline) and structural changes of the economies of cities and urban regions is still at an early stage, which implies that we must turn to other theoretical contributions to understand the underlying dynamics (Henderson and Venables, 2009). In the early 1990s, the American economist Paul Krugman introduced a new approach to analysing the economic development of regions – the so-called New Economic Geography (NEG) (Karlsson et al., 2006). The NEG models give new insights, particularly concerning the importance of

lowered transport costs, into understanding the changing spatial structures of economies. The fundamental insight in the NEG models is that
the combination of increasing returns to scale at the company level,
monopolistic competition and lowered transport costs for goods creates a
home market effect where companies *ceteris paribus* prefer to locate in
regions with a large market, that is, a large purchasing power. NEG
models do provide a consistent microeconomic foundation for the kind of
agglomeration economies that earlier were assumed only to exist in
models in urban economics. As in urban economics, these agglomeration
economies and in particular, the links between suppliers and customers,
lead to a clustering of mutually related activities (Krugman and Venables,
1995). At the same time, it is obvious that congestion, negative environmental effects and competition for land, labour and customers lead to a
tendency for dispersion of economic activities (Polenske, 2006). In
summary, it is the balance between centrifugal and centripetal forces that
determines the location of companies and households. Changes in
transport costs change the balance between these two forces and thus
change the overall spatial structure of economies.

Later contributions to NEG research have stressed that clustering
processes are characterized by feedback mechanisms, which implies that
existing agglomerations have a first-mover advantage. At the same time,
we can observe that technological advances and sectorial differences lead
to a reallocation of activities from high-cost to low-cost locations by
means of, for example, outsourcing activities and tasks. Many of today's
very complex production chains demand very careful coordination, which
often implies high search, transaction and management costs, which
implies that the location of management functions to large urban regions
is connected with substantial time and cost advantages.

What conclusions can we then draw from the above discussion about
the suitable spatial scale for industrial policy? A fundamental conclusion
is that differences between locations as well as national and regional
institutions tend to be enduring over time, which raises the question
about the ability of the political entrepreneurs to balance national as well
as regional economies over time. One further conclusion is that regional
economies are very complex with important and fundamental differences
between sectors, industries, functions and actors, which themselves
develop and change over time and furthermore are subject to unpredict-
able shocks. Clusters, cities and urban regions are often compared with
biological systems, since their development to a great extent is the result
of the self-organizing behaviour among companies and households. This

complexity implies for our political entrepreneurs that policy interventions at different levels of the economic system can generate quite unexpected results.

We continue now with the question of what cluster theory and empirical cluster studies can contribute to the discussion above. Here cluster theory means theories that have explicitly tried to explain cluster formation and the development of spatially concentrated groups of companies within one industry or a small number of related industries. We start with discussing Porter's cluster theory and continue with a more modern type of cluster theory.

Porter's Cluster Theory and Industrial Policy

The heart of Porter's cluster theory is his diamond-shaped economic model (Figure 4.1) developed in his book *The Competitive Advantage of Nations* (1990), which he claims identifies the sources of competitiveness in terms of demand conditions, production factor conditions, the degree of local competition between the companies, the presence of related and supporting companies and industries, government policy and chance events, all interacting with each other. Originally his theory was developed for countries but later it was applied to industrial clusters, since Porter claimed that the forces of the diamond were stronger when economic activities were spatially concentrated. According to Porter, clusters can emerge for historical as well as geographical reasons. To Porter, their role when it comes to creating competitiveness is obvious, since he claims that clusters drive economic development. They do that by improving the microeconomic business climate, which then helps to improve productivity, the ability to innovate and new firm formation and entrepreneurship (Porter, 1990, 2000; Karlsson, Johansson and Stough et al., 2014).

The application of the diamond model on clusters is very complex since it contains many elements, which all have a positive influence on each other. It is easy to understand that it is precisely the presence of positive feedback mechanisms that makes the model so attractive for the political entrepreneurs. To strengthen these positive feedback mechanisms is by itself positive and a motive for an active industrial policy in the form of cluster policies and for a long stream of innovative cluster development measures. Porter claims in fact that the national economic development policy should focus on clusters and abstain from vertical industrial policy that risks being kidnapped by narrow sector and industry interests. Porter thinks that the strategy that he recommends should be based on an identification and upgrading of existing clusters, which

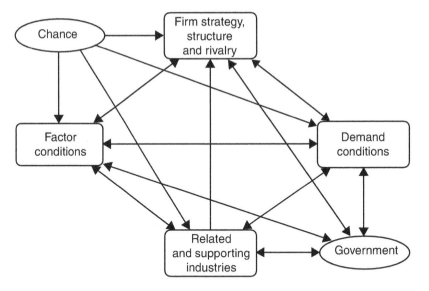

Source: Developed from Porter (1990).

Figure 4.1   Michael Porter's diamond model

involves a recognition that clusters exist and an elimination of hindrances and limitations for cluster development and an elimination of those inefficiencies that retard productivity growth and innovation.

Some of the policy measures suggested, such as improved contacts between companies and regional universities and improved intra- and inter-regional infrastructures, are quite reasonable. Other suggestions for policy efforts stand out as very speculative, such as, for example, free trade zones, export-promoting measures and the involvement of public authorities in clusters. Porter even stresses the importance of local measures for clusters to promote industries with high-value exports by, for example, developing the local market.

Even if Porter's cluster theory is very popular among political entre-preneurs, most regional scientists are sceptical and even outright negative to his theory (Duranton, 2011). The first and well-documented problem concerns the definition of a cluster. What actually is a cluster? The literature is rather vague at this point and Porter is very vague too. According to him, the determination of the borders of a cluster is a question of judgement that involves a creative process! Even if it is possible to create a reasonable definition, a number of difficult problems remain. The basic problem is that a well-developed theory is missing that highlights what problems the cluster policy is trying to solve. A common answer to the question of which role cluster policy should play is that it aims at improving local competitiveness or productivity. The problem with this answer is that it does not clearly specify the source of different possible inefficiencies and has consequently no answer to how they can be corrected. Porter's model can look complex, but the complexity is superficial since all elements influence each other positively through feedback mechanisms.

In reality, we also have to take into account negative feedback mechanisms of the kind that occur in the urban economics and NEG models. If one, for example, lowers the entry barriers in one industry, this may have the effect that some incumbent companies become more innovative, while others may choose to exit the market or to relocate. The total effect may be an increased number of innovations, but the net employment effects are unclear. This is of importance for the political entrepreneurs who are engaged in trying to increase the number of jobs available and the number of employed and who are interested in how the incumbent firms are doing.

A third problem with Porter's diamond model is that despite its complexity it disregards a number of fundamental economic driving forces. What is assumed, for example, concerning the mobility of households and firms? If the companies are mobile, but not the employees, how can one then be sure that encouraging large clusters in certain locations is a good idea? In addition, what is assumed concerning the market for land? In fact, there is a substantial risk that increased size of a cluster will only lead to increased incomes for landowners. The models that are developed within urban economics show that the answers to these questions are of fundamental importance when it comes to understanding how the spatial economy functions and to judge if there is any need for cluster policy measures. Interestingly enough the Porter model gives no answers to these issues.

Finally, even if there are positive feedbacks between the different factors in the Porter model, this does not imply by itself that there is a motivation for cluster policy interventions. Such a motivation must build upon a careful identification of the reasons why the market forces neglect these positive feedbacks and thus generate an inefficient result. This implies that there is a need for the political entrepreneurs to analyse the prevailing market failures and design a cluster policy that focuses these failures in a relevant way. However, we must observe here the presence of a multitude of different market failures, which makes it very difficult to know which cluster policies to introduce and how to design and implement them. Those political entrepreneurs that implement cluster policies based upon the Porter model ignore this fundamental problem and thus have no firm basis for the cluster policies they implement.

There are two other related problems for those political entrepreneurs that try to pursue cluster policies based upon Porter's diamond. First, the stress of local or regional cluster policy interventions encourages policy measures that are easy to implement but such a policy orientation risks missing the more urgent challenges that the actual companies are facing. Second, Porter is totally silent on how the policy measures he suggests should be delivered, including at what level in the political system the policy measures should be implemented. Given the conceptual, measurement and managerial problems that Porter's cluster model involves, there are substantial risks that emerge with competing cluster policy initiatives, coordination problems and so on.

These conceptual problems would not play any role if the political entrepreneurs that advocate cluster policies could point to unambiguous empirical proofs that all feedbacks are positive, something that could function as a foundation for cluster policies. Unfortunately, this is not the case since Porter's cluster concepts are so vague and so difficult to measure that they have been the subject of very few solid empirical studies. Even this would be of lesser importance if proofs existed that carefully designed cluster policies had distinct treatment effects in terms of the size of clusters, the innovativeness of clusters and/or the competitiveness of clusters. Unfortunately, we have very little such empirical evidences (Kline and Moretti, 2012). On the contrary, the available empirical evidence indicates that the policy initiatives by the policy entrepreneurs are the least important initiatives when it comes to developing the competitiveness of clusters and the positive effects that have been found are small in relation to the costs. Attempts by political entrepreneurs to start clusters from scratch have generated even worse results.

Dynamic Cluster Models and Industrial Policy

Dissatisfaction with the simple Porter-type static cluster models has encouraged researchers to develop richer cluster models that focus on the dynamics of clusters. The foundation for the development of these cluster models has been the research on regional innovation systems and evolutionary economic geography. The thinking around regional innovation systems has developed based upon the research on national innovation systems (Karlsson et al., 2009a). A national innovation system is made up of organizations in the public and the private sectors, whose activities and interaction initiate, import, modify, diffuse and implement new technologies (Karlsson, Johansson and Norman, 2012). It also involves social networks and relations, R&D and education infrastructures, communication and transport infrastructures and the national institutional framework with those norms and rules that govern economic and social interaction. The approach with regional innovation systems adapts this conceptual framework to regions and to clusters. The basic question is that, given the existence of agglomeration economies, can local and regional institutions, framework conditions and industrial policies effectively influence the capabilities of companies in different respects? Five aspects govern the outcome at the local or regional level: geographical space, organizations, industrial policy and technologies but also local or regional interdependencies that govern the behaviour of local or regional economic agents.

Given the stress of institutions and interactions, it is natural that empirical analyses of regional innovation make substantial efforts to describe key agents in a cluster and their relations are seen as the connections that govern the development of the actual cluster. These key agents include universities, public authorities, networks and existing local or regional institutions (rules and norms, etc.). In addition to this, it is given that national institutions, national competitiveness and sector specificities create the basic conditions for how a cluster functions.

The research field of evolutionary economic geography has developed from quite different foundations, such as evolutionary economics and the thinking on the development of cities. The theoretical framework for evolutionary economic geography uses concepts and metaphors that to a great extent have been borrowed from biological sciences. Even if the research by no means only focuses on clusters, it is obvious that there has been a strong theoretical and empirical stress on attempts to understand how geographical clusters of related activities emerge and develop (Boschma and Frenken, 2011).

A central question in this research stream has been how the actual and/or historical economic structure of cities and regions influence their future development trajectories. Often this starts with the observation that the economic diversity in (larger) cities both protects cities from external shocks and facilitates knowledge diffusion both within and between industries. Over time, these knowledge flows allow entrepreneurs, incumbent companies and other economic agents to combine existing ideas, knowledge, goods and services with new types of goods and services (Karlsson et al., 2009b). However, it is not clear what mixes of related activities generate dynamic effects and which mixes give the best protection from external shocks. In this literature, the authors make a distinction between related variety within industries that is associated with location economies and unrelated variety that is associated with urbanization economies (Frenken et al., 2007).

Another key discussion in the literature on evolutionary economic geography concerns the character of cluster development. Evolutionary geographers claim that dynamic causality and path dependence are central concepts for understanding the spatial structure of an economy and the development of this structure over time. However, there is no agreement concerning the best model. Linear models for path dependence imply that clusters, cities and regions are placed on a specific development trajectory by random events, which can be broken only by external shocks. A more open approach allows a role for spatial factors concerning new firm formation, support systems and selection among economic agents that can give rise to new development trajectories. When this approach is applied to clusters, it is at odds with the dominating life cycle approach for clusters and in line with a model that treats clusters as complex adaptive systems that can develop a number of different development trajectories.

The dynamic cluster models stress the tensions between positive and negative feedback and include explicit dynamic relations. They provide a substantially richer conceptual and descriptive framework than the Porter-type cluster models. The literature on regional innovation systems stresses the internal advantages of a cluster as a socioeconomic system but also points to the potential disadvantages, such as the risk of lock-in effects because of the companies' exaggerated dependence on local networks and ideas. The researchers in evolutionary economic geography claim that a number of different growth and decline trajectories for clusters exist where the interaction between the different parts of the cluster system generates positive, negative or uncertain outcomes.

However, it is important to observe that since much of the literature on evolutionary economic geography treats places as central actors in the spatial economic system or uses metaphors, the theoretic framework gives very little guidance on what factors actually determine what results these different concurrent and counteracting forces create. The reliance on metaphors and analogies at a high level of abstraction functions as another barrier for clearly understanding microeconomic mechanisms, the direction of the causalities and actual feedback mechanisms. This leads to clear limitations concerning what it is possible to get out of empirical studies. There is a frustrating contrast between the very rich descriptive literature on regional innovation systems and models of evolutionary economic geography and the very few and limited empirical studies on how the different system components influence each other. Very few theoretical and empirical studies deal with the microeconomic channels that are involved (Storper, 2011). This implies that the dynamic cluster models are also very difficult to use for generating ideas for the political entrepreneurs about suitable policy interventions. In the limited share of the literature in evolutionary economic geography that stresses companies, employment and households as the fundamental economic actors, we meet the problem that the strong dynamic complexity implies that one is forced to use very simple models for individual behaviour. This makes it very difficult to understand the effects of policy interventions, since these effects depend upon how the economic actors react.

Another and related effect is that due to the focus on geographical places instead of a focus on companies and households, the actual dynamic cluster models tend to focus on geographically demarcated immobile objects and structures instead of the relatively spatially mobile economic agents that make up a cluster. The models within urban economics stress that at the same time as there are strong forces that create and support clusters there are also forces that drive dispersion, which implies that a cluster, that is, a concentration of companies and households, can dissolve over time due to closures of companies and the relocation of companies and households.

Because of their focus on specific clusters rather than their actors, we can say that the dynamic cluster models that have been discussed in this section are mainly silent concerning the underlying fundamental dynamics. In summary, this implies that the political entrepreneurs have very little to get from the literature that has been discussed in this section when it comes to the issue of how a spatial industrial policy should be designed and implemented.

SMART SPECIALIZATION AS INDUSTRIAL POLICY

EU's new smart specialization policy is an obvious example of how the more modern cluster literature has had a strong influence on a central industrial policy initiative, but it is not possible to describe this policy initiative in detail here. Today, there is an extensive literature that describes how EU's smart specialization policy has been developed, and the elements and procedures it contains (McCann and Ortega-Argilés, 2013). All regions within the EU that want to make use of EU structural funds must have a smart specialization strategy in place. We can describe this policy initiative as a sectorial spatial industrial policy that does not need to include any cluster elements.

Without going into details, we can say that a smart specialization strategy must include an integrated place-based transformation agenda, which is characterized by each region building on its own strengths, its own capacities and its own historical specialization (Foray et al., 2012). There are strong reasons to question the assumption that the same model suits all regions with development problems without consideration of the actual situation, including the competitive situation, historical development and prevailing regional institutions. There is a substantial risk that structural funds resources will be channelled to education, infrastructure, R&D, and so on, in industries with fewer prospects exactly because these are the industries that currently represent the specialization of the region. Regions under strong international competition from low-cost producers may need, for example, to find a new basis for their specialization.

Interestingly, cluster policy is suggested as a central component in the practical strategy development. The suggested policy design builds upon a Schumpeterian framework, ideas from the literature on regional innovation systems and evolutionary economic geography. Cities and regions develop through an entrepreneurial discovery process, which implies that cities and regions have to identify their own comparative advantages. Naturally, the urban and regional context is important for the evolution of the urban and regional systems. This is particularly true for the position that entrepreneurs have and for how the links function between the private and the public sectors as well as between universities and companies. Political entrepreneurs in cities and regions need to exploit potential positive agglomeration economies but also have a capacity to deal with the negative agglomeration effects in 'overheated' cities and regions. At the same time, political entrepreneurs must be able to widen the urban or regional industrial structure to include a larger number of related industries, technologies and knowledge bases.

Entrepreneurial search processes are characterized by an inherent uncertainty. This has important implications for what industrial policies the political entrepreneurs should and can deliver, and how they should be implemented and governed. The economic agents in the private as well as the public sector at the urban and regional level have in many cases an interest in cooperation but the political entrepreneurs must avoid being trapped by specific groups and narrow egoistic interests (Rodrik, 2004). The smart specialization approach builds upon the assumption that the development and the implementation of the spatial industrial policy should be made through negotiations between different interests in the private and the public sectors. However, it is very unclear to what extent such negotiation processes will lead to an outcome that is reasonably close to an optimal and efficient use of available resources, that is, to what extent it risks leading to suboptimization and an inefficient resource allocation. A partly related problem is that economic agents in the private and the public sectors act on different time scales. Political decision-making in political assemblies follow their given and rather slow rhythm, while economic agents in the private sector must often react immediately to new signals from the market.

The guidelines for smart specialization stress the importance of clear and transparent processes, deep and extensive evaluations both ex ante and ex post, which make it possible for the political entrepreneurs to abandon failed political interventions. However, they give substantially less guidance concerning the problems and risks that the political entrepreneurs face when they develop and implement a smart specialization policy. Against this background it is astonishing to find that cluster policies are presented as one of the important instruments to deliver a smart specialization policy. It is even claimed that due to its inherent ability to support cooperation, cluster policy is a powerful instrument to further industrial competitiveness, innovations and regional economic growth. In particular, it is claimed that clusters can be used both to design and to implement a local and a regional smart specialization policy and as a platform to bring together economic actors from the private and the public sectors. Smart specialization is an all-embracing policy approach unusually well founded in well-established regional science research. However, at the same time the advocates for this policy approach admit that the choice of building blocks makes it difficult to design an efficient regional policy.

We can identify a number of challenges for those political entrepreneurs that want to use the smart specialization approach to develop concrete industrial policy measures:

- Models for regional innovation systems and evolutionary economic geography provide very rich theoretical frameworks but tend to collapse in individual case studies from which it is very difficult to draw any general conclusions that political entrepreneurs can use to develop practical measures for industrial policy at the regional level.
- Cities and regions are not closed systems, which implies that the geographical demarcation of cities, urban regions and regions, which is a fundamental characteristic of these two theoretical frameworks, generates a double risk of geographically too limited interventions and insufficient initiatives at the comprehensive regional level.
- It is very uncertain if the political entrepreneurs at the regional level have all the information, knowledge and competence that is needed to identify the optimal spatial industrial policy for their own region.

There is a big risk that for reasons of prestige they will choose to focus on phenomena that are fashionable at the time, such as tourism, information technology, new materials and biotechnology, irrespective of what basic conditions the region has to develop and implement such industries or technologies.

● Finally, and most alarmingly for political entrepreneurs, is that we do not know which industrial policy initiatives function since there is very little empirical research concerning the connection between the actual political targets and the instruments for industrial policy that have been assigned.

Summarizing the discussion above it is very surprising that the advocates for smart specialization recommend cluster policy as a major industrial policy approach, since experience shows that such a policy approach is genuinely inefficient. The actual guides for smart specialization policy urge the political entrepreneurs to use the instruments for cluster mapping developed by the European Cluster Observatory despite these instruments only giving simple measures for co-location, rather than direct and indirect links and cooperation between co-located companies. They do not even identify clusters in the way that Porter recommends. One positive thing is that the guide recommends that political entrepreneurs avoid the initiation of new clusters and instead focus on strengthening existing clusters. It is obvious that even if a spatial industrial policy is anchored in fundamental regional science theory, the operationalization of this theory as a foundation for the actions of political entrepreneurs is extremely difficult.

SPATIAL INDUSTRIAL POLICY – SOME REFLECTIONS

It is a fundamental fact that economic activities are spatially concentrated. This implies that those clusters that are observed are real, which makes the cluster concept a useful descriptive instrument. Unfortunately, as illustrated above, the cluster concept is much less useful as an analytical instrument or as a tool for spatial industrial policy. Physical clusters are a result of what entrepreneurs and companies decide and do. Exactly because a cluster is an outcome of such behaviour and the interaction between these economic agents it is extremely difficult for political entrepreneurs to develop a spatial industrial policy that focuses on the cluster outcomes and to manipulate and govern the cluster as such.

How then could a more efficient spatial industrial policy be designed? Quite likely, it should consist of two basic elements. (1) Certain types of national industrial policies can become more effective if they are made more sensitive to geographical places when it comes to design and implementation. (2) Political entrepreneurs should focus more on horizontal industrial policy that aims to make cities, urban regions and regions function better and that facilitates entrepreneurship and the growth of firms. Thus, the concept of cluster policy should be substituted with the concept of agglomeration policy.

If we accept that political entrepreneurs cannot manipulate and govern cluster outcomes, a better starting point for a spatial industrial policy is to focus on those market failures that influence and limit individual companies and households in a cluster. Such an approach can start from general proof of market failures, such as, for example, the difficulties for many (smaller) companies to finance their activities and in particular their growth ambitions, but that can benefit from a deeper understanding of an individual economic actor's situation in the cluster. Then the political entrepreneurs can develop several different industrial policy interventions using this information together with a fundamental analysis using regional science methods. These may include encouragement of entrepreneurship, subsidies/financing of companies in earlier stages, strengthening of the competence of the labour force and the management capacity of the companies and support of the companies to establish international links for exports and imports. For start-ups and very young companies the establishment of incubators and accelerators can be a very valuable and meaningful industrial policy initiative.

However, it is here essential to make a number of comments:

- Even if the spatial industrial policy outlined above can take advantage of a more detailed understanding of local and regional conditions, it is obvious that it needs much less information than many of the complex suggestions for cluster policies. It should also be stressed that even concerning those areas for industrial policy that have been outlined above it is difficult for political entrepreneurs to design and implement efficient policy measures. Robust empirical evidence for the efficiency of different specific industrial policy interventions is lacking and there is a very substantial need for continued research to identify clearly causal effects. This lack of empirical evidence points in the direction of more experimentation with industrial policy at the local and the regional levels but also highlights a need for careful and serious evaluations.
- It is important to observe that in situations with several interacting market failures it is not at all certain that elimination of one of them will lead to increased efficiency. Thus, there are no guarantees that

the elimination of market failures will automatically increase employment or productivity in clusters. Furthermore, the existence of different technological externalities makes it possible that some clusters are too big.

- Certain important industrial policy measures are controlled at the national level, which limits the freedom of action for political entrepreneurs at the local and the regional levels and this can induce them to use second- or third-best interventions, which leads to suboptimization. There are many reasons to reflect radically over which industrial policy measures should be available at different spatial levels in the political system.
- Important here is that many of the possible industrial policy interventions that are discussed don't need to be specific for those sectors or geographical places that the political entrepreneurs are most interested in. A majority of the small and medium-sized firms could take advantage of the interventions sketched above independent of industry location. This has two further implications for the design and implementation of spatial industrial policy. The effects of industrial policy can often spill over between industries and between locations and regions.

Given that industrial policy interventions can spill over to other companies both in other industries and in other clusters the question arises whether it is desirable that the spatial industrial policy should have any sectorial components overall. This depends in turn upon whether market failures are common in particular in certain industries. This can mean, for example, that for activities that are at or close to the technological frontier, entrepreneurship and company growth meet specific challenges due to market structure, information asymmetries and externalities that can lead to too low investment. In the new digital economy, the costs of entering the market are low but at the same time many of the companies in the new economy can have difficulties solving their financing problems and hiring highly qualified labour from the international labour market (Johansson et al., 2006). If political entrepreneurs want to encourage the development and the growth of the digital and other knowledge-intensive industries – as these industries generate a high value-added per employee and/or socioeconomic benefits that are higher than the private benefits – there are good arguments for focusing on acute problems in these industries beyond the advantages these industries can get from a horizontal industrial policy. To the extent that these industrial policy interventions target specific industries, a spatially blind industrial policy can mean that certain industrial clusters are favoured.

The discussion above leads to a second conclusion: horizontal industrial policy that focuses on geographical aspects rather than industries to stimulate economic growth can be considerably more effective than purely cluster-based industrial policy interventions. Furthermore, it is the case that the goals of horizontal industrial policy can be better achieved by focusing on specific geographical places rather than by applying a spatially blind industrial policy. The basic argument is that cities and urban regions generate productivity advantages, which implies that if political entrepreneurs by using industrial policy improve the functioning of cities and urban regions the result will be that the total national economy is strengthened. An agglomeration-focused industrial policy has this as its starting point and tries to develop industrial policy interventions that increase the advantages of an urban location of companies and households in terms of productivity and innovativeness at the same time as it reduces the disadvantages of an urban location in terms of higher costs. Empirical evidence points, for example, in the direction that political entrepreneurs at the local and regional levels in particular should focus on investments in infrastructure and the knowledge and skills of the labour force but also at a more market-oriented housing policy. Finally, it is important to stress that it is important to re-evaluate industrial policy and analyse which spatial level is optimal for different policy instruments.

CONCLUSIONS

The above discussion raises four main points. (1) It is important that, with political entrepreneurs' increasing interest in industrial policy, they devote substantial attention to the spatial economy and for the spatial outcome of industrial policy interventions. (2) The cluster cookery books deliver an interesting mixture of industrial policy measures at a superficial level, which unfortunately generally leads to an inefficient industrial policy as illustrated in the above text. (3) More focused horizontal industrial policy interventions and a stronger focus on furthering agglomeration economies have a great potential to deliver substantially better results than cluster policy. (4) The empirical knowledge to design and implement spatial industrial policy is insufficient and there is a very substantial need for future experiments with associated serious evaluations. The political entrepreneurs that want to pursue a spatial industrial policy must be aware that this is partly unknown terrain and not fall for simple suggestions about cluster policies but instead have patience and take the time to carry through experiments, have the experiments evaluated and be prepared to learn from the evaluation results.

REFERENCES

Aghion, P. (2012), 'Growth policy and the state: implications for the design of a European growth package', London: LSE.

Boschma, R. and K. Frenken (2011), 'The emerging empirics of evolutionary economic geography', *Journal of Economic Geography*, **11**(2), 295–307.

Cheshire, P.C., M. Nathan and H.G. Overman (2014), *Urban Economics and Urban Policy. Challenging Conventional Policy Wisdom*, Cheltenham, UK and Northampton, MA, USA: Edward Elgar Publishing.

Duranton, G. (2011), '"California dreaming": the feeble case for cluster policies', *Review of Economic Analysis*, **3**(1), 3–45.

Foray, D., D.C. Mowery and R.R. Nelson (2012), 'Public R&D and social challenges: what lessons from mission R&D programs?', *Research Policy*, **41**(10), 1697–702.

Frenken, K., F. van Oort and T. Verburg (2007), 'Related variety, unrelated variety and regional economic growth', *Regional Studies*, **41**(5), 685–97.

Glaeser, E. (2011), *The Triumph of the City*, London: Pan Macmillan.

Henderson, J.V. and A.J. Venables (2009), 'The dynamics of city formation', *Review of Economic Dynamics*, **12**(2), 233–54.

Johansson, B., C. Karlsson and R. Stough (eds) (2001), *Theories of Endogenous Regional Growth. Lessons for Regional Policies*, Berlin/Heidelberg: Springer.

Johansson, B., C. Karlsson and R. Stough (eds) (2006), *The Emerging Digital Economy. Entrepreneurship, Clusters and Policy*, Berlin/Heidelberg: Springer.

Karlsson, C. (ed.) (2008a), *Handbook of Research on Cluster Theory*, Cheltenham, UK and Northampton, MA, USA: Edward Elgar Publishing.

Karlsson, C. (ed.) (2008b), *Handbook of Research on Innovation and Clusters. Cases and Policies*, Cheltenham, UK and Northampton, MA, USA: Edward Elgar Publishing.

Karlsson, C. and R. Stough (eds) (2005), *Industrial Clusters and Inter-Firm Networks*, Cheltenham, UK and Northampton, MA, USA: Edward Elgar Publishing.

Karlsson, C., B. Johansson and T. Norman (eds) (2012), *Innovation, Technology and Knowledge*, London: Routledge.

Karlsson, C., B. Johansson and R.R. Stough (eds) (2006), *Entrepreneurship and Dynamics in the Knowledge Economy*, New York: Routledge.

Karlsson, C., B. Johansson and R.R. Stough (eds) (2009a), *Innovation, Agglomeration and Regional Competition*, Cheltenham, UK and Northampton, MA, USA: Edward Elgar Publishing.

Karlsson, C., B. Johansson and R.R. Stough (eds) (2009b), *Entrepreneurship and Innovations in Functional Regions*, Cheltenham, UK and Northampton, MA, USA: Edward Elgar Publishing.

Karlsson, C., B. Johansson and R.R. Stough (eds) (2010), *Entrepreneurship and Regional Development. Local Processes and Global Patterns*, Cheltenham, UK and Northampton, MA, USA: Edward Elgar Publishing.

Karlsson, C., B. Johansson and R.R. Stough (eds) (2012a), *The Regional Economics of Knowledge and Talent. Local Advantage in a Global Context*, Cheltenham, UK and Northampton, MA, USA: Edward Elgar Publishing.

Karlsson, C., B. Johansson and R.R. Stough (eds) (2012b), *Entrepreneurship, Social Capital and Governance. Directions for the Sustainable Development and Competitiveness of Regions*, Cheltenham, UK and Northampton, MA, USA: Edward Elgar Publishing.

Karlsson, C., B. Johansson and R.R. Stough (eds) (2013), *Entrepreneurial Knowledge, Technology and the Transformation of Regions*, London: Routledge.

Karlsson, C., B. Johansson and R.R. Stough (eds) (2014), *Agglomeration, Clusters and Entrepreneurship. Studies in Regional Economic Development*, Cheltenham, UK and Northampton, MA, USA: Edward Elgar Publishing.

Karlsson, C., K. Kobayashi and R.R. Stough (eds) (2014), *Knowledge, Innovation and Space*, Cheltenham, UK and Northampton, MA, USA: Edward Elgar Publishing.

Klaesson, J., B. Johansson and C. Karlsson (eds) (2013), *Metropolitan Regions. Knowledge Infrastructures of the Global Economy*, Berlin/Heidelberg: Springer.

Kline, P. and E. Moretti (2012), 'Local economic development, agglomeration economies and the big push: 100 years of evidence from the Tennessee Valley Authority', *NBER Working Paper No. 10993*.

Krugman, P. and A.J. Venables (1995), 'Globalization and the inequality of nations', *Quarterly Journal of Economics*, **110**(4), 857–80.

Martin, R. and P. Sunley (2003), 'Deconstructing clusters: chaotic concept or policy panacea?', *Journal of Economic Geography*, **3**(1), 199–210.

McCann, P. and R. Ortega-Argilés (2013), 'Transforming European regional policy: a results-driven agenda and smart specialization', *Oxford Review of Economic Policy*, **29**(2), 405–31.

Overman, H. and T. Leunig (2008), 'Spatial patterns of development and the British housing market', *Oxford Review of Economic Policy*, **24**(1), 1–33.

Owen, G. (2012), 'Industrial policy in Europe since the Second World War: what has been learnt?', *ECIPE Occasional Paper No. 1/2012*, Brussels: European Centre for International Political Economy.

Polenske, K.R. (2006), 'Clustering in space versus dispersing over space', in B. Johansson, C. Karlsson and R.R. Stough (eds), *The Emerging Digital Economy*, Berlin/Heidelberg: Springer.

Porter, M.E. (1990), *The Competitive Advantage of Nations*, New York: Free Press.

Porter, M.E. (2000), 'Location, competition, and economic development: local clusters in the global economy', *Economic Development Quarterly*, **14**(1), 15–34.

Rodrik, D. (2004), 'Industrial policy in the twenty-first century', *CEPR Discussion Paper No. 4767*, London Centre for Economic Policy Research.

Storper, M. (2011), 'Why do regions develop and change? The challenge for geography and economics', *Journal of Economic Geography*, **11**(2), 333–46.

Weiss, J. (2011), 'Industrial policy in the twenty-first century', *UNU-WIDER Research Paper No. WP 2011/55*, Helsinki: UN-Wider.

5. Political entrepreneurship, infrastructure and regional development

David E. Andersson and Åke E. Andersson

This chapter deals with entrepreneurial factors that support the long-term development of a region. The analysis focuses on decisions on investment in durable public resources that constitute the regional and economic infrastructure. The word infrastructure is derived from the Latin *infra* (under) and *structura* (structure). Politicians and planners mostly use the term to refer to physical network links such as roads, railways and utility networks. Here, we use it in the broader sense of all durable and shared systems that support the regional economy. The infrastructure thus includes material public capital such as roads, but also non-material public capital, including regional accessibility to knowledge and markets and a region's formal and informal institutions.

The first section includes a discussion on the infrastructural conditions and their geographical extension for economic development and what constitutes the material and non-material dimensions of infrastructure that favour economic development. It is followed by a historical approach to the role of infrastructure in the Swedish Industrial Revolution and the transformation into a creative knowledge society. This section identifies how the Swedish infrastructure planning and policies of the 1970s onwards have changed from national towards regional perspectives and also how the private sector has come to play an active role in pushing for new initiatives on infrastructure development. Two illustrative examples of material public capital are presented in the Arlanda Express line linking Arlanda Airport to downtown Stockholm and the Öresund Bridge, linking the third largest city in Sweden, Malmö, to the Danish capital Copenhagen. It is followed by two examples of non-material infrastructure expansion and regional reorganization of Sweden's science infrastructure in terms of knowledge and networks in the establishment of

Umeå University and the Jönköping International Business School. At the end, the main arguments are concluded.

INFRASTRUCTURE AS LIMITATION AND OPPORTUNITY

The most important causes of the economic development of a region are its infrastructural systems and their geographical extension. There are two fundamental attributes of infrastructure: (1) it is a public good that many firms and households can use at the same time and (2) it is much more durable than other capital. These two attributes make it possible to employ the novel dynamics approach of synergetics (Haken, 1983) to model the impact of infrastructure on other economic variables.

The synergetic modelling strategy mainly involves a subdivision of variables according to different relevant time scales. Applying the synergetic approach to the modelling of non-linear interdependencies in economic growth and development requires two types of separation: first, separation of time scales and second, separation of variables according to their individual (or private) versus collective (or public) effects.

Table 5.1 illustrates a useful subdivision of different goods for a synergetic analysis of a dynamic economic system.

Table 5.1   Different goods by rate of change and scope of effects

Effects/Rate of Change	Fast	Slow
Individual (private)	Ordinary market goods	Private capital goods: machinery, buildings
Collective (public)	Information	Material and non-material infrastructure: networks, knowledge, institutions

The following equation represents individual market good dynamics:

$$dp/dt = f(\mathbf{p}, \mathbf{k}, y, \mathbf{z}); \qquad (5.1)$$

where $\mathbf{p}$ is a vector of non-negative prices of ordinary market goods (including factor services), $\mathbf{k}$ is a vector of given quantities of private capital goods, y is information and $\mathbf{z}$ is a vector of predetermined infrastructure, including markets, knowledge networks and institutions governing the exchange of goods. Equation (5.1) gives rise to a fixed-point solution under standard conditions as specified in general equilibrium theory. The following equation represents investment or capital accumulation:

$$s(k) \, dk/dt = g(\mathbf{p}, \mathbf{k}, y, \mathbf{z}); \qquad (5.2)$$

where $s(k)$ is a constant that represents the time-scale conversion between ordinary market goods and capital goods, that is, $s(k) = t/T(k)$. If t equals one year and $T(k)$ equals ten years we would have $s(k) = 0.1$. With $\mathbf{p}$ in equilibrium and y as well as $\mathbf{z}$ at given levels, $\mathbf{k}$ would be approximately constant.

Information is modelled as:

$$s(y)dy/dt = h(\mathbf{p}, \mathbf{k}, y, \mathbf{z}); \qquad (5.3)$$

where $s(y)$ is greater than or equal to one, signifying a rapid time scale. Information would thus reach its equilibrium state almost instantaneously.

Finally, the following equation represents infrastructure development:

$$s(z)dz/dt = m(\mathbf{p}, \mathbf{k}, y, \mathbf{z}); \qquad (5.4)$$

where $s(z) = t/T(z)$. $T(z)$ is a very slow (although positive) time scale, indicating that $s(z)$ is a very small positive number, possibly of the order of 0.01 or even lower. This implies that in the timeframe of the other variables in this system, dz/dt approximately equals zero most of the time. We thus have a dynamic system:

$$dp/dt = f(\mathbf{p}, \mathbf{k}, y, \mathbf{z}^*)$$
$$s(y) \, dy/dt = h(\mathbf{p}, \mathbf{k}, y, \mathbf{z}^*); \qquad (5.5)$$
$$s(k) \, dk/dt = g(\mathbf{p}, \mathbf{k}, y, \mathbf{z}^*)$$

to be solved subject to the constraint:

$$m(\mathbf{p}, \mathbf{k}, y, \mathbf{z}^*) = 0; \qquad (5.6)$$

For systems of this kind, we can apply Tikhonov's theorem (Sugakov, 1998). Assume a dynamic system of N ordinary differential equations that can be divided into two groups of equations. The first group consists of m fast equations; the second group consists of $m + 1, \ldots, N$ slow equations. Tikhonov's theorem states that the system:

$$dx_i/dt = f_i(x,g); \ i = 1, \ldots, m \ \text{(fast equations)}$$

$$f_j(x,g) = 0; \ j = m + 1, \ldots, N \ \text{(slow equations)}$$

has a solution if the following conditions are satisfied: (1) the values of x are isolated roots; (2) the solutions of x constitute a stable stationary point of $f_j = 0$ for any x, and the initial conditions are in the attraction domain of this point. For each position of the slow subsystem, the fast subsystem has plenty of time to stabilize. Such an approximation is called 'adiabatic' (Haken, 1983; Sugakov, 1998).

In the very short run, the fixed-point solution of the first two equations, $f^*(\mathbf{p}, y) = 0$ and $h^*(\mathbf{p}, y) = 0$, results in market equilibrium, keeping the approximate values of $dk/dt = 0$ and $dz/dt = 0$. This solution corresponds to a conventional 'general market equilibrium' of the Cassel-Wald-Debreu type. In the medium term, we would have an expansion of capital, implying that $s(k)dk/dt = h^{**}(\mathbf{k})$, where the double star indicates that $\mathbf{z}$ is approximately constant and x and y are kept at their equilibrium values (*mutatis mutandis*). The solution is thus a fixed-point solution of $dk/dt/k = g$, where g is the balanced rate of growth.

In the very long run, the slow change of the infrastructure cannot be assumed to be zero, as given by (5.6), and the system as a whole would then cease to be as well behaved as in the short and medium terms. It would in the very long run have all the bifurcation properties that are typical of non-linear and interactive dynamic systems. Between periods of structural change induced by infrastructural discontinuities, there would be equilibrating periods of stable economic growth. This implies that general equilibrium theory, as conventionally formulated by Wald, Debreu and others, is not general enough to account for dynamic systems (or combined spatial and dynamic systems).

Modelling spatial economic development in terms of employment, production, capital formation and interregional trade requires a clear understanding of the ways in which the infrastructure is changing and at what rate. Sometimes the infrastructure serves as a catalyst for regional restructuring. Changes in the infrastructure can thereby trigger sudden transformations of the location patterns of production and employment as well as transport, communication and trade flows.

Infrastructural Dimensions

As stated above, infrastructure may be material or non-material. The road and rail networks are the most economically important of the transportation networks, which constitute a subset of the material infrastructure. This infrastructure is geographically delimited and territorial. It affects the spatial distribution of property rights, private capital and land prices. The consequence is that a material infrastructural good has three generic characteristics:

- It is a public good for large parts of the population within a geographically delimited area.
- Its use creates rivalry among consumers to the extent that it becomes congested.
- Its use may be open access or limited to individuals or organizations that have been endowed with enforceable property rights.

The non-material infrastructure includes the shared knowledge and values of a community or region as well as constitutional and other dynamically stable rules, such as legal systems or voting rules. The transportation networks are useful for most people as long as the flow of traffic does not exceed the capacity of the network. The non-material infrastructure does not have the same capacity limitations. An illustration is the Pythagorean Theorem, which countless students and engineers have used for almost three millennia without the congestion problems typical of the material infrastructure. Even so, some inventors view the absence of natural limitations in the use of knowledge as undesirable. An artificial capacity constraint is the prerequisite for the creation of new knowledge as a scarce good with monopoly pricing. Intellectual property rights create such artificial constraints. They thus enable property rights holders to use money prices to ration the use of knowledge and information with intrinsic public good attributes.

THE ROLE OF INFRASTRUCTURE IN SWEDEN'S INDUSTRIAL REVOLUTION

In less than 100 years, beginning in about 1870, Sweden underwent an economic transformation from one of the poorest countries in Europe, with a lingering hierarchical monarchy, into an advanced industrial economy. It industrialized much later than Britain, the north-eastern part of the United States and the centre of continental Europe. Together with

Japan, Italy and the peripheral parts of North America, Sweden belonged to the third wave of industrialization, thus benefiting from the experiences of earlier industrializers, copying their solutions and speeding up the rate of change.

Massive investments in new railroads and the introduction of compulsory primary education preceded the Swedish version of the Industrial Revolution. New economic legislation that was introduced in the 1850s was even more important for the country's take-off. These new laws and regulations were at least partly inspired by classical liberal reforms that had proven successful in Britain and elsewhere.

Sweden's growth mainly occurred in the largest cities and a number of new industrial towns, all of which had above-average accessibility to natural resources and markets. The transport and communication systems of early industrialism were mostly large scale and confined to a few key routes. Large firms dominated the shipping industry, which provided transport services that were designed for slow bulk transportation of raw materials. National railway networks only provided useful capacity along selected development corridors. Telephone and telex communication systems linked the world's main political and financial centres. All these infrastructure networks relied on large-scale operations and hierarchically organized decision-making. Monopolies and cartels were hence the predominant market forms in the main industries that supplied tangible infrastructure. Scale economies and the technological advantages of hub-and-spoke networks restricted competition.

From Industrial Society to the Creative Knowledge Society

A slow and steady improvement of the transport and communication networks, sooner or later, leads to radical improvements in nodal accessibility to markets, information and knowledge. At a critical threshold, these improvements cause the economic structure to undergo a process of creative destruction that paves the way for the transformative establishment of a new economic system. Such transformations are rare occurrences. The transformation of early capitalism into a full-fledged industrial society is the most well-known transformative change of this sort.

Sweden, like most other parts of Western Europe and North America at the beginning of the twenty-first century, is facing a new transformation of this disruptive type. Investments in extensive new computerized communication and transportation networks together with parallel massive investments in research and higher education are creating the conditions for a post-industrial economic system. Post-industrial infrastructure networks are usually not conducive to the formation of monopolies or oligopolistic cartels. A practical consequence has been the phasing out or liberalization of regulations that governed many of the obsolescent monopolistic or oligopolistic industries, beginning with the deregulation of the US airline and trucking industries in the late 1970s. Similar deregulatory reforms affected large swathes of the Swedish economy in the 1980s and 1990s. New competitive road, aviation and telecommunications networks have become the three pillars of the material infrastructure that supports the emerging post-industrial society, largely replacing the railway, shipping and surface mail networks of the preceding era. This new 'road-air-telecom system' has evolved into a type of interdependent multi-layered network that offers up a continuous ability to adjust and adapt to new logistical demands.

THE SUPPLY OF NEW MATERIAL INFRASTRUCTURE

During the twentieth century, the Swedish government, like the governments of many other industrialized countries, focused its infrastructure building efforts on extensions to networks that were first built in the nineteenth century. Railroads were expanding, but at a slowing pace until the 1960s, after which railroad spending was limited to routine maintenance and repairs. The relative economic importance of the railroads started declining already at the turn of the twentieth century. Figure 5.1 shows that railroads had declined to the extent that they only accounted for half a per cent of Sweden's GDP in 1976.

Source: Krantz (1986).

*Figure 5.1   The percentage contribution of railroad transportation
             services to GDP, 1856–1976*

Meanwhile, investments in the road network increased, peaking in the early 1930s and again in the period from 1950 to 1965 (Figure 5.2).

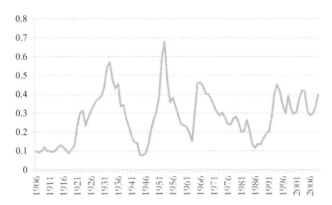

Sources: *Statistics Sweden (SCB); Trafikanalys (2011).*

Figure 5.2   Swedish road investments as percentage of GDP, 1906–2006

From the 1970s onward the contribution of road investments to GDP has remained at approximately three-tenths of 1 per cent. The post-war shift from rail to road transportation made possible the adoption of new computer-aided logistics by Sweden's leading global firms, such as IKEA, H&M, Spotify, Skype and Ericsson. Two new tendencies in infrastructure planning and policy have emerged in Sweden after the 1970s. First, there has been a shift from national toward regional perspectives and second, the private sector has become increasingly active in lobbying for and taking an active part in the planning of large road, bridge and railroad projects. Two important examples are the Arlanda Express line, connecting Arlanda Airport to downtown Stockholm and the Öresund Bridge, which connects the city centres of Malmö and Copenhagen.

Arlanda Express
The opening of the Arlanda Express line in November 1999 made it possible to reach Arlanda Airport in only 20 minutes from central Stockholm (Table 5.2). The impetus for the new line was three-fold: the rapid increase in the number of airline passengers in the 1980s, the subsequent construction of a third runway at Arlanda and political pressures to substitute rail for road transport for environmental reasons. The Arlanda Express line was the first major railway project in more than 100 years and it was for the most part innovated, designed and funded by

private entrepreneurs. The national government did, however, become part of the innovation process when it persuaded a number of international banks to invest in the line in exchange for future ticket revenues. Australia's Macquarie Bank owned Arlanda Express for a decade and is a good example of how infrastructure provision now involves global markets. However, following approval of the change of ownership by Arlandabanan Infrastructure AB, there is now a new owner of Arlanda Express. This owner consists of a consortium of institutional investors, with Australian superannuation funds as the dominant shareholders. Annual passenger volumes increased by over two million between 2004 and 2014, reaching a total of five million passengers per year in 2014.

Table 5.2 Transportation options for travel between downtown Stockholm and Arlanda Airport (42 km), 2014

Travel Option	Travel Time (Minutes)	Fare (SEK)	Frequency (Per Hour)
Arlanda Express	20	200	4
Commuter train (SL)	37	145	2
Long-distance train (SJ)	21	206	0.5
Airport Shuttle Bus	45	99	4
Taxi	40	500	–

Source: Rodriguez (2015).

The Öresund Bridge – connecting two metropolitan regions in two nations

Southern Sweden used to be part of the Kingdom of Denmark. With the 1658 Treaty of Roskilde, the Skåneland region was transferred from Denmark to Sweden and the University of Lund was established with the explicit mission to reshape Skåneland into a culturally integrated part of Sweden. The growth of the pan-Scandinavian movement in the nineteenth century gave rise to the idea of attaining cultural and economic gains from building a bridge across the Öresund (the Öresund is the sound that separates the Danish island of Zealand from the southern Swedish province of Scania).

In the 1970s, the decline of traditional manufacturing and the closure of the region's shipyards and textile factories increased unemployment on both sides of the sound. Many policy-makers saw the need for an updated infrastructure and regarded it as a necessary condition for renewed economic growth. The prospect of a bridge that would connect Sweden and Denmark became part of the agenda of the European Round Table of Industrialists, which was established in 1983 with the CEO of Volvo, Pehr G. Gyllenhammar, as an important member. The Chamber of Commerce and Industry of Southern Sweden became the most forceful regional interest group that argued in favour of a new bridge, allying closely with pro-bridge politicians in Copenhagen and Malmö. The decision process that eventually led to the construction of the bridge coincided with the Swedish European Union (EU) accession process, causing major political conflicts.

At the same time, Swedish public opinion was strongly against the building of a bridge as well as against membership of the EU, as is shown by responses to a typical opinion poll from the early 1990s in Table 5.3.

Table 5.3   *Swedish attitudes about EU membership and a bridge to Denmark, early 1990s*

Attitudes	In favour of EU membership (%)	Against EU membership (%)	Total (%)
In favour of bridge to Denmark (%)	28	10	38
Against bridge to Denmark (%)	14	48	62
Total (%)	42	58	100

Source: Falkemark and Gilljam (undated).

As Table 5.3 shows, a majority of the Swedish population was against joining the EU, and an even larger majority was against building a bridge to Denmark. Interestingly, Sweden's two largest political parties, the centre-left Social Democrats and the centre-right Moderates, were strongly in favour of building the Öresund bridge; these two parties also advocated full EU membership for Sweden.

The question of whether to build a bridge was a bone of contention between and within the political parties before the final decision was reached. In the end, the political conflicts within the centre-right coalition government caused the leader of the small Centre Party, Olof Johansson, to leave the coalition, asserting that this bridge would only be built over his dead body. Surprisingly, the bridge was completed in the year 2000 and Olof Johansson was still alive at the time of writing this chapter in 2016.

The Öresund Bridge actually comprises an island, a bridge, and a tunnel; it is therefore sometimes also called the Öresund Connection. The construction cost amounted to approximately DKK20 billion. This is the longest bridge connection in Europe that carries both motor vehicles and trains. The bridge serves over 60 000 travellers per day, most of whom are daily commuters between the two sides of Öresund.

The consequences of the Öresund Bridge have been substantial:

- The traffic across the bridge has grown beyond forecasts in spite of the monopolistic pricing strategy. Since the opening of the bridge, the total number of crossings by cars exceeds 70 million. In 2012 18 500 vehicles crossed the bridge daily; 41 per cent of these were commuter trips. Railway traffic hit a record in 2012, with an average of 30 000 passengers crossing the bridge per day, or a total of 11 million for the year. Sixty per cent of these were regular commuters (Hasselgren and Lundgren, 2014, p. 14).
- Commuting has partly integrated the housing market in the cross-border region, creating a new property market that encompasses a region with a total population of 3.7 million.
- The link has caused the cities of Copenhagen and Malmö to reorganize their urban planning. A case in point is a major housing and business corridor between downtown Copenhagen and Copen-hagen International Airport. In Malmö, the redevelopment of the old docks has created a new mixed residential and commercial neighbourhood that includes Scandinavia's only skyscraper – 'Turn-ing Torso'.
- The Öresund Region market for knowledge-intensive business services has been growing rapidly after the completion of the bridge, especially on the Swedish side of the sound.
- An integrated science region is being established, including major European investments in large-scale facilities for experimental physics – European Spallation Source and the Max 4 facilities in the Malmö region.

- Copenhagen International Airport has become the major Scandinavian air transportation hub, eclipsing both Oslo (Gardemoen) and Stockholm (Arlanda).

NON-MATERIAL INFRASTRUCTURE EXPANSION

Extensions of material infrastructure in the form of new transport links, as in the case of the Öresund Bridge, can cause dramatic economic effects within a time frame of a decade or two. Non-material infrastructure investments rarely cause such rapid productivity gains. Legal reforms or new value structures seldom have short-term economic consequences. Still, there are many reasons to believe that the transformation of the non-material infrastructure has had an even greater impact on regional and national development than most investments in the material infrastructure.

The non-material infrastructure is mostly public knowledge, both old and new. Sometimes this is shared among the residents of a region or nation. Sometimes, as in the case of the Pythagorean Theorem, people everywhere share the benefits. Economists have coined the term 'human capital' as an analogy to physical capital, in order to sum up the aggregate economic effects of investments in scientific research, education and learning. Some of this human capital earns private returns, such as when knowledge is embodied as a not easily transferable personal skill. The ability to conduct surgery, play soccer or teach economics are all examples of private human capital. Other knowledge affects everyone in various ways, ranging from mathematical formulas of global reach to the articulated or tacit institutions that govern behaviour for a geographically or socially delimited community of people.

Most of us can appreciate the skill difference between someone who performs a demanding task after having invested in several years of training and someone who tries to perform the same action without having invested substantial time in an effort to master the actions that the task in question requires. This difference is especially evident in scientific or artistic endeavours. Innate musicality without several years of practice could never suffice for playing one of Mozart's piano or violin concertos at the level of the type of expert that is usually called a 'virtuoso' in this context. It is equally impossible to perform surgery without a long medical education and practical training by experienced surgeons. Knowledge is simultaneously embodied in the skills of a person and disembodied as a resource that can be transmitted through books and academic papers. This latter type of knowledge, which is sometimes called articulated knowledge, often serves as an important type of research input that generates new ideas, experiments and hypotheses, especially when articulated-knowledge artefacts from different sources are combined in novel ways.

Creative knowledge expansion sometimes creates economic benefits over long time spans, indeed long after the creator of the knowledge has received all of the private economic payments from the buyers of his or her individual knowledge services. One example is the output of Mozart, who created more than 600 musical compositions. Many of these compositions are still being performed regularly, thereby affecting the livelihoods of thousands of musicians, record companies, music publishers, film producers and other users of this durable and collectively accessible human capital. That is to say that this type of human capital is now part of the non-material infrastructure. In this case it is part of the global infrastructure, in the same way as the Pythagorean Theorem. Every new theorem, every new production technique, and every new product design eventually becomes part of our collective knowledge capital as long as there is someone who benefits from using the 'blueprint' in question. It goes without saying that the value of a specific instance of infrastructural knowledge capital depends on the number of people that directly or indirectly can make use of it, and ultimately on the aggregate benefit to all those people as a 'blueprint-using' group.

Networking is a term that usually refers to multilateral exchange, open-ended cooperation and flows between nodes. It is evident that scientific and other creative and innovative networking presupposes the existence of a serviceable network. In other words, human interaction requires networks. In this way investments in material and non-material infrastructure interact dynamically. If you want to cooperate or socialize with someone in a neighbouring place or region, it is necessary that a transportation or communication link already exists so as to connect the two locations. But such interaction also depends on a number of less obvious, non-material prerequisites.

If mobility is restricted by passport and visa requirements it may not matter much if the road is in excellent condition. Such institutional restrictions sometimes amount to as much of an obstacle as a potholed road during a hurricane. On a more subtle level, it is often necessary to have a shared value system, a shared language and a shared interest in order to attain smooth and meaningful cooperation, as is the case in the Öresund region covering parts of Sweden and Denmark. Shared laws, customs and values create invisible networks that shape the economic and social interplay that occurs on physical networks. Some human values and institutions are more supportive of market exchange and social cooperation than others. For example, the values and institutions of science, English, peer reviews and replicable hypothesis testing, have doubtless facilitated much greater long-distance interaction volumes than are common in, say, politics, law or journalism.

The non-material infrastructure evolves at a very slow pace by means of a combination of social processes such as gradual cohort replacement, legal verdicts and legislative reforms. Though this evolution may be slow, continuous accumulation of dispositional and behavioural regularities produces enormous collective impacts as centuries of group-specific history pile up. Most of this infrastructure is embodied in human minds. It changes in tandem with the demographic and socioeconomic composition of the relevant group. The individual both helps shape and is shaped by his or her institutional structure (Berger and Luckmann, 1967).

The classical economists explained the emerging industrial society by making use of three resources as the building blocks for understanding the supply of goods. These resources were labour, land and (physical) capital such as machines and buildings. Nineteenth-century politicians and industrialists tended to regard these resources as virtually inexhaustible. They regarded the exploitation of natural resources as a question of having a recognized right to use the required amount and quality of land, as well as having the purchasing power to buy enough capital and rent sufficient amounts of labour services. To the extent that resource limitations became obvious, they hoped that geographical discoveries would soon overcome apparent resource bottlenecks.

After centuries of industrial growth this view is, of course, no longer realistic. Natural limits to the supply of minerals and mineral-derived energy sources are becoming increasingly evident. Some parts of the world face additional water shortages. Many natural resources have for this reason become relatively expensive. In a growing, but structurally static society, it is inevitable that exhaustible natural resources will command increasing scarcity prices.

The supply of labour, if measured as the total number of gainfully employed individuals, has grown dramatically over the past century in the industrialized world. The real increase in the supply of labour is, however, much smaller. Women were only to a limited extent counted as economically active members of the workforce in early industrial societies, although the great majority of women took part in labour-intensive (but unpaid) agricultural production and the time-consuming domestic chores associated with large households. At the same time, those in the formal economy worked about twice as many hours compared with current levels. All in all, this amounts to a total increase in the labour supply, measured in the number of hours worked, of no more than one-half to two-thirds of 1 per cent per year over the past century (Maddison, 1982, 2003).

The main causes for the economic growth of the past 100 years have been the improvements to the infrastructure for personal transportation and communication and, in particular, the growth of knowledge in terms of formal education. If the aggregate number of formal education years is a good proxy for the aggregate knowledge of a population, then the annual growth rate of the 'knowledge capital' of most industrialized countries has been in the vicinity of 2 or 3 per cent per year over the past century. In a typical developed Western country, this would imply that the total stock of knowledge is between 10 and 15 times greater than at the onset of the Industrial Revolution.

The long-term development of industrialized regions thus points to ever-scarcer natural resources and working time coupled with a growing supply of knowledge, communication and information resources. Nowadays, and even more so in the future, the idea that land, labour and capital are the fundamental resources is obsolete. Future economic development instead depends on expanding computer-enabled information networks and on the creation, coordination and dissemination of knowledge.

Knowledge amounts to a productive resource, which as articulated knowledge gradually extends beyond its private human capital origins to become part of the non-material infrastructure, often first among small communities of specialists but later as a ubiquitous and unlimited global resource. In many ways, the evolution of each specific piece of knowledge resembles the product life cycle of a typical consumer good. In its 'mature stage', a previously private knowledge item has become an infrastructural resource in the form of a generally accessible theory, method, or composition. The sum of all infrastructural knowledge items is then the stock of knowledge. This stock is in part scientific or technical. But it is also in part aesthetic, as well as containing legal, linguistic, political, religious and symbolic parts. It manifests itself as a composite resource from which individuals can extract selected parts in accordance with their personal skills and proclivities.

The collective and individual attributes of knowledge are interrelated and they jointly influence the long-term development trajectory of the relevant group, whether a community of practice or a political jurisdiction. These developmental consequences have increasingly made knowledge policy a national and regional political priority. A growth-promoting knowledge policy often encompasses the following measures:

- investments in education at all levels;
- importation of science-based industrial knowledge;

- imitation of best practice by global benchmarking of relevant industries;
- creation of new knowledge through scientific research, industrial R&D and artistic endeavours.

The global supply of new knowledge is increasing at a slow pace but with irreversible effects. It is an accumulative process. The history of mathematics is a good example of this. Euclid invented geometry more than two millennia ago. Together with the extensions and generalizations of the seventeenth to nineteenth centuries, Euclidian geometry is still the irreplaceable foundation for much applied engineering work. Even state-of-the-art high technology derives many of its results from theories that physicists and other scientists formulated in the seventeenth, eighteenth and nineteenth centuries. Scientific research incessantly activates and recombines elements of the knowledge stock, while education contributes to its maintenance and dissemination.

The Regional Reorganization of Sweden's Science Infrastructure – Two Examples

Umeå University
In the 1950s all of Sweden's universities and most of its scientific research were located in the three main metropolitan regions of Stockholm/Uppsala, Gothenburg and Malmö/Lund. Certain influential politicians in northern Sweden were critical of this spatial concentration, most notably the Social Democrat politician and Minister of Transport and Communications, Gösta Skoglund. In the Swedish parliament, Skoglund had regularly argued for the need to create a new university in the north of Sweden. His argument was that a northern university would address the persistent shortage of teachers and physicians in the north. As a member of parliament, Skoglund repeatedly introduced bills that would establish a northern national university, but these bills were defeated by parliamentary opponents. Insistent lobbying slowly changed the views of the central government, however, and after being appointed to a Social Democrat cabinet Skoglund could exert his influence from within the government. The private sector was rather passive and did not play a major role in lobbying for or against the proposed university. On the other hand, northern politicians from different political parties – both centre-left and centre-right – collaborated with Skoglund in forming a forceful northern interest group within the parliament.

The first step in the gradual process of establishing a new university was the location of an odontology institute in Umeå, which had the explicit aim of addressing the shortage of dentists in northern Sweden. Next was the establishment of a medical institute in 1959 and a social science institute in 1963. Fairly soon thereafter the Swedish parliament decided to integrate these institutes and a number of science centres as faculties of a new university, Umeå University, which was inaugurated in 1965. The subsequent growth of this new university was remarkable by Swedish standards, so that in 2016 its budgeted annual expenditures reached €540 million – a level that is near the average of leading European research universities.

The regional impact of Umeå University has been large and sustained. At the outset, around 1960, two towns in the north of Sweden were seen as suitable candidates – Härnösand and Umeå. Both towns had similar population sizes of 18 300 and 22 500, respectively. In 2015 the town that lost the contest for hosting Sweden's first northern university, Härnösand, had seen its population decline to less than 18 000, while Umeå had grown from 22 500 to 120 000, implying a population growth of 3 per cent per year over the 50 years that had elapsed since the formal establishment of the university.

Jönköping International Business School (JIBS)

Most infrastructure investments that aim at creating better conditions for economic development focused on northern Sweden between 1960 and 1990. It was thus with an increasing sense of frustration that the governor of Jönköping County, Gösta Gunnarsson, a Centre Party politician and previous undersecretary in the Prime Minister's Office, in the mid-1980s expressed his view that the flow of infrastructure investments for regional development was biased in favour of counties in central and northern Sweden.

Even though Jönköping County, in the south of Sweden, had many features in common with the country's north, it received almost no national resources for developing its material or non-material infrastructure. Governor Gunnarsson became convinced that this situation had to change through concerted regional efforts.[1] One of the underdeveloped areas was higher education, with Jönköping not offering any higher education apart from a few courses organized by a small community college. At the same time, the surrounding region of Småland was afflicted with generally low levels of education among most of its workers, especially in the manufacturing sector. This was a situation that might have evolved into typical rustbelt stagnation, as had happened in so many regions in Europe and the United States from the 1970s onward. As is now widely known, this was a consequence of progress elsewhere: the rapid development of some economies with low labour costs and incessantly improving information and communication technology that accelerated the integration of financial markets in different parts of the world.

In 1990, the time was ripe to present the results on the importance of higher education and research for Jönköping's future development. A concrete proposal was to establish a business school. The proposed business school would occupy a new niche by focusing on European business models and the development of small and medium-sized enterprises (SMEs). A genuine international focus had not been present in Sweden's existing business schools. Another potential advantage of this approach was that the other Swedish business schools had strong ties with Sweden's large multinational corporations rather than with entrepreneurial start-ups. Since the economy of Jönköping County was unusually well endowed with SMEs, the combination seemed perfect. The new business education model not only reflected the economic structure in the region, but also contributed with an approach that was entirely new in the Swedish context. The county governor endorsed the proposal with great enthusiasm and thus the local government and the local business community decided to embark on an ambitious education and research infrastructure project.[2]

Funding remained a major challenge. Starting a new international top-level business school could never be a low-cost proposition. After a period of persuasive fund-raising, some of the public and private organizations in the region decided to allocate the necessary resources for the initial investments. The Chamber of Commerce took on the leading role in the private sector. The Chamber of Commerce became responsible for persuading member firms to invest money in the new business school. A board of directors overseeing the implementation of the project was created, with the county governor as chair and with representatives from both regional and national industry, public organizations and educational institutions.

Within three years the project should attain its first goal of a parliamentary decision that would transform the vision into reality. An Act of Parliament in 1993 stated that a new higher education institution was to be created in Jönköping. Apart from enabling the business school to get off the ground, it was also decided that the entire university would be transformed into a private foundation. A fortuitous turn of events was that the national government, with Per Unckel as Conservative/Liberal Minister of Education, had decided to introduce privatization experiments in higher education at the same time as the Jönköping project was being pursued. The objective of the centre-right coalition government was to liberate a few higher education institutions from state control by re-establishing them as independent private foundations. The reform did not attract much interest from the existing educational institutions; hence only the Chalmers Institute of Technology and Jönköping University College were to be governed by private foundations.

The parliamentary vote on the proposed vision was eventually opposed by the opposition centre-left Social Democrats. But since the Social Democrat representatives from Jönköping County disagreed with the party line and decided to abstain from voting, it became possible to realize the vision. The new business school stressed a close connection between classroom theory and business practice, cooperation between academia and industry and a research-led school. With the authorization to launch PhD programmes it became possible for creative and innovative professors to participate in shaping the history of Swedish intellectual life. A new business school was born and by 2015 JIBS had obtained both AACSB[3] and European EQUIS[4] accreditation.

The regional consequences have been substantial. The city has been reorganized spatially with a rapid growth of services and knowledge-based industry and government institutions. Population stagnation has been followed by growth. In the 1970s and 1980s Jönköping's population had been stagnant at about 105 000 residents. By 2016 that figure had increased by 30 per cent.

CONCLUSIONS

We have presented a brief overview with four examples of Swedish infrastructural strategies in this chapter. Two are examples of material infrastructure investments, the Arlanda Express rail link in Stockholm and the Öresund Bridge that connects the downtowns of Malmö and Copenhagen with each other as well as Scandinavia's main international airport about halfway between the two cities. In passing, we mentioned EU membership as an example of intangible, institutional infrastructure improvement, focusing instead on two examples of new knowledge infrastructures. The first example was the establishment of Umeå University, as Sweden's first university in a geographically peripheral region, while the second example was the creation of the first business school with English as the medium of instruction in a lagging manufacturing town in south-central Sweden. From these examples we draw the following general conclusions:

- Synergetic time scale differences work: successful infrastructure innovators seem to have been aware of the necessary long delays between the decision to embark on a new infrastructure strategy and its lasting regional economic consequences.

- Simple or advanced cost–benefit calculations were not used as a preparation for the infrastructure projects that were presented in this chapter.
- There was always a small group of visionaries near the core of each project; they formulated a vision of the long-term regional development outcomes that they ascribed to the initial investment.
- A majority of the general public were always initially opposed to or sceptical about new infrastructure investments.
- Over time regional interest groups and regional lobbying efforts have become more important. Most of the resistance to new infrastructure has come from government ministers and other national representatives based in the Swedish capital of Stockholm.

NOTES

1. The idea among Jönköping's politicians was to give Åke E. Andersson (co-author of this chapter and then Head of the Institute for Futures Studies in Stockholm) the task of analysing the situation in the region and on the basis of that analysis formulate a vision and strategy for the region's future development. With such an inquiry, the local politicians thought it would become easier to persuade the national government that Jönköping County also needed resources so as not to slip further behind in the competition among different regions in Sweden.
2. Professor Charlie Karlsson (editor of this volume) was hired as the new leader of the implementation phase of the project. His role was to put into action both concrete and abstract ideas of what a new international business school in Jönköping should entail. The reactions were decidedly mixed. Some were very enthusiastic, but others were much more sceptical. A common reaction was 'Are we able to pull this off?' A decisive factor was the statement by the CEO of a dominant regional company Herenco AB, Stig Fredriksson, who strongly approved the project together with the CEO of Saab Combitech, Per Risberg, who was another enthusiast.
3. Association to Advance Collegiate Schools of Business.
4. EFMD [European Foundation for Management Development] Quality Improvement System.

REFERENCES

Berger, P. and T. Luckmann (1967), *The Social Construction of Reality: A Treatise on the Sociology of Knowledge*, New York: Anchor.
Falkemark, G. and M. Gilljam (undated), 'Opinionen i Öresundsbrofrågan' [Public opinion on the Öresund bridge], accessed 16 May 2016 at http://som.gu.se/digitalAssets/1282/1282865_5_opinionen_i_oresundsbrofragan.pdf.
Haken, H. (1983), *Synergetics, an Introduction: Nonequilibrium Phase Transitions and Self-Organization in Physics, Chemistry, and Biology*, 3rd edition, New York: Springer-Verlag.

Hasselgren, B. and A. Lundgren (2014), *TransGovernance Öresund – Experiences and Future Development in Transport Infrastructure Development and Governance in the Öresund Region*, Stockholm: KTH Royal Institute of Technology.

Krantz, O. (1986), *Historiska nationalräkenskaper för Sverige: Transporter och kommunikationer 1800–1980* [Historical National Accounts of Sweden: Transport and Communications 1800–1980], Lund: Media Press.

Maddison, A. (1982), *Phases of Capitalist Development*, Oxford: Oxford University Press.

Maddison, A. (2003), *The World Economy: Historical Statistics, Development Centre Studies*, Paris: OECD.

Rodriguez, C.M. (2015), *Development of the Connectivity of Arlanda Airport*, Stockholm: Department of Transport Science, KTH.

Sugakov, V. (1998), *Lectures in Synergetics*, Singapore: World Scientific.

Trafikanalys (2011), *Dynamiskt samspel mellan utvecklingen av infrastruktur och BNP* [Dynamic Interaction Between the Development of Infrastructure and GDP], Report No. 2011:2, Stockholm: Trafikanalys.

6. Political entrepreneurship and sustainable growth in rural areas

Per Assmo and Elin Wihlborg

The Swedish countryside can be viewed as a peaceful place with a beautiful fresh environment. Another picture can be painted of large, sparsely populated areas with a declining economy, shrinking communities, ageing population and poor welfare and market services. The complex reality is that a local rural area often displays both these images. However, each local area is in many ways unique and the local actors find different ways to use resources and overcome constraints to make a living and build the local community. Rural resources differ from urban settings and thus there is a particular need to make them visible. These processes to overcome constraints and make resources visible and available are often promoted by local political entrepreneurs. Hence, this chapter focuses on local political entrepreneurs' search for alternative ways to enhance locally anchored development processes in the rural context.

In the rural context, there is a close interplay among arenas of political and related welfare services, the market and, not least, civil society. Welfare in broad terms is provided in a greater mix to meet the unique local demands of development and make them sustainable (Westholm, 2010; Wihlborg, 2015b). However, the small size and low densities of rural communities also challenge networked governance structures since they involve fewer actors and there are fewer resources available for development. The contemporary economic and social challenges are visible in rural areas in different ways from urban settings, but the consequences are still as great if not more so. The rural context is often less open to political entrepreneurs who dare to challenge traditional norms and values and models of local policy-making in search of innovative solutions (Olausson, 2015). Openness to allowing actors to promote entrepreneurship and new ideas differs from more turbulent and dynamic urban contexts (Florida, 2005).

Political entrepreneurs in the local rural setting play a partly different, but still crucial role for local development. Here the prospects for development are more constrained – there are fewer resources and people, a limited local market and transportation constraints. Thus, political entrepreneurs have to use specific time-spatial power strategies to make changes (Wihlborg, 2011b). However, the political entrepreneur concept includes a variety of roles, actions and characteristics. Thus, the term 'political entrepreneur', as Narbutaité Aflaki et al. (2015) argue, could be seen as an 'umbrella term'. We will thus elaborate on the meaning of political entrepreneurs in their local time-spatial setting of the rural community. If local political entrepreneurs are to become crucial actors in policy-making and local development, we have to get to know them, no longer consider them as anomalies in the policy process, and use them for improved local development.

This chapter contributes in three ways to the general aim of the book to demonstrate the role that the political entrepreneur might play in promoting entrepreneurship, enterprise and entrepreneurial diversity. First, we will show the importance of the time-spatial setting of the political entrepreneur by using a time-geographical approach (Häger-strand, 1953 [1967], 1985). Second, we elaborate different types of political entrepreneurs. Finally, we will show how differently political entrepreneurs can promote local development by presenting three illus-trations based on extensive bottom-up qualitative field studies.

The aim of this chapter is to contribute to the conceptualization of political entrepreneurs from a time-spatial perspective and analyse their role in three rural settings in striving for sustainable growth in different ways. The chapter proceeds in three steps. In the next section the local setting and conceptualization of political entrepreneurs is discussed and anchored in the time-spatial theoretical approach. Thereafter, three exam-ples from different rural areas in Sweden are used to illustrate different forms of sustainable growth in a local context. The theoretical modelling, outlined in the chapter, is used to analyse the implications of the cases. Finally, the chapter is summarized and some implications for research as well as for practical policy-making are discussed.

POLITICAL ENTREPRENEURS IN A TIME-SPATIAL SETTING

The local conditions at a specific place at a given time are crucial for political entrepreneurs. They have to have the power to make changes and encourage others to make changes then and there. The general idea in the contemporary setting of networked governance (Sørensen and Torfing, 2008; Löffler, 2009; Pierre, 2009) is that there is a demand for actors that locally knit these networks together, thereby supporting and coordinating different interests, resources, local conditions and managing the ensuing constraints (Von Bergmann-Winberg and Wihlborg, 2011). Another more constructive approach to the same process is to say that the political entrepreneurs translate ideas and visions into local manageable projects (Wihlborg, 2015a). This section begins with a wider discussion on the meaning of political entrepreneur in order to discuss two types of political entrepreneur. Second, their local framing is discussed by relating it to the time-geographical approach and look at a more distinct interpretation of power. This develops into an analytical model that will be used in the next section.

Political Entrepreneurs with Different Ambitions

The term 'political entrepreneur' is used as a broad term for those actors searching for alternative (new) policies to create political change that can enhance development processes. Political entrepreneurs challenge existing norms and values to contribute to new innovative practices. There is diversity in the field of entrepreneurial practice. The term political entrepreneur is an umbrella term including a wide range of actors (Narbutaité Aflaki et al., 2015), however, in this chapter we want to distinguish two types of political entrepreneurial actor to highlight the need to address structural changes as well as single issues. We call those focusing on structural changes 'policy entrepreneurs' and the ones focusing on single issues 'issue entrepreneurs'. Both these types of actor are included in the overall concept of political entrepreneurs as they are conceptualized here, but there is a need to refine the concepts to see the nuances in analyses of their practices (Wihlborg, 2011b, 2015b). Bernhard and Wihlborg (2014, 2015) have used a similar but slightly different model where the policy entrepreneur is the overall concept and issue and political entrepreneurs are subordinated concepts, however, the adjustment here is made to fit into the overall discussions of the volume.

The conceptualization here is based in the networked governance setting and will thus build on Rhodes and Marsh's (1992) almost ideal-typical division of policy networks into 'issue networks' and 'policy communities'. Issue networks gather actors who have a certain opinion on a specific question or problem. The specific issue motivates the actors to become engaged and involved in the issue network. Their self-interest is most often in focus and a main motivation. An issue network can aim to arrange a local music festival or to open an elderly-care home. This kind of network is open to anyone interested in engaging in the issue and functions as long as the issue has to be addressed. When the music festival is over, the issue network dissolves. The political entrepreneurs in these networks are called issue entrepreneurs. On the other hand, a policy community is stable over a longer time and kept together by strategic and structural policy-making. These types of networks are more focused on the political game as such and strive to address basic norms and value systems in society rather than a single issue. The entrepreneurs in these networks are called policy entrepreneurs.

The policy entrepreneur takes on a wider scope of engagement and addresses more basic issues, thus focusing on the political game of policy-making (cf. Erlingsson, 2009) and aiming to change structures for development. They thus express competencies such as goodwill, community trust and contribution to social capital, knitting the network together. Such entrepreneurial profits are here seen in much wider terms, which, apart from formal structures, also include private, civil and all other areas as possible contexts for the streams of local policy change to take place (Mintrom and Norman, 2009; Wampler, 2009). The policy entrepreneur is a type of actor focusing on the political game and addresses the structures made up by policies.

To summarize this section, within the umbrella concept of political entrepreneurship, we distinguish the policy entrepreneur who addresses structural policy challenges from the issue entrepreneur who focuses on a single political issue. Both these types of political entrepreneurs are challenging existing norms and values, promoting entrepreneurship in new, innovative ways but they have different focuses and thus they contribute to local sustainability in different ways. If and how the political entrepreneur focuses on the policy or the issue depends on the local context they are acting within.

A Local Time-spatial Approach

Both types of political entrepreneurs, as discussed above, act in local contexts. A fundamental component is thereby to highlight the importance and uniqueness of the 'place'. The physical location forms the basis for people's livelihood, something that is largely neglected or taken for granted in conventional development perspectives (Giddings et al., 2002; Widgren, 2012; Head and Stenseke, 2014; Assmo and Wihlborg, 2014b). However, here we argue that all local development is situational, based on the available resources and the constraints the actors experience then and there. Hence, the term 'local' is primarily given a spatial meaning, formed in the interplay of formal and informal structures and networks.

In local rural communities development is much more than economic growth and involves different values from general models of (economic) growth (Gibson-Graham, 2006; Assmo and Wihlborg, 2014b). Hence, we need to explore an analytical approach that focuses on local resources, constraints and activities in a time-spatial context and later on relate to how different types of political entrepreneurs manage development beyond economic growth.

Inspired by Hägerstrand's work on time-geography (Hägerstrand, 1953, 1985), we will set the analyses of policy entrepreneurs in their local time-spatial settings. A time-geographical approach strives to enhance an understanding of how people perform activities throughout their path through time-space. The focus is on how the path is formed by using available resources and managing constraints to fulfil the projects one takes on. Hence, formal and informal rules and regulations create constraints that make people act in specific ways. Hägerstrand (1985) created the concept of 'pockets of local order' to show how local contexts are physical as well as outcomes of the power relations among the actors in the pocket. A pocket of local order is a pocket of time-space formed to arrange different resources and constraints so the actors passing through the pocket can fulfil their projects.

To highlight the notion that places change over time in a pocket of local order, think, for example, about the different character of a railway station on a Monday morning at 7am and a Saturday night at 11pm. Different pockets of order are formed. The powers to constrain or enable different activities are obvious in this example. On a Monday morning there are commuter trains and there are people following daily routines to catch trains. A basic constraint is that the train leaves on time and you have to catch it. There is support for this busy morning schedule in the form of announcements on loudspeakers and billboards with the times and tracks. In the same place on Saturday night on the other hand most people are less busy and routinized; they may stop for a drink and chat. There are also other risks of crime and violence in the Saturday night pocket, so there might be police officers or security guards patrolling to maintain order. There are probably fewer police in the Monday morning pocket. This idea of pockets of local order opens up an analysis of specific time-space activity patterns, but it also opens up an analysis of the powers that keep the order in order.

The available resources and constraints that the actors experience here form the order. Hägerstrand (1985) defined three types of constraints. The first type is the capability constraints within the (human) actor. The second type is the coupling constraints that constrain the actor's ability to connect to others, like catching the train on time. The third type of constraint, which Hägerstrand only paid limited attention to, is the authority constraints. These are constraints based on other actors' power to steer the activities in one way or another. Even if all types of constraints are about power in broad terms the power relations become more obvious when it comes to authority constraints and thus there is a need to elaborate on these more.

Authority constraints can be related to theories on power and can thereby be divided into three perspectives on power (Wihlborg, 2011a). First, there are individual authority constraints expressed as other individuals' power relations in single meetings, a relational form of power. Second, there are formal authority constraints through formal institutions like laws and regulations, an institutional approach to power. Third, there are informal institutions such as discourses, cultural practices and social arrangements based on a more discursive interpretation of power.

The activities conducted in the time-spatial pocket of local order are constrained by these types of constraints. The processes within the pockets rearrange and reproduce the order, based on people's aims and ambitions and management of the constraints. An analysis of a pocket of local order includes the interplay of both the natural preconditions and the technical, social and mental arrangements of the resources and constraints. The pocket of local order concept thereby aims to capture the interplay of actors and structure to analyse local practices (Assmo and Wihlborg, 2014b).

The analytical pocket of local order concept can be applied on different time-spatial levels. The orders do, however, influence each other. The structural setting in a larger time-spatial pocket of local order may (and most likely will) define and/or influence the authoritative constraints in the more limited local pockets of order that are continuously formed within a larger order. However, people structure their activities based on the local order where they take place. Thus the activity patterns also influence and develop pockets of local order in relation to changes of structures or norms as well as local practices (ibid.). The orders are formed through practices, which can be promoted by the political entrepreneur. The issue entrepreneur focuses on the issue of the order, in contrast to the policy entrepreneur who addresses more structural orders formed by authority constraints. We will show here how the political entrepreneurs in three cases address different authority constraints to promote sustainable growth in rural areas.

POLITICAL ENTREPRENEURS IN LOCAL SETTINGS –
THREE EXAMPLES FOR RURAL CHANGE

The chapter now turns to its second part where we analyse three extensive bottom-up qualitative field studies focusing on local development in rural areas in Sweden where political entrepreneurs have appeared to play crucial roles. Since our field studies take a bottom-up approach we address competing understandings of the policy process (Pedersen, 2007). The analyses elaborate on the two functions of political entrepreneurs: the policy entrepreneur focusing on policy-making and on the other hand the issue entrepreneur emphasizing specific issues. None of these case studies have been purely inductive, but move beyond predefined categories and focus on how actors actively construct and reconstruct meanings and may even open up new categories (Bogason, 2000, p. 159). All case studies comprise broad qualitative methods, like interviews, participatory observations, document studies and focus group discussions. We have worked from empirical impressions and constructed narratives of the local development processes in a rural community, in interplay with theories in the policy field.

The analyses are thus a construction of two categories of policy entrepreneur, mirrored through different forms of authoritative constraints, in relation to local development in specific time-spatial settings. The different local case studies have been conducted with a focus on certain issues or problems, but are in this chapter primarily used to highlight the roles of policy entrepreneurs. The first case discusses the closure of two local schools in a small rural municipality in south-eastern Sweden, which was included in a study on how municipalities struggle to meet budget cuts in public services. The second case on community work in a village in the mountains in northern Sweden was part of a study on broadband infrastructure investments and provision. The overall focus of the third example was to analyse opportunities and constraints to expand and improve local ecological farm production for local development in rural areas of south-western Sweden.

Saving the Community School – Illustration from Ydre

Local schools are often considered as the local hub of the community, in particular where, as in Sweden, schooling is compulsory and publicly funded. Municipalities are responsible for ensuring that all children, regardless of where they live, have access to education in line with the national legislation and curriculum. Rural communities are often sparsely populated with few children scattered over large areas (Cedering, 2016).

In the contemporary Swedish public administration setting of new public management, local small schools are seen as economically inefficient and expensive for the municipality. The issue of local schools is therefore an interesting example of how difficult it can be for small municipalities to deliver services to its citizens when the template is designed for larger urban municipalities.

In the municipality of Ydre in southern Sweden about 3600 inhabitants are scattered across the countryside and in four small village-like towns. Schools in the municipality have been merged as the population declined since elementary school was introduced in 1842. In the early 2000s, the municipality decided that the existing four schools were to be reduced and merged into two schools. Consequently, the children in the two villages that lost their local school were to travel instead by school bus to one of the remaining two schools. This decision prompted the people in both affected villages to act (Cedering, 2012; Assmo and Wihlborg, 2012a). A policy window opened up for the issue entrepreneurs regarding the schools and they extended their discussions to focus on local community development as policy entrepreneurs.

In both villages where the schools would be closed, alternative proposals from residents and parents were put forward. A network was established where different interests were united in the goal of saving the local schools. The parents' network highlighted other benefits than strictly economic, including closeness to the school, reducing travel costs and risk of accidents, trust through togetherness between pupils and parents, using existing facilities, voluntary parents' work and so on.

In response to the municipal decision, the network used these ideas and applied to start a cooperative private school in place of the ones being closed. In this way the network and its spokespersons acted as issue entrepreneurs by addressing formal institutional constraints and using the window of opportunity to start an independent school. The application aimed to circumvent the municipality's decision, as they wanted to show that other values were more important (Cedering, 2012; Assmo and Wihlborg, 2012b). They tried to point out general values in the community by enlarging the school issue into a general development policy – by acting rather as a political entrepreneur. However, the alternative arguments to see beyond the conventional standards were not accepted, and these alternative ideas of local development policies were not realized. The application was rejected by the Swedish National Agency for Education, primarily based on the municipal decision not to support the application (Assmo and Wihlborg, 2012a). The municipality could not, in other words, think outside the box.

Some of those who were active in the school issue in Ydre also formed a local political party group, an association within the Green Party. For the first time in a number of years, the Green Party thereby obtained representation on the municipal council. It took on a formal function as a political entrepreneur. Despite these efforts, the association eventually failed to save the local schools. No permission to open private schools was given, and the majority in the municipal council confirmed the political decision to merge the four schools into two. The community work on local opinions and development plans were neglected (Berry, 2013).

Even so, the question about sustaining the local schools became an important and sensitive issue, on which most people in the local area had an opinion. The issue became a symbol of keeping the local countryside alive, and it triggered confidence and opportunities to enhance local development. The initiative showed that cooperation could involve co-production of shared services in new ways.

Developing Local Ecological Farming Business – Illustration from Grästorp

Grästorp municipality in south-western Sweden is located in what is traditionally known as the bread basket of Sweden. The municipality is mainly a rural area with a strong tradition in farming. However, as in most rural areas of Sweden, many of the (smaller) farms have in recent decades closed down or been merged into larger production units. With fewer people living and working in these areas, community services have become increasingly difficult to maintain. At the same time, there is a growing interest in locally (ecological) produced food.

In these rural areas, farmers have begun to improve and expand various forms of locally produced ecological farm products. This not only includes the actual production of basic foods, but is also connected to local manufacturing processes. For some years, a non-profit association called 'Närproducerat' has promoted the production and marketing of locally produced farm products. The association, among other things, runs a local shop and catering facility. Within the local area, they use a wide variety of locally produced food such as beef, chicken, turkey, pork, game, egg, fish, grain, bread, vegetables, fruit, berries and mushrooms.

In Sweden in general there is an increasing interest among both producers and consumers in locally produced ecological food (Natur-vårdsverket, 2004; Jordbruksverket, 2010, 2013). As noted by the association, the main constraints are related to other formal and informal structures. One problem is competition from the supermarkets. Being located close to larger (urban) consumer groups selling cheaper (imported) products tends to make consumers choose to buy all their food from these places. Hereby, the local association as an issue entrepreneur has resources to associate their local marketing to a more general discourse.

Furthermore, to buy and sell products from the local producers, the supermarkets require large quantities, at a competitive price, with long-term delivery. These are requirements that almost none of the local producers can meet. Another problem highlighted by the association is the municipal and regional/state bureaucracy surrounding regulations for local ecological farming. This can, for example, include different health regulations that for small-scale producers become quite expensive and increase the price of the end product. The municipality is also one of the biggest consumers of food, used for schools, elderly-care homes, kinder-gartens and so on. However, even if the municipality claims to adhere to and support local ecological production, one finds that the municipality rarely buys any locally produced food products. Following the conven-tional market-oriented view, the municipality instead purchases almost all food from the cheapest provider. These conventionally produced non-ecological food products are largely imported from outside Sweden.

The association for locally produced food has in various ways tried to influence the municipality. This opportunity arose after the municipal board opened up discussions about the importance of saving the country-side, as well as a focus on better food quality in local public institutions. From the association's point of view, there has been less focus on the issue that local ecological food products are more expensive than conventional products. Instead, it has been argued that quality, in terms of health, security and knowledge about the origin of the products have been more important aspects to promoting the local products. Hereby, the association has to address both formal constraints in public procurement and the competition of market prices.

The chairperson of the association is also a member of the municipal board. In this way, the chairperson has taken on the role of a local political entrepreneur by promoting the municipality to adopt policies to encourage more locally produced ecological food to be bought and used in public institutions. Furthermore, money spent on locally produced food, at locally owned shops, remains in the community, creating jobs and increasing incomes, and thereby also the community tax base. It is the chairperson's dual role – in the formal policy-making structure and in the association – that opens up such a unique policy window in the specific pocket of local order. Highlighting the constraints identified by the people concerned provides a deeper understanding and a more complex explanatory picture of problems and solutions related to local ecological farm production and trade.

Broadband Opens up Opportunities for Sustainable Growth – Illustration from Åre

Rural areas often have insufficient, or even a total lack of, infrastructure. This is mainly due to the fact that the economic investments (by public or private means) for development and maintenance of infrastructural systems is seen as too costly in relation to the few and scattered number of users. Location is thus crucial for how and by whom infrastructure is provided. Physical infrastructure is indeed connected to the local physical setting, and thereby a basic condition in the pocket of local order.

The expansion of broadband, including fibre-optic cables for the Internet and other information technologies, is the latest example of infrastructure investments. Since the use of online services and the Internet is increasing, the disadvantages for rural areas are increasing. There is indeed a policy problem that needs to be addressed and there are openings for policy entrepreneurs to act. The implementation of broadband infrastructure is made in explicit development policies both at European level and nationally in Sweden. From these higher levels of the governmental system there is also economic support provided through different forms of co-funding. In practice, this means that the government co-finances local investments in broadband together with local resources from municipalities, industry and, not least, local civil society.

There is a need for local networks to take on the responsibility and actually form the new settings for innovation. The structure requires local entrepreneurs with the competence to knit such networks together. The state simply requires that local actors work together to create development, but it is the local actors themselves who have to find out how to do it.

Kall village is located north of the skiing mountain resort Åreskutan, in the municipality of Åre in Jämtland. Through an active village association many different stakeholders joined together around the need for broadband for local development. The association has been involved in trying to save the school, the shop and the ability to refuel cars and, not least, snow mobiles in the village, but it was due to the issue of expanding broadband to everyone in the village that the collaboration really took off. By coming together and helping each other, they have expanded and connected broadband throughout the elongated village. The village community has acted as an association and coordinated the work.

The different components have been implemented in collaboration with local companies and a lot of volunteer work. Even if broadband was a single issue, addressed by issue entrepreneurs with the technical know-how, there were also several opportunities to set the issue in more general terms of local development that local political entrepreneurs took up.

The improved opportunities for communication to, from and in the village have provided households and companies with better opportunities to develop. Due to the broadband connection, they managed to save the school, keep the library open, and even some new companies and businesses have moved into the village. In other words, one could say that the new innovation created in the village Kall in Åre municipality produced ripples of flourishing development that enhanced the possibility to sustain and even expand local livelihoods in the village.

The key work here has been done by a few people taking on a role of issue entrepreneurs with different focuses and competences in the process. Some of them took on the role of planning and formal mapping, while other had the excavators and machinery to actually dig the ditches and roll out the broadband cable. Hereby the formal constraints were addressed by local existing attributes and also a new order in the community. The chairperson of the community group took on the explicit role as political entrepreneur. He had the competence and resources to actually connect the ideas with the municipal administration as well as the county board (Länsstyrelsen) and the regional managers of the EU funding for broadband investments. Through the division of responsibilities among the policy entrepreneurs in the community they managed to address a complex challenge with practical as well as political-administrative competences. Networking was the solution for the local development policy, and broadband was the solution that would address the many challenges in the local community. By promoting broadband they were not just simply arranging the infrastructure, they were opening up new opportunities for the community and people living there – now as well as in the future.

CONCLUSIONS

This chapter contributes to the conceptualization of political entrepreneurs, related to local (rural) development, by focusing on what characterizes different types of political entrepreneurs and how they enhance locally anchored development processes. A policy entrepreneur is viewed in broader terms, extending from the conventional idea that entrepreneurs promote business with the main aim to make (economic) profit. Local policy entrepreneurs act to expand action spaces for others in a local context to promote development (in all its meanings). The issue entrepreneur, on the other hand, creates opportunities relating to the issue in contrast to the policy entrepreneur who rather opens up opportunities of a more structural nature. The cases above have showed the different needs and approaches of how political entrepreneurs can either address issues or structural constraints of regional development, and thus there is a need to elaborate on and distinguish (at least) these two types of actors. Development can be promoted in entrepreneurial ways both regarding single issues and more structural changes.

Since the constraints and opportunities for entrepreneurial practices are localized in a specific place at a specific time, the time-spatial analytical approach helped us to understand and analyse how, why and where actions of political entrepreneurs appear. Local development is embedded in pockets of local order where local norms and values are addressed, in these cases to promote development. To change norms and values, as the main aim of political entrepreneurs, the local order has to be addressed. In each pocket of local order there are different challenges demanding different solutions from political entrepreneurs. The local issue entrepreneur, on the one hand, focuses on a single issue to pave the way for new innovations that favour entrepreneurship regarding the specific issue. The local policy entrepreneur, on the other hand, addresses structural settings for regional development and reaches beyond conventional financially measured development approaches. In so doing, a more local development process is obtained, which integrates the social, ecological and economic dimensions of local development.

In the three cases of local rural development, local changes took place when local actors took on roles as political entrepreneurs. They were far from alone, but their engagement and innovative approaches were essential to bring together networks, allocate resources and make use of the opportunities. In Ydre, the problem of school closure was initially an opportunity that focused on the issue of education and the children's future. However, due to the failure of saving the local schools, the issue became more political in character when the interest group formed a political coalition. Thus the issue entrepreneurs turned into policy entrepreneurs with broader ambition and scope to address structural changes. A similar process was seen in Grästorp, where the association focusing on local ecological production also managed to broaden the question to include general municipal politics. Concerning broadband infrastructure in Åre, several local problems were addressed with the single solution of improved infrastructure. Based in the pocket of local order, specific solutions were found to manage the issue of broadband. Hence, in all cases, the local settings of the pocket of local order defined what types of problems were addressed and how political entrepreneurs played the political game.

Based on these analytical illustrations, this chapter enhances a conceptual discussion on local political entrepreneurs. Interest in political entrepreneurship has both analytical and practical grounds and implications. There is a need to examine the new roles of entrepreneurial actors and to elaborate and distinguish the different aspects of their actions and motives. There is also a need to take into consideration their localization, how they act to expand action spaces for themselves as well as others in the local community. Here this was addressed through the concept of pockets of local order. If local political entrepreneurs are to become crucial actors in policy-making and local development, we have to get to know them and no longer consider them as anomalies in the policy process and use them for improved local development.

REFERENCES

Assmo, P. and E. Wihlborg (2012a), 'Ydre 2.0 An alternative time-spatial approach towards post-monetarism', in B. Johansson, C. Karlsson and R.R. Stough (eds), *Entrepreneurship, Social Capital and Governance – Directions for the Sustainable Development and Competitiveness of Regions*, Cheltenham, UK and Northampton, MA, USA: Edward Elgar Publishing.

Assmo, P. and E. Wihlborg (2012b), 'Public services choices when there are no alternatives? A paradox of new public management in rural areas', *Journal of Rural and Community Development*, **7**(2), 1–17.

Assmo, P. and E. Wihlborg (2014a), *En annan kommunal ekonomi. Om andra sätt att värdera lokala resurser och aktiviteter. Bilder från Ydre kommun* [Another Local Economy. Other Ways to Value Local Resources and Activities. Illustrations from Ydre], Linköping: LIU Tryck.

Assmo, P. and E. Wihlborg (2014b), 'Home: an alternative time-spatial concept for sustainable development', in D. Humphreys and S. Stober (eds), *Transitions to Sustainability: Theoretical Debates for a Changing Planet*, Champaign, IL: Common Ground Publishing LLC.

Bernhard, I. and E. Wihlborg (2014), 'Policy entrepreneurs in networks: implementation of two municipal contact centres from an actor perspective', *International Journal of Entrepreneurship and Small Business*, **21**(3), 288–302.

Bernhard, I. and E. Wihlborg (2015), 'Municipal contact centres: a slower approach towards sustainable local development by e-government', *European Planning Studies*, **23**(11), 2292–309.

Berry, M. (2013), 'Sockentänk: En studie av två deltagardemokratiska experiment i Ydre kommun' [Community thinking. A study of two participatory experiments in Ydre Municipality], thesis, Linköpings universitet.

Bogason, P. (2000), *Public Policy and Local Governance: Institutions in Postmodern Society*, Cheltenham, UK and Northampton, MA, USA: Edward Elgar Publishing.

Bovaird, T. and J. Tizard (2009), 'Partnership working in the public domain', in A.G. Bovaird and E. Löffler (eds), *Public Management and Governance*, 2nd edition, New York: Routledge.

Cedering, M. (2012), 'Skolnedläggningar på landsbygden: konsekvenser för vardagsliv och lokalsamhälle' [School closures in rural areas: impact on daily life and the local community], dissertation, Department of Human Geography, Uppsala University.

Cedering, M. (2016), 'Konsekvenser av skolnedläggningar: En studie av barns och barnfamiljers vardagsliv i samband med skolnedläggningar i Ydre kommun' [Impact of school closures: a study of the daily life of children and families in connection with school closures in Ydre], dissertation, Department of Human Geography, Uppsala University.

Erlingsson, G. (2009), 'The spatial diffusion of party-entrepreneurs in Swedish local politics', *Political Geography*, **28**(7), 654–73.

Florida, R. (2005), *Cities and the Creative Class*, New York: Routledge.

Gibson-Graham, J.K. (2006), *A Postcapitalist Politics*, Minneapolis, MN: University of Minnesota Press.

Giddings, B., B. Hopwood and G. O'Brien (2002), 'Environment, economy and society: fitting them together into sustainable development', *Sustainable Development*, **10**(4), 187–96.

Hägerstrand, T. (1953 [1967]), *Innovationsförloppet ur korologisk synpunkt* [Innovation Diffusion as a Spatial Process. Postscript and translation by Allan Pred, Chicago, IL, Chicago University Press], Lund: Gleerups.

Hägerstrand, T. (1985), 'Time-geography: focus on the corporeality of man, society, and environment', in *The Science and Praxis of Complexity*, Tokyo: The United Nations University.

Head, L. and M. Stenseke (2014), 'Humanvetenskapen står för djup och förståelse' [Humanities stands for depth and interpretations], in E. Mineur and B. Myrman (eds), *Hela vetenskapen! 15 forskare om Integrerad forskning*, Stockholm: Swedish Research Council, pp. 26–33.

Jordbruksverket (2010), *Hållbar konsumtion av jordbruksvaror – vad får du som konsument när du köper närproducerat?* [Sustainable Consumption of Agricultural Goods – What do You do as a Consumer When You Buy Locally?], Report No. 2010:19, Jönköping: Jordbruksverket.

Jordbruksverket (2013), *Landsbygdens utveckling i norra Sverige under 2012* [Rural Development in Northern Sweden in 2012], Report No. 2013:17, Jönköping: Jordbruksverket.

Löffler, E. (2009), 'Public governance in a network society', in T. Bovaird and E. Löffler (eds), *Public Management and Governance*, 2nd edition, New York: Routledge.

Mintrom, M. and P. Norman (2009), 'Policy entrepreneurship and policy change', *The Policy Studies Journal*, **37**(4), 649–67.

Narbutaité Aflaki, I., E. Petridou and L. Miles (eds) (2015), *Entrepreneurship in the Polis. Understanding Political Entrepreneurship*, Farnham, UK: Ashgate.

Naturvårdsverket (2004), *Hållbar produktion och konsumtion i Sverige* [Sustainable Production and Consumption in Sweden], Report No. 432, Stockholm: Naturvårdsverket.

Olausson, P. (2015), 'Regional autonomy and regional entrepreneurship', in I. Narbutaité Aflaki, E. Petridou and L. Miles (eds), *Entrepreneurship in the Polis. Understanding Political Entrepreneurship*, Farnham, UK: Ashgate.

Pedersen, A.R. (2007), 'Constructing narrative health policies', in E. Sørensen and G. Gjelstrup (eds), *Public Administration in Transition: Theory, Practice, Methodology*, Copenhagen: DJØF.

Pierre, J. (2009), 'Reinventing governance, reinventing democracy?' *Policy & Politics*, **37**(4), 591–609.

Rhodes, R.A.W. and D. Marsh (1992), 'New directions in the study of policy networks', *European Journal of Political Research*, **21**(1–2), 181–205.

Sørensen, E. and J. Torfing (eds) (2008), *Theories of Democratic Network Governance*, Basingstoke, UK: Palgrave Macmillan.

Von Bergmann-Winberg, M.-L. and E. Wihlborg (eds) (2011), *Politikens entreprenörskap. Kreativ problemlösning och förändring* [Political Entrepreneurship. Creative Problem Solving and Change], Malmö: Liber förlag.

Wampler, B. (2009), 'Following in the footsteps of policy entrepreneurs: policy advocates and pro forma adopters', *Journal of Development Studies*, **45**(4), 572–92.

Westholm, E. (2010), 'Spatial perspectives on the welfare state', in *Placing Human Geography: Sweden Through Time and Space, YMER Yearbook 2010*, Svenska Sällskapet för Geografi och Antropologi.

Widgren, M. (2012), 'Landscape research in a world of domesticated landscapes: the role of values, theory, and concepts', *Quaternary International*, **251**(February), 117–24.

Wihlborg, E. (2011a), 'Makt att äga rum. En essä om tidsgeografisk epistemologi' [Power to take place. An essay on the epistemology of time geography], in J. Palm and E. Wihlborg (eds), *Sammanvävt. Det goda livet i vardagslivsforskningen. En vänbok till Kajsa Ellegård på 60-årsdagen*, Linköping: Almlöfs förlag.

Wihlborg, E. (2011b), 'Entreprenörer på plats' [Entrepreneurs in place], in M.L. von Bergmann-Winberg and E. Wihlborg (eds), *Politikens entreprenörskap. Kreativ problemlösning och förändring*, Malmö: Liber förlag.

Wihlborg, E. (2015a), 'Policy entrepreneurs meeting mediators – a conceptual extension', in I. Aflaki, L. Miles and E. Petridou (eds), *Entrepreneurship in the Polis*, London: Ashgate.

Wihlborg, E. (2015b), 'Utvecklingspolitik på lokal nivå' [Development policy at the local level], in N. Bolin, S. Nyhlén and P. Olausson (eds), *Lokalt beslutsfattande*, Lund: Studentlitteratur.

PART III

Political entrepreneurship and entrepreneurial diversity

7. Political entrepreneurs and women's entrepreneurship

Charlotte Silander and Caroline Berggren

Women as entrepreneurs are on the political agenda in most European countries. The creation of businesses is considered to be an important way to keep the economy growing. Women are especially targeted as a potential group in order to increase the number of self-employed on the labour market since they are comparatively few (European Commission, 2010a). Since the Treaty of Maastricht in 1993, the European Union (EU) has strengthened its role as agenda-setter and policy-maker in the area of employment policy (Rhodes, 2010), emphasizing the role of women's entrepreneurship in strategies for European growth (European Commission, 2010a). Policies to promote entrepreneurship have rapidly been more and more directed towards higher education (Karlsson and Nystrom, 2007; European Commission, 2010a). This approach has resulted in an increase in the number of entrepreneurship education programmes at universities (see Chapter 10) and a higher expectation for graduates to become self-employed (Olofsson, 2012).

There are various views on the promotion of women's entrepreneurship. Many argue that special support systems for women entrepreneurs are necessary (Braidford and Stone, 2008) as a way to strengthen and promote social inclusion for women (Rouse and Kitching, 2006). Terjesen et al. (2015) argue that there is no 'one-size-fits-all' entrepreneurship policy but, instead, that it is necessary to consider the distinct nature of different types of entrepreneurship in order to realize effective public policies. Critical reflections on these policies are, however, limited and there seems to be a gap between policy rhetoric and the actual numbers of self-employed with tertiary education (Berggren and Olofsson, 2011).

Political entrepreneurs are both actors within and creators of policies of promoting entrepreneurship. In this chapter we use self-employment, owning a business and entrepreneurship as exchangeable concepts. In the first part of this chapter, we set out to describe policies and programmes promoting women entrepreneurs from a gender perspective; for example, which arguments are used, how are the programmes designed and how do they position the woman as an entrepreneur (Ahl, 2006)? EU policy and major initiatives to promote women's entrepreneurship are described, as well as Swedish policies and the major initiatives for promoting women's entrepreneurship. In the second part, we turn to the empirical analysis of the number and proportion of women entrepreneurs with a tertiary degree according to the educational field. To what extent do men and women in Sweden with a higher education degree become self-employed? Finally, we comment on the promotion of women entrepreneurs from a gender perspective and discuss possible explanations that relate to the empirical results.

POLICY FOR WOMEN'S ENTREPRENEURSHIP – THE EU

Defining Entrepreneurship and Proportion of Women among Entrepreneurs

According to the European Commission's definition entrepreneurs are individuals who are 15 years old and older who work in their own business, farm or professional practice in order to make a profit. Further, by definition such individuals spend time in the operation of a business or are in the process of setting up a business. These entrepreneurs consider the running of their enterprises to be their main activity. The Commission differentiates between solo entrepreneurs, entrepreneurs who are employers, and part-time entrepreneurs (European Commission, 2014, p. 7).

Women entrepreneurs can be measured as the percentage of women entrepreneurs out of the total number of entrepreneurs or as the percentage of women entrepreneurs out of the total labour force, and the latter is referred to as the entrepreneurship rate. In 2012, there were 10.3 million women entrepreneurs who were active in the 28 EU countries, which equates to 31 per cent of the total number of entrepreneurs. This share varied considerably between countries: Liechtenstein had the highest share of women (43 per cent) and Malta had the lowest (18 per cent) (ibid.). The percentage of women entrepreneurs out of the total active labour force was 10 per cent in 2012; this can be compared to 19 per cent among men. The highest entrepreneurship rate among women was found in Greece (24 per cent) and the lowest in Norway (4 per cent) (European Commission, 2014, p. 8). During the period 2003–12, the entrepreneurship rate for women stayed around 10 per cent (European

Commission, 2014). However, when comparing entrepreneurship rates between different countries, the type of welfare state and financial situation need to be taken in consideration – for example, the size of the public sector and the availability of unemployment benefits. Women and men in the EU are active in different sectors. In 2012, a majority (around 60 per cent) of the entrepreneurs active in the human health, social work, services and education sector were women, while in sectors including construction, transport and storage, water supply, information and communication and manufacturing, they were in the minority (European Commission, 2014, p. 8).

The EU's Employment Policy

The EU has become an actor of major importance in terms of policy and promotion of women's entrepreneurship. Up until 1992 the area of employment policy and job creation was considered the business of individual states. Since 2000, however, employment policies and issues concerning job creation and entrepreneurship have shifted from a more marginalized position to become a central question on the EU agenda (Rhodes, 2010). Policy guidelines and recommendations from the EU affect national policies in the area of employment. Swedish programmes on promoting women's entrepreneurship and on entrepreneurship education are, to a large extent, influenced by EU rhetoric and can be viewed as a part of an EU strategy to influence national policies.

With the introduction of the Lisbon Process in 2000, the EU took on a new role in the area of employment policy. At the summit, the EU set the goal for the next decade: 'to become the most competitive and dynamic knowledge-based economy in the world capable of sustainable economic growth with more and better jobs and greater social cohesion' (European Council, 2000). This goal served to create an important link between education and employment policies that legitimizes the Union's ability to act in the area of employment and education in order to create jobs and growth, areas that have traditionally had limited provisions for action on the EU level according to the treaties (Rhodes, 2010). This meant that the EU, for the first time, could influence policies in the areas of employment and education.

A focus for action was placed on education, raising employment, and strengthening equal opportunities, including reducing occupational segregation and creating a friendly environment for starting up and developing innovative businesses, especially small and medium-sized enterprises (SMEs) (European Council, 2000). In 2010, as a continuation of the Lisbon Process, the Council adopted a new ten-year strategy for the

Union entitled 'Europe 2020'. Education and entrepreneurship were now further emphasized as important for the solution to Europe's problems (European Commission, 2010d). Central to the area of employment and as a part of the Europe 2020 strategy is the European Employment Strategy (EES). Its main objective is to create more and better jobs (ibid.). The EES is an example of soft law, which means that the EU shapes policy through non-binding decisions and recommendations, rather than binding regulations and directives, through the so-called Open Method of Coordination (OMC). The OMC is one of several methods based on voluntary and informal ways for policy through discussion and negotiation. The OMC is mainly used in areas where the EU only has the power to support, coordinate or supplement member states' actions (Alexiadou, 2010). The process was introduced at the European Council in Lisbon in 2000 when the EU had reached a point where the economic integration process began to approach issues at the very core of the welfare state, such as employment policy and social policy and where member states were reluctant to give up sovereignty. Thus, it took an alternative to the traditional community method by which the EU could continue to play a role without being perceived as a threat to sensitive issues at the national level (Borrás and Jacobsson, 2004). Within the framework of the OMC, the Council invites the EU member states and the Commission to identify policy issues and to set common goals to address these issues. Instead of binding decisions, policy impact is expected to occur by learning processes or policy learning (Alexiadou, 2010). If the policy learning works, it will enable the convergence of the objectives of employment policy in the member states. The OMC can be seen as a compromise solution, as it maintains member states' responsibility for the policy area while giving the EU a coordinating and policy-making role that member states can accept.

Support for Women's Entrepreneurship

EU support for entrepreneurship and education is, to a large extent, framed within the discourse of the European economic crisis. The EU regards the promotion of entrepreneurship and self-employment as essential to increase employment rates (European Commission, 2010d, p. 3). In Europe, where self-employment is relatively low, there is a clear aim to increase the number of self-employed (European Commission, 2012, p. 4; European Parliament, 2013). Since 2008, the economic crisis has brought the employment rate down and the unemployment rate up. The general director for the Directorate General for Employment, Social Affairs and Inclusion at the European Commission stated that:

> [p]romoting a climate of entrepreneurship is essential in terms of job creation. It is a means to respond to the current employment crisis and to fight social exclusion. The impact of the global financial and economic crisis calls for giving entrepreneurship and self-employment a stronger role in economic and social development policies. (OECD and the European Commission, 2014, p. 4)

The important components of the EES aim to create a better education and training system in order to promote job creation: 'It is not enough to ensure that people remain active and acquire the right skills to get a job: the recovery must be based on job-creation' (European Commission, 2010d, p. 16). One way to increase the employment rate in Europe is by raising the involvement of women (ibid.). The EU attributes to women a special role as an underexploited source of growth (European Commission, 2016). Other groups are young people, older people and immigrants (European Commission, 2010a). Women's employment rates are lower than men's (59.6 per cent for women compared to 70.1 per cent for men) (Eurostat, 2014). The strategy is to 'raise employment rates substantially, particularly for women and young and older workers' (European Commission, 2010a, p. 2) as '[i]t is clear that more women need to be part of the workforce to reach that goal and to get Europe's economic engine moving again. Europe should make better use of women's talents' (European Commission, 2010b, p. 5). Here, EU growth policy becomes connected to gender equality as a way to strengthen the European economy: 'gender equality is a necessary condition for the achievement of the EU objectives of growth, employment and social cohesion' (European Commission, 2006, p. 2). Women are further viewed as a group with a high potential for increasing the share of self-employed in Europe since they comprise only 31 per cent of self-employed European citizens (European Commission, 2014), which provides room for an increasing number of women to choose self-employment (European Commission, 2010b).

Entrepreneurship and Higher Education

In order to increase the number of entrepreneurs, entrepreneurial education and training to support growth and business creation play an important role. The traditional assumption is that cooperation between governments, industry and higher education supports innovation and provides growth (Etzkowitz, 2005). This 'triple helix' model primarily focuses on research, which is supposed to be a crucial component in order to stimulate entrepreneurship (ibid.). Recent research has also highlighted the role of education in promoting innovation and entrepreneurship (Wilson et al., 2007; Herrmann, 2008; Nabi and Holden, 2008; Daghbashyan, 2013). Higher education is increasingly viewed as crucial for the creation of new SMEs (Karlsson and Nystrom, 2007; European Commission, 2010a). This means that universities should not only offer education and research, but also innovation and entrepreneurship (Yusuf and Nabeshima, 2007). Nabi and Holden (2008) further argue that higher education is crucial to students' career choices and whether or not they deem it possible and attractive to start businesses. The role of the educational system is to support entrepreneurial skills by teaching these skills to students (European Commission, 2013). The Commission states that:

> [e]ntrepreneurship should become a more widespread means of creating jobs, as well as fighting social exclusion. The accent must be put on training to ensure that education systems truly provide the basis to stimulate the appearance of new entrepreneurs, and that those willing to start and manage an SME acquire the right skills to do so. Member States should develop entrepreneurship in school curricula to create a critical mass of entrepreneurship teachers, and to promote cross-border universities and research centres' collaborations in the area of innovation and entrepreneurship. (European Commission 2010d, p. 18)

A special focus is on teaching women, as 'young women should also benefit from the growing emphasis on entrepreneurship as one of the basic skills that schools should teach all pupils' (European Commission, 2010b, p. 12).

EU Activities to Promote Women Entrepreneurs

EU actions to support women's entrepreneurship occur through rules and directives, strategic documents and actions via the OMC. In addition to binding regulations, there are a number of strategic documents, such as strategies, guidelines and recommendations, in which the EU has established the strategies and directions with regard to women's entrepreneurship. These documents provide the basis for action, which mainly takes place through the OMC. The EU also provides financial support to programmes that foster women entrepreneurs through European Social Funds (ESFs).

In 2008, the Commission launched the Small Business Act in order to support entrepreneurship in the EU. The act established an overarching framework for the EU policy on SMEs aiming to improve possibilities for entrepreneurship, stating the need for the member states to address the gender gap in terms of entrepreneurship, by fostering entrepreneurial interest and talent among young people and women, and ensuring that the system of education provides the basic skills for entrepreneurs. The act sets out to establish an EU network of female entrepreneur ambassadors, promote mentoring schemes to inspire women to set up their own businesses and promote entrepreneurship among women graduates (European Commission, 2008, p. 6). Further, it furthers invites member states to provide mentoring and support for female entrepreneurs (ibid.).

Other examples of actions are programmes directed towards supporting women entrepreneurs at EU level. One example is the Competitiveness and Innovation Framework Programme (CIP), which aims to support the competitiveness of SMEs. The main objective of the programme is to provide better access to finance for SMEs through venture capital investment and loan guarantee instruments, business and innovation support services delivered through a network of regional centres and provide support for policy-making that encourages entrepreneurship and innovation in Europe (European Commission, 2013). A more concrete example of EU actions on supporting women entrepreneurs at the EU level is the European Network to Promote Women's Entrepreneurship (WES), which was set up in 2009. This is a policy network with members from 31 European countries. The delegates represent national governments and institutions and are responsible for promoting and supporting women's entrepreneurship at the national level. WES members provide advice, support, information and contacts regarding existing support measures for female entrepreneurs, as well as help to identify good practices (European Commission, 2012).

POLICY FOR WOMEN'S ENTREPRENEURSHIP – SWEDEN

In Sweden, public authorities regard the development and promotion of entrepreneurial activity as an engine for innovation, employment and economic growth. Sweden has a comparatively small proportion of entrepreneurs – just fewer than 10 per cent (Ekonomifakta, 2014) – compared to an average of around 15 per cent in the EU (European Commission, 2010c). A great number (75 per cent) of the businesses consist of only one person and the remaining 25 per cent have less than ten employees (Ekonomifakta, 2014).

Women and men's self-employment reflects the gender-segregated division within the Swedish labour market (Holmquist and Wennberg, 2010). The group 'self-employed women' is just like 'self-employed men' – characterized by great variety. However, there are significant gender differences that are mostly related to the field of the business. Women are commonly engaged in culture, entertainment, leisure and services. Self-employed women are also found in agriculture, forestry, trade and cleaning services (Statistics Sweden, 2012a). Lower initial costs and lower or no investments in machinery characterize these areas. Men are usually active in agriculture, forestry, animal breeding and crop production, followed by the construction sector (Statistics Sweden, 2012b). Self-employed women are, on average, younger and have a higher level of education than self-employed men. Businesses run by women often have few or no employees (Holmquist and Wennberg, 2010).

The Swedish government encourages more women to be self-employed (Swedish Government, 2012b). The argument is based on gender equality (i.e., that women should have the same opportunities as men to be entrepreneurs) and the need for economic growth. By increasing the number of self-employed entrepreneurs, Sweden seeks to secure employment and increase its competitiveness (Government Communication, 2007). The government emphasizes the connection between the potential of gender equality and efficient uses of resources in the society: 'The more women that run a business, the more jobs, tax revenue and innovations are generated' (Swedish Government, 2012b, p. 2).

Support for women entrepreneurs in Sweden takes place in two different forms. One form is through direct financing subsidies, and another is by a specially designed support programme targeted towards women. In addition to this, there are a number of indirect interventions that promote enterprise, such as changes in the social security system and legislation aimed at promoting both men's and women's entrepreneurship. Major policy changes have occurred in the healthcare and school sectors, which have been opened up for private interest (Government Bill, 2008). Reforms in tax regulations in the household service sector have partly been motivated by reasons to create more jobs in the private sector for women (ibid.). Changes have also been made in the social security systems, such as including entrepreneurs in unemployment, sickness and maternity benefits (Government Bill, 2008; Social Code SFS, 2010:110).

In Sweden, there has been a policy to promote women's entrepreneurship since the mid-1990s, initially in the form of business advisers for women (between 1996 and 2000) (Nutek, 2001). There are a number of public actors that operate at the regional level and in different ways aim to support women to start up and run businesses. Examples of important political entrepreneurs are the Regional Council, the County Administrative Board and ALMI (a government agency providing advisory services, loans and venture capital) (ALMI, undated). Political entrepreneurs play an important role in supporting women's entrepreneurship by acting at the regional level. Many of the actors promoting women's entrepreneurship are municipalities, business entities and municipal companies. Several projects are co-funded by several actors: the Agency for Economic and Regional Growth and regional EU funds. Most of the political entrepreneurs act at the county or regional level. The evaluations also showed that, for example, officials at the regional level were crucial to achieving quality in the projects (Ramböll Management Consulting, 2011).

Since 2007, the Swedish Agency for Economic and Regional Growth has run a programme called 'Promoting Women's Entrepreneurship'. The major action directed towards women's entrepreneurship in Sweden has taken place within the framework of this programme (Swedish Agency for Economic and Regional Growth, 2015). The programme was conducted over two programming periods – the first in 2007–10 and the second in 2011–14 (Ramböll Management Consulting, 2011; Swedish Agency for Economic and Regional Growth, 2015). The main objective of the first period was to strengthen economic development through affecting both women's entrepreneurship and the system of business promotion in general (Swedish Agency for Economic and Regional Growth, 2013). The purpose was to:

> [...] contribute to higher employment and economic growth in Sweden by more women establishing, operating, taking over and developing companies. It increases the dynamics and competitiveness of Swedish enterprise. Entrepreneurship can also entail new career paths for women who want to find new ways of using their expertise, creativity and capacity. (Swedish Agency for Economic and Regional Growth, 2009, p. 10)

The objective was to get more women to run a business and to capitalize on new business opportunities, which would generate increased employment and economic development (Government Decision, 2012). The programme was directed towards (1) women who run, wish to start or develop, or are willing to run a business, (2) the business promotion system, consisting of actors working to promote entrepreneurship and business development and (3) the public, politicians and other groups in society related to women's entrepreneurship (Swedish Agency for Economic and Regional Growth, 2013).

The first period (2007–10) involved a total of 340 million SEK. The programme was made up of four sub-programmes, the largest of which, the Business and Innovation Development Programme (195 million SEK), was directed towards strengthening individual women's ability to run a business (Swedish Agency for Economic and Regional Growth, 2011). By means of education and knowledge, this programme was to support women in taking the step to start up a new business or to develop an existing business. By participating in courses and seminars, consulting, coaching, training (including sales training, marketing training, leadership training) mentoring projects, networking and network meetings, women would learn to develop their business ideas (Ramböll Management Consulting, 2011, p. 24).

In the second-largest sub-programme, The Entrepreneurship Programme (17 million SEK), the aim was to encourage female university students to 'see entrepreneurship as an equivalent alternative to employment' (Nutek, 2007, p. 16). As a large proportion of women are students, but only a small share of women are entrepreneurs, the programme operations were directed towards the universities. By incorporating the element of entrepreneurship in programmes and courses, the programme was to encourage the higher education institutions to adapt their programmes and activities in order to stimulate entrepreneurship and influence students to start businesses.

In the third-largest sub-programme, The Ambassadors for Women's Entrepreneurship Programme (12 million SEK), more than 800 women were appointed as ambassadors and served as role models by holding lectures in schools and universities and by acting in various networks, all with the purpose of making women's entrepreneurship visible and to inspire women to see entrepreneurship as a natural career choice (Ramböll Management Consulting, 2011).

A second period of promoting women's entrepreneurship followed in 2011–14. This was largely a continuation of previous programmes and cost 65 million SEK per year (Swedish Agency for Economic and Regional Growth, 2015). The basic policy objectives were the same, but with a special focus on green industries, the service sector, the creative and cultural sector, health care and education. During this period the programme especially emphasized the ambassador's programme, immigrants, business and innovation development and activities directed towards higher education (ibid.).

There are also other policy initiatives and actions towards women's entrepreneurship in Sweden, many of which are partly related to the national programme. A recent policy is the government's Action Plan for Gender Equality and Regional Growth 2012–14, which aimed to contribute to gender equality related to regional growth. In the period 2013–14, the Agency for Economic and Regional Growth ran the Golden Rules of

Leadership initiative commissioned by the Swedish government with the aim to increase the opportunities for women to attain and take on leadership positions (ibid.).

A GENDER ANALYSIS OF POLICY TO PROMOTE WOMEN'S ENTREPRENEURSHIP

Policy and promotion of women's entrepreneurship can be analysed through different perspectives. Pettersson (2012, 2015) uses three different points of view: a neoliberal growth-oriented perspective, a woman-oriented perspective and a gender perspective. According to the neoliberal growth-oriented perspective, women's entrepreneurship is promoted in order to contribute to economic growth. Women are seen as an underused resource and activities to promote women's entrepreneurship are directed towards the individual level, rather than making structural changes (Pettersson, 2015). The woman-oriented perspective focuses on special programmes directed towards women that aim to strengthen their opportunity to compete with men, rather than changing the underlying structures (Pettersson, 2015, p. 18). The gender perspective focuses more on gender-segregated structures in the educational system and on the labour market in general and regards the change in gender structures in society as necessary in order to give women entrepreneurs the same opportunities as their male counterparts (ibid.).

An analysis of strategies, guidelines and targets in the EU and in Sweden shows that policy and the promotion of women's entrepreneurship overall fit the neoliberal perspective. Promotion of women's entrepreneurship is framed in economic terms, especially in relation to combating the European economic crisis where women, up to now, have been underused. The view of women as 'new' potential for job creation is also found in Swedish documents (Swedish Government, 2012b; Swedish Agency for Economic and Regional Growth, 2015). Higher education is an important way to change the negative perspectives of self-employment and to teach students the entrepreneurial skills necessary for starting a business (Nutek, 2007; Swedish Agency for Economic and Regional Growth, 2013).

The Promoting Women's Entrepreneurship 2007–14 programme primarily embraced an economic growth perspective and, to some extent, contained a woman-focused perspective. The gender perspective was less present. The overall goal was to create jobs and economic growth by providing new opportunities for professional development for women.

Publications from the programme occasionally address gender segregation in education and on the labour market, but the overall spending of funding and activities are clearly growth oriented. The majority of the funding was directed towards the business and innovation development sub-programme. A majority of the funding for both periods was allocated for business and innovation development (Swedish Agency for Economic and Regional Growth, 2011, 2015; Silander and Berggren, 2015).

Policy and promotion activities are directed towards the individual, rather than changing underlying structures. The Business and Innovation Development Programme project was motivated by the view that women are not adequately reached by business advice and that increased counselling would benefit people starting businesses; the Agency for Economic and Regional Growth funds activities such as sales training, development of business ideas, mentoring and coaching. The programme was directed towards the individual level and supported a woman-focused perspective that positioned women as 'deficient' and in need of counselling and business development. This risked positioning women as inferior and different entrepreneurs, instead of linking the under-representation of women entrepreneurs to gendered structures in society as a whole (Pettersson, 2012).

The European network of female entrepreneurship ambassadors and the ambassadors' programme in Sweden both serve as examples of the emphasis that the EU and Sweden place on women entrepreneurs as role models for other women. Important ideas are about inspiration, visibility and role models, clearly in line with the 'best practice' tradition found in the field of entrepreneurship with the intention to increase employment by showing good examples (Ahl, 2006). There is a risk that the ambassadors' programme and the strong focus on business development projects serve to position women as inferior entrepreneurs to men. From a gender analytical perspective, it seems to focus on women's lack of role models, knowledge and interest in becoming entrepreneurs, although the problem could rather be that the gendered structures of the labour market, in education and in terms of family responsibilities, prevent women from becoming entrepreneurs.

SELF-EMPLOYED WOMEN WITH A HIGHER EDUCATION DEGREE IN SWEDEN

In the previous section we demonstrated that an important focus of EU and national policy towards women's entrepreneurship is directed towards higher education. By integrating entrepreneurship into higher education, students should be encouraged to view self-employment as a natural choice besides employment. In this section we discuss previous research on self-employment among university graduates and investigate to what extent graduates do become self-employed in Sweden.

Previous Research on Higher Education and Women Entrepreneurs

Starting a business is a possible career for individuals with an advanced degree; however, previous research on self-employment among those who are university educated is contradictory. On the one hand, there are studies that claim a connection between higher education and business creation (Shane, 2008; Teruel Carrizosa and De Wit, 2011; Backman, 2013). This would indicate a high interest in self-employment. This is, however, challenged by the modest proportion of graduates who actually become self-employed. Berggren and Olofsson (2011) have shown that only a small percentage of university graduates (4 per cent) start their own business, indicating that self-employment is not the first choice for university graduates. This shows a gap between expectations and actual results. Andersson and Hammarstedt (2011) suggest that it is primarily individuals who have difficulties in finding employment who choose to become entrepreneurs. If a student is attractive on the labour market, then his or her interest in entrepreneurship is expected to be lower. This could indicate the paradox: high quality in higher education results in students with less interest in entrepreneurship and self-employment (Lindahl and Regnér, 2005; Lundin, 2007).

Our analysis will focus on gender and the fields of study of those who are self-employed. The gender factor is relevant within entrepreneurship, as gender and educational choices differ depending on gender (Holmquist and Wennberg, 2010). Field of study is important, as women and men traditionally choose different fields of education (Leathwood and Read, 2009; Lindberg et al., 2011) and because female-dominated sectors, in terms of self-employment, diverge from female-dominated sectors of education. Those who start their own businesses often do this in the same sector as their field of knowledge. This further accentuates the gender differentiation within an already gender-segregated labour market. A larger share of women have a higher education degree in areas where employment is found in the public sector. Women often work in health care, education and public administration, which provide them with stable and often permanent job contracts. A previous study (Berggren and Olofsson, 2011) shows that, in terms of number, it is primarily men with a technical education that become self-employed. If we look instead to the proportions of students in different educational fields, it is graduates within agriculture, forestry or art who are most likely to become self-employed, with more men in agriculture and forestry and more women in the arts. Individuals who have studied within traditional female-dominated fields are likely to find work in the public sector and individuals with technical training are likely to find jobs in the private sector. The field of education is therefore expected to impact whether or not an individual becomes self-employed.

Length of education is also important for the predisposition to become self-employed. People with shorter education are more likely to start their own business. Men generally have a shorter education, poorer school performance and higher dropout rates than women (Wernersson, 2010). A Swedish survey, based only on male employees, shows that it was common among the groups with either a high or a low income to start a business and less likely for the group in the middle (Andersson Joona and Wadensjö, 2013)

Data on Self-Employment among Graduates

To what extent do men and women in Sweden with a higher education degree become self-employed and within which fields of education do men compared to women become self-employed? The data analysed in this section came from Swedish registers (Gothenburg Educational Longitudinal Database) and include information on tertiary degree, employment and income two and five years after finishing higher education studies. The analysed population consists of those individuals born in 1973–82 who had obtained any of the selected common professional degrees and who were active on the labour market during the period 1994–2011. They are all individuals in these birth cohorts who meet the above stated criteria; they are not a sample. The age of the individuals when their employment status was analysed two years after was within the range of 21–38 years, and five years after within the range of 24–35 years. This means there are fewer individuals measured five years after completion than two years after. The time point for the measure also varies; what is stable is the time the graduates have had to establish themselves as employed or self-employed. Since the statistics between two and five years are not comparable in numbers, the results will mainly be discussed in percentages. There are 63 per cent of women and 37 per cent of men, since more women study at higher education institutions and more women complete a degree. Information on income from employment and self-employment is not shown in Table 7.1, but creates the basis for the calculations of how many individuals are employed, self-employed or both (hybrids and combiners). The professions listed are

Table 7.1 *Descriptive statistics of the graduates, employment and self-employment, numbers and percentages*

Degree	Gender	Number Employed Two Years After	Number Self-employed Two Years After	% Self-employed Two Years After	Number Hybrid Two Years After	% Hybrid Two Years After	Number Employed Five Years After	Number Self-employed Five Years After	% Self-employed Five Years After	Number Hybrid Five Years After	% Hybrid Five Years After
Physician	Men	2 045	50	2.4	49	98.0	1 178	71	5.7	66	93.0
	Women	2 819	23	0.8	22	95.7	1 543	30	1.9	28	93.3
Dentist	Men	243	14	5.4	8	57.1	118	11	8.5	8	72.7
	Women	457	4	0.9	3	75.0	214	8	3.6	5	62.5
Nurse	Men	1 553	21	1.3	20	95.2	673	17	2.5	16	94.1
	Women	10 824	66	0.6	62	93.9	5 700	46	0.8	39	84.8
Physiotherapist	Men	474	46	8.8	33	71.7	202	22	9.8	13	59.1
	Women	1 595	74	4.4	52	70.2	933	47	4.8	32	68.1
Psychologist	Men	245	35	12.5	33	94.3	76	15	16.5	13	86.7
	Women	715	30	4.0	25	83.3	264	19	6.7	14	73.7
Social worker	Men	522	5	0.9	3	60.0	243	3	1.2	2	66.7
	Women	4 775	43	0.9	37	86.0	2 523	33	1.3	29	87.9
Teacher	Men	6 795	186	2.7	177	95.2	3 689	135	3.5	125	92.6
	Women	28 981	226	0.8	205	90.7	17 894	189	1.0	162	85.7
Lawyer	Men	2 496	63	2.5	53	84.1	1 510	36	2.3	30	83.3
	Women	3 947	38	0.9	28	73.7	2 444	22	0.9	18	81.8
Engineer	Men	30 818	760	2.4	637	83.8	21 107	606	2.8	505	83.3
	Women	11 300	112	1.0	99	88.4	7 359	87	1.2	76	87.4
Agriculture	Men	657	144	18.0	106	73.6	465	145	23.8	95	65.5
	Women	981	47	4.6	42	89.4	580	47	7.5	34	72.3

Table 7.1 (continued)

Degree	Gender	Number Employed Two Years After	Number Self-employed Two Years After	% Self-employed Two Years After	Number Hybrid Two Years After	% Hybrid Two Years After	Number Employed Five Years After	Number Self-employed Five Years After	% Self-employed Five Years After	Number Hybrid Five Years After	% Hybrid Five Years After
Veterinary	Men	43	4	8.5	4	100.0	21	3	12.5	2	66.7
	Women	293	30	9.3	27	90.0	144	24	14.3	18	75.0
Forestry	Men	282	18	6.0	14	77.8	173	15	8.0	13	86.7
	Women	70	2	2.3	2	100.0	33	3	8.3	3	100.0
Arts	Men	861	225	20.7	170	75.6	492	168	25.5	119	70.8
	Women	1101	217	16.5	155	71.4	611	120	16.4	90	75.0

aggregations of different specializations. For example, nurse includes all specializations; psychologist includes psychotherapists; teacher includes pre-school to upper secondary school teachers; agriculture consists of a variety of professions such as horticulturist, agronomist and farm manager; forestry consists of forest warden, forester and forest technician; and arts are those who have earned a degree in the field of fine arts.

Table 7.1 shows that, two years after completing higher education, more men than women have income from self-employment. The only field where women were almost as likely as men to become self-employed was within the field of fine arts. Employment within this field is often project-based (e.g., acting). Generally, the proportion of self-employment was low – in several professions, it was only 1 per cent. Universities have traditionally had the purpose of educating for work and service within governmental institutions and this is still the case. For professions within teaching and health care, which comprise a large part of the student population, their education is directed towards positions in the public sector. Tertiary-educated students within engineering are expected to be the drivers of innovations and to start businesses. Since engineers are a large group, many have income as self-employed; however, the proportion of self-employment in relation to employment is low. Many graduates within engineering find employment within companies such as Ericsson, Volvo and Skanska. Five years after completing tertiary studies, the proportion of self-employed has just increased slightly in some professions – physicians, psychologists, agriculturalists, veterinarians and foresters and male artists. As can be seen from Table 7.1, there were few professionals within some categories, which means that some of the conclusions can only be drawn tentatively.

Looking at those graduates who are combining their employment with self-employment, they make up a large majority. It seems that most of the graduates are running their business on the side. However, these figures might be somewhat underestimated as the estimation is based on the main income source and not on time invested. It is difficult to estimate income among those who are self-employed. Often they do not have regular income and have the possibility to influence the finances of their business, meaning that some of the turnover could be used for reinvestment before being estimated for tax authorities.

We have also studied the proportion of the main sources of income among the 'hybrids': from self-employment or employment (not shown in the table). In the literature, it is often assumed that women will become self-employed to be able to combine career and care of their family. Interestingly, there was no clear gender differences concerning main source of income among the hybrids. Among the physiotherapists,

30–45 per cent had their main income from self-employment, around 40 per cent among men within agriculture (< 20 per cent women), 30 per cent among women veterinarians (too few men to estimate), 12–18 per cent among engineers and 30–37 per cent among artists. Among male psychologists 12 per cent, and five years later 16 per cent, have income from self-employment; however, those who have self-employment as their main source of income are only single individuals. From this we cannot conclude that women become self-employed to manage career and family. Women (and men) are not likely to become self-employed unless the labour market requires it, such as in the case of artists who are engaged on a project basis or farmers who have their own land to care for.

CONCLUSIONS

A study of the Promoting Women's Entrepreneurship programme shows that it primarily embraces economic growth and to some extent from a woman-focused perspective. Activities are mainly oriented towards the individual level. The Business and Innovation Development Programme was motivated by the view that women are not adequately reached by business advice and that increased counselling would encourage them to start a business; the focus on business development and women as role models risks positioning women as lacking the will or knowledge for entrepreneurship. The Swedish policy for promoting women's entre-preneurship has addressed what could be interpreted as 'wrong' attitudes to entrepreneurship. The 'problem' is further presented as tertiary-educated women choosing employment instead of becoming self-employed because they do not see (or understand) self-employment as a natural form of employment since universities do not teach them entre-preneurship. The presumption is that there is a large market of opportun-ity out there and if women do not take part in it, they will lose out. Policy and programmes run by the EU and Swedish Agency for Economic and Regional Growth have primarily focused on attitudes held by women or students and, to a lesser extent, the actors in the support system.

This study shows that the proportion of self-employment is low – neither women nor men with a university degree seem to choose self-employment unless the labour market requires it. If university graduates become self-employed, they do it in combination with their employment. Considering the structure in the educational sector and on the labour market, women with higher education are more likely to get a better job with a higher salary when employed versus self-employed.

There is little incentive for tertiary-educated women to start businesses. Entrepreneurship education aiming at inspiring women to see entrepreneurship as a natural alternative to employment seems to be less realistic. Nevertheless, the policy on promoting women's entrepreneurship shows that the focus is on the individual level. Actions are directed towards changing the individual entrepreneur when the problem is really rooted in the structural conditions at the time the entrepreneurship programme was studied.

There is limited empirical research into how political entrepreneurs in Sweden pushed for, and succeeded in promoting employment and entrepreneurship among women. Political entrepreneurs in the area of women's entrepreneurship act within a policy frame that almost exclusively limits policy and action to the individual; that is, it focuses on 'changing the women' in order to fit them into the expectations of society, and lacks structurally oriented actions to really change the possibilities for women's entrepreneurship. How these political entrepreneurs act and interact to support female entrepreneurship needs to be studied more closely in the future in empirical studies at the micro level to provide greater knowledge of political entrepreneurship.

REFERENCES

Ahl, H. (2006), 'Why research on women entrepreneurs needs new directions', *Entrepreneurship Theory and Practice*, **30**(5), 595–621.

Alexiadou, N. (2010), 'Policy learning and governance of educational policy in EU', *Journal of Education Policy*, 25(4), 443–63.

ALMI (undated), 'About ALMI', accessed 18 May 2016 at http://www.almi.se/ English/.

Andersson Joona, P. and E. Wadensjö (2013), 'The best and the brightest or the least successful? Self-employment entry among male wage-earners in Sweden', *Small Business Economics*, **40**(1), 155–72.

Andersson, L. and M. Hammarstedt (2011), 'Invandrares egenföretagande – trender, brancher, storlek och resultat' [Immigrant entrepreneurship – trends, industries, size and performance], *Ekonomisk debatt*, **39**(2), 31–9.

Backman, M. (2013), 'Regions, human capital and new firm formation', dissertation, Jönköping: Jönköping International Business School.

Berggren, C. and A. Olofsson (2011), 'From higher education studies to self-employment – a matter of discipline and gender?', paper presented at the European Conference on Educational Research (ECER), Berlin.

Borrás, S. and K. Jacobsson (2004), 'The open method of coordination and new governance patterns in the EU', *Journal of European Public Policy*, **11**(2), 185–208.

Braidford, P. and I. Stone (2008), 'Women's business centres – lessons learned from USA, Sweden and Canada', *Proceedings, Institute for Small Business and Entrepreneurship*, Belfast, 5–7 November.

Daghbashyan, Z. (2013), *Essays on University Efficiency Analysis and Entrepreneurship among University Graduates*, Stockholm: KTH Royal Institute of Technology.

Ekonomifakta (2014), 'Företagare' [Entrepreneur], accessed 18 May 2016 at www.ekonomifakta.se/sv/Fakta/Foretagande/Naringslivet/Foretagare/.

Etzkowitz, H. (2005), *Trippelhelix – den nya innovationsmodellen: högskola, näringsliv och myndigheter i samverkan* [Triple Helix: The New Model of Innovation: Education, Industry and Authorities in Cooperation], Stockholm: SNS förlag.

European Commission (2006), *Roadmap for Equality Between Women and Men (2006–2010)*, Luxembourg: Publications Office of the European Union.

European Commission (2008), *Think Small First – A Small Business Act for Europe*, Brussels: European Commission.

European Commission (2010a), *Europe 2020 – A Strategy for Smart, Sustainable and Inclusive Growth*, Brussels: European Commission.

European Commission (2010b), *Strategy for Equality Between Women and Men 2010–2015*, Luxembourg: Brussels: European Commission.

European Commission (2010c), *European Employment Observatory Review – Self-employment in Europe*, Brussels: European Commission.

European Commission (2010d), *An Agenda for New Skills and Jobs: A European Contribution Towards Full Employment*, Luxembourg: Publications Office of the European Union.

European Commission (2012), *European Network to Promote Women's Entrepreneurship: Activity Report 2012*, Brussels: European Commission.

European Commission (2013), *Entrepreneurship 2020 Action Plan*, Brussels: European Commission.

European Commission (2014), *Statistical Data on Women Entrepreneurs in Europe*, Luxembourg: Publications Office of the European Union.

European Commission (2016), 'Female entrepreneurs', accessed 18 May 2016 at http://ec.europa.eu/growth/smes/promoting-entrepreneurship/we-work-for/women/index_en.htm.

European Council (2000), *Presidency Conclusions 23 an 24 March 2000*, Brussels, European Council.

European Parliament (2013), *Women's Entrepreneurship in the EU*, Brussels: European Parliament.

Eurostat (2014), 'Gender statistics', accessed 25 May 2016 at http://ec.europa.eu/eurostat/statistics-explained/index.php/Gender_statistics.

Government Bill (2008), *Utredningen om trygghetssystemen för företagare* [The Investigation of Social Security Systems for Entrepreneurs], Stockholm: Fritze.

Government Communication (2007), *Sveriges företagande och konkurrenskraft* [Swedish Entrepreneurship and Competitiveness], DS 2007:37, Stockholm: Näringsdepartementet.

Government Decision (2012), *N2011/1250/ENT, Regleringsbrev för budgetåret 2013 avseende Tillväxtverket inom utgiftsområde 19 Regional tillväxt och utgiftsområde 24 Näringsliv* [Appropriation for Financial Year 2013 in Relation to Tillväxtverket in Category 19 Regional Growth and Expenditure 24 Business], 13 December.

Herrmann, K. (2008), *Developing Entrepreneurial Graduates: Putting Entrepreneurship at the Centre of Higher Education*, London: NESTA.

Holmquist, C. and K. Wennberg (2010), *Många miljarder blir det ... Fakta och nyckeltal om kvinnors företag* [Many Billions will be ... Facts and Figures on Women's Business], Stockholm: Tillväxtverket.

Karlsson, C. and K. Nyström (2007), *Nyföretagande, näringslivsdynamik och tillväxt i den nya världsekonomin* [Business Creation, Business Dynamism and Growth in the New Global Economy], Stockholm: Globaliseringsrådet.

Leathwood, C. and B. Read (2009), *Gender and the Changing Face of Higher Education. A Feminized Future?*, Maidenhead, UK: Open University Press.

Lindahl, L. and H. Regnér (2005), 'College choice and subsequent earnings: results using Swedish sibling data', *The Scandinavian Journal of Economics*, **107**(3), 437–57.

Lindberg, L., U. Riis and C. Silander (2011), 'Gender equality in Swedish higher education: patterns and shifts', *Scandinavian Journal of Educational Research*, **55**(2), 165–79.

Lundin, M. (2007), 'Effects of college choice on incomes in Sweden', *Working Paper No. R2007:016*, Swedish Institute for Growth Policy Studies.

Nabi, G. and R. Holden (2008), 'Graduate entrepreneurship: intentions, education, and training', *Education and Training*, **50**(7), 545–51.

Nutek (2001), *Att främja näringslivsutveckling – En framtidsinriktad utvärdering av affärsrådgivning för kvinnor* [Promoting Business Development – A Future-oriented Evaluation of Business Advice for Women], Stockholm: Nutek.

Nutek (2007), *Främja kvinnors företagande – programmet i korthet* [Promoting Women in Business – Programme in Brief], Stockholm: Nutek.

OECD and the European Commission (2014), *The Missing Entrepreneurs: Policies for Inclusive Entrepreneurship in Europe*, Paris: OECD Publishing.

Olofsson, A. (2012), 'Konflikten mellan kontroll och förändring – exemplet entreprenör (skapsutbildning) i det svenska utbildningssystemet' [The conflict between control and change – the example of entrepreneurship (community education) in Swedish education], in M. Stigmar and T. Sandstedt (eds), *Kvalitet och kollegialitet – vänbok till Leif Lindberg*, Växjö: Linnaeus University Press.

Pettersson, K. (2012), 'Support for women's entrepreneurship: a Nordic spectrum', *International Journal of Gender and Entrepreneurship*, **4**(1), 4–19.

Pettersson, K. (2015), *Två steg fram och ett tillbaka? En genusanalys av policy för kvinnors företagande i Norden* [Two Steps Forward and One Back? A Gender Analysis of Policies for Women's Entrepreneurship in the Nordic Countries], Stockholm: Tillväxtverket.

Ramböll Management Consulting (2011), *Slututvärdering – Främja kvinnors företagande* [Final Evaluation – Promoting Women's Entrepreneurship], Stockholm: Ramböll.

Rhodes, M. (2010), 'Employment policy – between efficacy and experimentation', in H. Wallace, M.A. Pollack and A.R. Young (eds), *Policy-making in the European Union*, Oxford: Oxford University Press.

Rouse, J. and J. Kitching (2006), 'Do enterprise support programmes leave women holding the baby?' *Environment and Planning C: Government and Policy*, **24**(1), 5–19.

Shane, S.A. (2008), *The Illusions of Entrepreneurship: The Costly Myths that Entrepreneurs, Investors, and Policy Makers Live By*, New Haven, CT: Yale University Press.

Silander, C. and C. Berggren (2015), *Politiska entreprenörer och kvinnors företagande*, Stockholm: Santérus Förlag.

Social Code SFS (2010:110), *Svensk författningssamling* [Swedish Code of Statutes].

Statistics Sweden (2012a), '5 vanligaste yrkena för egenföretagande kvinnor' [5 most common occupations for self-employed women], accessed 18 May 2016 at www.scb.se/sv_/Hitta-statistik/Statistik-efter-amne/Arbetsmarknad/Sysselsattning-forvarvsarbete-och-arbetstider/Yrkesregistret-med-yrkesstatistik/59064/59071/358148/.

Statistics Sweden (2012b), '5 vanligaste yrkena för egenföretagande män' [5 most common occupations for self-employed men], accessed 18 May 2016 at www.scb.se/sv_/Hitta-statistik/Statistik-efter-amne/Arbetsmarknad/Sysselsattning-forvarvsarbete-och-arbetstider/Yrkesregistret-med-yrkesstatistik/59064/59071/358150/.

Swedish Agency for Economic and Regional Growth (2009), *Programme to Promote Women's Entrepreneurship*, Nutek Info. 0071.

Swedish Agency for Economic and Regional Growth (2011), *Fler kvinnor driver och utvecklar företag!* [More Women Run and Develop Companies!], Stockholm: Tillväxtverket.

Swedish Agency for Economic and Regional Growth (2013), *Vision: hållbar tillväxt – Tillväxtanalys 2013 delrapport 1* [Vision: Sustainable Growth – Growth Analysis 2013 1st Interim Report], Stockholm: Tillväxtverket.

Swedish Agency for Economic and Regional Growth (2015), *8 Years Promoting Women's Entrepreneurship in Sweden. Promoting Women's Entrepreneurship in Sweden 2007–2014 – Results and Lessons Learned in Brief*, Stockholm: Swedish Agency for Economic and Regional Growth.

Swedish Government (2012a), *Regeringens satsningar på kvinnors företagande. Bilaga till beslut vid regeringens sammanträde den 8 mars 2012. N2012/1365/RT, Handlingsplan för en jämställd regional tillväxt 2012–2014* [Government Initiatives on Women's Entrepreneurship. Annex to the Decision at the Government's Meeting on 8 March 2012. M2012/1365/RT, the Action Plan for an Equal Regional Growth 2012–14], Stockholm: Tillväxtverket.

Swedish Government (2012b), *Handlingsplan för en jämställd regional tillväxt 2012–14* [Action Plan for an Equal Regional Growth 2012–14], Stockholm: Tillväxtverket.

Terjesen, S., N. Bosma and E. Stam (2015), 'Advanced public policy for high growth, female and social entrepreneurship', *Public Administration Review*, **76**(2), 230–39.

Teruel Carrizosa, M. and G. de Wit (2011), 'Determinants of high-growth firms: why do some countries have more high-growth firms than others?' *EIM Research Reports*, Universitat Rovira i Virgili.

Wernersson, I. (2010), *Könsskillnader i skolprestationer – idéer om orsaker?* [Gender Differences in School Performance – Ideas About the Causes], Stockholm: Fritze.

Wilson, F., J. Kickul and F. Marlino (2007), 'Gender, entrepreneurial self-efficacy, and entrepreneurial career intentions: implications for entrepreneurship education', *Entrepreneurship: Theory and Practice*, **31**(3), 387–406.

Yusuf, S. and K. Nabeshima (2007), *How Universities Promote Economic Growth*, Washington, DC: The World Bank.

8. Political entrepreneurs, networking women entrepreneurs and business growth

Marie-Louise von Bergmann-Winberg and Yvonne von Friedrichs

Women as business entrepreneurs have been the subject of more intensive research in the last decades, not the least in connection with European Union (EU) projects and inter-state comparisons. However, regional comparisons within Nordic states in general and within Sweden in particular are rare. In this study, we investigate whether regional business traditions and regional structures influence women entrepreneurs and if so, how and to what extent. We have chosen the counties of Mid-Sweden, that is, the counties of Västernorrland and Jämtland, where both regions are well known for rising numbers of women business entrepreneurs, with, however, varying structural and cultural backgrounds. Our aim is to investigate the role of business networks (networking) and political entrepreneurship on the regional and local levels, where the differences between these two counties could be described as follows.

Västernorrland is a traditional industrial county with forestry, paper, pulp and heavy industry. Around the beginning of the twentieth century it was one of the richest counties per capita in Sweden. The role of women entrepreneurs is by tradition rather small and the access to business organizations and networks limited. However, with changing business structures in the last decades, the role pattern has started to change, which has paved the way for strong female networks in different lines of business. The opposite regional structure is found in Jämtland, previously part of Norway, with a traditional lion's share of jobs in the public sector and in small farms connected with forestry and tourism. With the dominance of the public sector, jobs were gradually created in connection with small business firms with private owners, or even within the voluntary sector. The cooperation within the local communities or with larger regions has been tight, because of the problems of the smallest county of Sweden compared to the large geographical area. This has called for solutions that might be called variants of political entrepreneurship, enabling possibilities for female entrepreneurs, who without the Kirzner (1973) type of crossing borders, or stretching legislative procedures, creating possibilities and space, would probably not have been as prosperous.

The analysis of our regional case studies verifies the original hypothesis: without the corresponding support of political entrepreneurship, women business entrepreneurs in Västernorrland have built and strengthened their networks, thus creating more and stable firms, whereas the small-scale women entrepreneurs in Jämtland have benefitted from the various local and regional public support of political entrepreneurship, in some cases quite remarkably when creating internationally known businesses. To some extent, the county of Jämtland has also benefitted from the comparatively large number of regional and local EU projects from 1995 onwards, which paved the way for multi-actor cooperation, not the least the inclusion of municipal political entrepreneurship.

The research questions are as follows: Under what conditions and with which criteria is political entrepreneurship of crucial importance as counterweight to strong business networks, or are they to be considered complementary? Does political entrepreneurship matter and if so what would be the criteria for women business entrepreneurship? Do some forms of networks replace the absence of political entrepreneurship or are they to be considered as complementary? How is this affected by the local or regional business climate and corresponding historical traditions?

POLITICAL ENTREPRENEURS: WHO, HOW AND WITH WHAT EFFECTS?

Who are to be considered political entrepreneurs and how do they act in order to enhance economic growth and better conditions for women as business leaders? In our study we concentrate on two mid-Sweden regions, low-density population areas, but extensive in size, compared to other Swedish regions. Nevertheless, the archetypal political entrepreneur in the Swedish type of multilevel government is about the same: a politician, a bureaucrat, an officer, or even department within the public-funded sector who with innovative approaches encourages entrepreneurship or business with the goal of growth and employment – the common basis for this anthology.

Beyond this, we think some clarification and operationalization is needed for our purpose of comparing regions. Not only should we focus on political entrepreneurs as defined above, but also on *how* and *why* they act to enhance the growth of women business enterprises. According to McCaffrey and Salerno (2011, p. 552) political entrepreneurship is considered an underdeveloped area of economics, but is played out in the political arena. The starting point is sometimes attributed to Joseph Schumpeter (1934), though he never used the term political entrepreneurship in his writings, although his theories of democracy as an elite competition between political parties and individuals for political governance are in line with later thinking on political entrepreneurship (Swedberg, 2008; Von Bergmann-Winberg, 2014, p. 313). McCaffrey and Salerno (2011) echo the early theories of Robert Dahl, who almost 50 years ago tackled political entrepreneurship in *Who Governs?* (Dahl, 1961). The question is of topical interest in our study, in much the same way as in Kirzner (1973, p. 39) who focuses on creative destruction and innovation in entrepreneurial behaviour and organization (Coffé and Geys, 2006; Kiewicz, 2007; Parker, 2008). Petridou et al. (2015, p. 2), on the other hand, find an emphasis in this theorization on political entrepreneurs, understood as state actors, as owners of resources, along the lines of McCaffrey and Salerno, disciples of the so-called Austrian school of entrepreneurial thinking. Thus, we might even draw a line between political entrepreneurs and entrepreneurial politicians (Nyhlén, 2013), to distinguish between those actors who set the goals for enhancing growth in women business enterprises, and those who as officials or bureaucrats have to implement them.

In many Western countries, formal government structures have long had elements of multi-actor negotiations and networking, but over time a governance structure was established with cooperation between several groups of actors. The actual shift of paradigm had taken place already with the creation of the EU internal market in 1992, as its regional cohesion plans have shaped the construction of partnerships and networking for regional governance.

How do the political entrepreneurs use their abilities as either entrepreneurial politicians or officials and bureaucrats? The ways and means according to entrepreneurship theories, are either innovative measures or, according to Kirzner (1973, p. 73) regaining stability after change, where the entrepreneur functions as a stabilizing agent. Kingdon (1984 [2003]) developed the metaphor of 'windows of opportunity', referring to the space for action created, and which could be used for new methods. Schneider and Teske (1992) discuss how the political entrepreneurs advertise their policy ideas in the political arena, which according to Holcombe (2002, p. 153) encompasses cooperation or competition. All in all, political entrepreneurs in public administration seem to use their resources and means to do things differently, create space for new initiatives, stretching legal borders in the multi-level governance that characterizes current Swedish regions.

When political entrepreneurs are given more freedom of action, and act innovatively to make a real difference, the effects can be measured in business growth over time. In our study of women business enterprises in two regions, this might prove the necessity of regional prosperity and change for political entrepreneurs. According to Petridou and Ioannides (2013), this can be the effect of so-called 'creative milieu', in line with Florida's (2002) work on creativity, innovation and economic development. Defining regions, or even sub-regions, as creative geography might be a difficult path to follow for a regional comparison. However, it might be possible to identify creative sub-milieus, and creative women starting business enterprises in a networking environment, where the support from political entrepreneurs is vital. Or the obvious lack of political entrepreneurship on regional and local levels might prove that sustainable internal networking leads to comparable effects, in this case diminishing the role of potential political entrepreneurs. All in all, we will investigate whether political entrepreneurs make a difference, compared to inactive public officials, whether the starting points are different or not. Our criteria as far as *how* and *with what effects* are concerned, are the means, that is, the public policies on regional or local level to facilitate for the creation of new women business enterprises or the support of existing companies, to enhance further growth, or new lines of business.

NETWORKING ENTREPRENEURS AS MEANS FOR GROWTH

The importance of women's entrepreneurship for a country's economic development has increasingly attracted global attention (Ahl, 2006) and women are the fastest-growing group of entrepreneurs (Brush et al., 2006). It is further shown that women entrepreneurs in different respects are significant contributors to the welfare of society development, as innovators as well as employers. But the opportunity for women to be entrepreneurs or business owners varies from country to country and within a country. Recent statistics from the European Commission (2014) show that the number of entrepreneurs in the total active labour force varies a lot between countries in Europe and that the Scandinavian countries are among the countries in Europe with the lowest entrepreneurship rate. The entrepreneurship rate for women (percentage of women entrepreneurs out of the total number of women in the active labour force) is half the entrepreneurship rate for men in Europe, and Sweden is one of the countries with the lowest rate of women entrepreneurs (ibid.). As a response to this, Nordic countries like Sweden have expressed a strong political will to increase women's participation in the business sector in order to enhance local and regional growth and development (Sundin and Holmquist, 2015). The Institute for Growth Policy Studies (ITPS, 2007) has studied the policy of promoting women's entrepreneurship in Denmark, Netherlands, UK, USA and Sweden. It argues that consistently important measures for the promotion of women entrepreneurship in all countries studied are access to (public and private) business services, financing in the form of micro-credit, mentoring and networking promotion.

Previous research shows that women and men's different conditions create differences in their ability to both start and develop their businesses (Hamilton, 2013). Further, it is argued that these differences might be related to the fact that men and women work in different industries, but also that entrepreneurship is largely gendered. For example, Johansson and Malmström (2008) show that men have better access to venture capital and public support compared to women entrepreneurs.

Holmquist and Wennberg (2010, p. 21) together with Marlow and McAdam (2013) argue that the main reason for the difference between men and women entrepreneurs lies in the traditional distribution of family responsibilities and that another reason is that women are trained in the service, care and humanities sectors previously managed by the public sector in welfare countries like Sweden. Welfare policy has thus led to segregation in the labour market and has been reinforced by women increasingly working in the regulated public sector, with the men working in the competitive private sector (Andersson-Skog, 2008). Holmquist and Wennberg (2010) argue that women are constantly forced to make choices about how they balance family obligations with their entrepreneurship and that this combined with their gender leads to great challenges in pursuing and developing their businesses. Women entrepreneurs generally have a 'family first' orientation (Fitzgerald and Folker, 2005), which means that women more often choose other business strategies than men to cope with everyday life, for example, choose a flexible working model where family obligations can be combined with entrepreneurship. Balancing between individual circumstances and the contextual conditions for running businesses is therefore of great importance to women's opportunities to develop their business and entrepreneurship.

To promote women entrepreneurs to start and grow their business in Sweden a special programme, 'Promoting Women's Entrepreneurship', has been set up by the Swedish government. About 63 million euros have been invested in the programme during 2007–14. The aim of the programme was to 'help create growth and renewal in Swedish industry by increasing the number of companies run and developed by women' (Tillväxtverket, 2012). The main focus of the programme was to reinforce networking activities between entrepreneurs in order to enhance relationships between individuals and as an outcome of this enable access to resources and business support. It is believed that resources and support for business growth are more problematic for women entrepreneurs to access compared to men entrepreneurs (Malmström and Johansson, 2015).

Interpersonal networks and networking have been highlighted as having a major impact on entrepreneurial success (e.g., Malecki, 1994). Researchers such as Martinez and Aldrich (2011) argue that networking strategies among entrepreneurs are important means to enhance business activity and growth. Networks are important vehicles for entrepreneurs to access useful information and knowledge to better perceive business opportunities (Malecki, 1994; Gurrieri, 2013), but also to influence local and regional entrepreneurship policies. One of the obstacles for women entrepreneurs' growth is the often-limited access to professional networks (Holmquist and Wennberg, 2010), which hinders them from accessing information and knowledge. One explanation for this is that network formations of entrepreneurs are homophilous – the tendency of individuals to associate and bond with similar others – that is, 'men tend to have more sex homophilous networks than do women, especially in establishments where they are a strong majority' (McPherson et al., 2001, p. 424). This will prevent women from accessing powerful local and regional networks and influencing the contextual conditions for their own business development. Sorenson et al. (2008, p. 615) claim that women compared to men 'prefer to organize in networks that include a broad range of people and to create collaborative and cooperative relationships within those networks' and that these networks enable women entrepreneurs to acquire resources to meet business needs.

TWO REGIONS IN COMPARISON: VÄSTERNORRLAND AND JÄMTLAND

Västernorrland

Västernorrland County was founded in its present form in 1654, with Härnösand as its capital city.[1] Today Västernorrland is the sixth in size of the Swedish counties, but only 16th in terms of population with approximately 12 persons per sq km, and the decrease in population by 16.4 per cent was the most pronounced of all Swedish counties during the period 1970–2005. Today there are around 245 000 inhabitants. A slight increase in population has taken place since 2013. Its major cities and towns are Härnösand, Sundsvall, Örnsköldsvik, Sollefteå and Kramfors.

The age of timber and wood processing made Västernorrland the most affluent county, in terms of income per capita, at the beginning of the twentieth century. The economic growth of the county was considerably larger than the rest of Sweden. Other major heavy industries such as metal, construction of vehicles, and hydroelectric power, to mention a few, were to follow the development of forestry and wood processing, thus creating employment in the bigger cities but also in the countryside where agricultural farms coexisted with various plants and business enterprises. Today, tourism plays a considerable role, not only city tourism but also to the famous UNESCO World Heritage site Höga Kusten (High Coast) with the spectacular bridge over Ångerman River. In the last decades, public organizations and civil service departments have either been transferred from Stockholm, or established in Västernorrland, with the result that a large share of the workforce has been able to find work there. More than half of all women working in the county work in the public sector while more than 80 per cent of the men work in the business sector. Compared with the rest of Sweden there are more women and men working in the public sector than in other counties. Almost a third of women in the county work in health care and social services, and along with those in the education sector 47 per cent of the women work in the public sector. The corresponding proportion for men in the county in these sectors is only 11 per cent. In the male-dominated industries like manufacturing, mining and construction a third of the men are working in those sectors, but only 6 per cent of the women (Länsstyrelsen Västernorrland, 2016).

Banking and insurance companies are well developed sectors and make Sundsvall a major Swedish actor because of their mutual cooperation. Mid Sweden University, which became a fully fledged university in 2005 (founded in 1977 as a university college) has been a powerful resource to regional development through research and education of a skilled labour force. The establishment of Mid Sweden University's research centres of international prominence together with the large forestry companies, and electronics networking nationally and internationally have affected the new labour market in the larger cities considerably, and paved the way for new highly skilled inhabitants. As for lines of business for both men and women in Västernorrland in general, the production or sales of goods accounts for 42.3 per cent (Swedish average 33 per cent) and services 57.7 per cent (Swedish average 67 per cent). As for companies with women CEOs the picture for women is 27.8 per cent production and sales of goods, which is well above the Swedish average (16.2 per cent) while for services it is 72.2 per cent, below the Swedish average (83.8 per cent) (Tillväxtverket, 2015a).

Table 8.1 shows in more detail the percentages of women in different lines of business compared with the national average.

Table 8.1   Lines of business for women leaders in Västernorrland (cf. national average) (%)

Line of Business/Sector	%
Agriculture, hunting, fishing and forestry	23 (15)
Construction and housing	17 (17)
Trade	14 (14)
Law, technology and economics	10 (14)
Manufacturing and handicrafts	8 (7)
Hotels and restaurants	4 (4)
Real estate	4 (4)
Culture, leisure, entertainment	4 (4)
Information and communication	4(6)
Nursing and care	2 (3)
Education	1 (2)

Source: Tillväxtverket (2015a) (smaller sectors are not presented).

Västernorrland is by tradition a county with a structure of large industries and the proportion of business owners among those who work (16–74 years) is 10.5 per cent, which is lower than the Swedish average (11.6 per cent) (Tillväxtverket, 2016). All in all, the economic structure of Väster-norrland has changed a lot during the past decades, which also reflects the changing role of women in the labour market. The small companies in Västernorrland, many of which have women leaders, have, together with the well-known county of Jönköping, the strongest desire for growth. By as much as 30 per cent, the biggest hindrance to growth is perceived to be the lack of suitable workforce, also a national perspective. Yet, fewer persons in this county than the Swedish average want to be a leader or self-employed owner of a business (Tillväxtverket, 2015a).

In the county of Västernorrland 2933 women are in charge of business enterprises. The share of business owners or leaders in general (16–74 years) is 10.5 per cent (Swedish average 11.6 per cent), and the share of men business leaders is 15 per cent (Swedish average 15.9 per cent), and women business leaders 5.5 per cent (Swedish average 6.9 per cent) (Tillväxtverket, 2015a). Women business leaders in the county have higher education than the Swedish average: 85.6 per cent of them have college or university education, whereas 14.4 per cent have completed compulsory education (nine years) or less.

There are both local and regional networks. The regional network for women business owners, with national affiliation, is Winnet Västernorrland. The overall aim of the organization is to make women's conditions and the empowerment of women visible, especially through structured and strategic work, for entrepreneurship on equal terms. The strategy is knowledge driven and strategically focused. Winnet Västernorrland consists of three local organizations: Winnet Örnsköldsvik, Winnet Härnösand and Winnet Sundsvall/Timrå. The local organizations aim to promote structural issues at the local level. Winnet Västernorrlands' work is aimed at developing mainly the following areas: entrepreneurship and innovative environments, and strategic cross-border cooperation. Specifically, this involves the following:

- Regional development must be followed up once a year on the basis of gender and gender equality perspective.
- Public regional programme descriptions from 2016 should have clear objectives and measures of gender equality.
- More actors are needed in business support, innovation support and capital support, for example, banking, insurance, venture capital, seed funding and incubators, to participate in the dialogue and reach a better understanding of gender and structures.
- Knowledge should be intensified among the actors involved in regional growth, among the actors within the Winnet partnership, among the actors in the Winnet network and among women who run companies.
- Venues are to be created for Winnet for knowledge transfer and to perform needs analysis evenly throughout the county.
- There must be cooperation to share knowledge across national and regional boundaries between at least two resource centres and organizations working on similar issues.

One of the goals for Winnet Västernorrland is to promote at least one local network for women entrepreneurs and leaders in every municipality. One such network is Winnet KlöverDam, a volunteer association that has been around a long time and has established itself as a strong party in

Örnsköldsvik industry. An important aim of the network is that members will have viable businesses. As it is claimed that about 70 per cent of all contracts in Sweden are distributed through contacts and networks, KlöverDam aims to help the members get more business. The network meets frequently, which is important for trust building and creates opportunities for the members to recommend each other and advise on opportunities.

The Q-nätverket (Q Network) for women entrepreneurs and leaders in Sollefteå is another locally based volunteer association. This network is also working for a more dynamic society where more women run viable businesses and more women can be found at senior level. The members are women who run companies or are leaders of companies or organizations. The network aims to expand women entrepreneur networking, to help entrepreneurs to do business, to develop women's entrepreneurship and leadership, and create venues for entrepreneurs to meet, discuss and exchange experiences.

Futura Kramfors is an organization for women in business in Kramfors municipality. The members in the association are entrepreneurs in various industries and sectors and it is open to active businesswomen, women in leadership positions and women who are about to take over a company. The goal is to create meeting places for entrepreneurs to learn and develop. They collaborate and act as a sounding board to Kramfors municipality's business unit, the market development department.

Mittnätverket Vendela (MidNetwork Vendela) is a network with the mission to promote gender-equal entrepreneurship in the municipality of Härnösand. The network creates communities for women entrepreneurs and initiates and implements activities and courses, projects and development activities, and offers advice and support to entrepreneurs.

The resource centre in Sundsvall-Timrå is an organization working together with other actors in the municipality for gender-equal entrepreneurship. In the municipality, as well as a number of networks in different municipal districts such as Kvitter, there is a network for enterprising women in Njurunda. It meets once every month to have fun and generate positive energy but also experiences are shared and members are updated on matters of importance for entrepreneurs. Women entrepreneurs from Matfors have also formed a local network, Wia, bringing together women from a range of professions.

In the municipality of Ånge is an initiative to engage women entrepreneurs to cooperate in a network – Ljungandalens initiativrika kvinnor (Ljungandalen Enterprising Women – LIF). The network is loose, the members are connected via Facebook and they cooperate with the regional organization Winnet Västernorrland.

Recent studies initiated by Winnet revealed a gender-biased business climate in the county (Sundin and Von Friedrichs, 2014; Von Friedrichs and Dalborg, 2016), which involved considerable negative consequences for women entrepreneurs in accessing important resources. The analysis reveals shortcomings in the work for gender equality in entrepreneurship in terms of both attitudes and actions.

In summary, the county of Västernorrland and the women's business networks are foremost formally organized and structured somewhat hierarchically within a regional organization that cooperates with most of the locally municipality based women business networks. The aim for these networks is foremost to engage women entrepreneurs in networking in order to increase the impact on regional policies and power structures. Another aim is to create meeting venues for knowledge and experience transfer between women entrepreneurs and business owners. In Winnet Västernorrland the ambition is to enhance the participation of women entrepreneurs and business owners in the regional and local formal (and informal) business networks and also to become a recognized powerful actor in regional and local policy-making. Winnet Västernorrland is represented in the County Administrative Boards 'county partnership', the collective, strategic regional development network in Västernorrland, with representatives of key organizations in the county.

Jämtland

Jämtland is a historical province in the centre of Sweden, where it borders on Västernorrland in the east, Västerbotten in the north and Trøndelag (Norway) in the west. Jämtland covers an area of 34 000 sq km, which is around 8 per cent of Sweden's total area, thus it is the second largest province in Sweden. It has a population of 128 000, the majority of whom live in Storsjöbygden, the area surrounding Lake Storsjön, where the only major city Östersund is situated, ranked as the 24th (of 290) most populous city in Sweden. The county is the least populated of all the 21 Swedish counties with a population density of 3.3 inhabitants per sq km. The city of Östersund was founded in 1786 in order to create a well-functioning regional administration after more than 100 years without a city. The number of people living outside an urban area is 34 per cent of the total population, making Jämtland one of the largest rural areas in Scandinavia. This clearly has to do with lifestyle choice, given the natural facilities and resources, specifically as a tourism resort. Jämtland is known as a year-round tourist destination with the peak in winter.[2]

The culture of Jämtland has been greatly affected by the fact that it has never had an upper class, since the population mostly consisted of farmers and entrepreneurs with wide connections and a strong regional identity, which prevails to this day. Jämtland was populated early. In fact, the first humans came to Jämtland after the last Ice Age, engaged in hunting and fishing, and eventually switched to a more agricultural lifestyle. Though sparsely populated, agriculture could not sustain the population, so it was combined with hunting, trading and iron production. With the rise of industrialization Jämtland was one of the few Swedish regions that never became fully industrialized, but supplied the Norrlandic coast with raw materials, mainly lumber. The focus in Jämtland's economy was directed towards tourism soon after the construction of the railroad, starting with the 'nature tourists' who came to experience the untouched nature and the fresh air and to see the snowy mountains, the waterfalls and the natural environment. Today the tourism industry is, together with forestry and engineering, the largest economic sector in the county. Tourism is now a year-round industry, offering outdoor sports like cross-country and alpine skiing in the winter and hiking and downhill biking in summer.

As Jämtland never fully industrialized, the share of agriculture is much larger than the Swedish average, that is, 4.4 per cent against the Swedish average of 1.8 per cent. The extent of the agricultural sector in the region has contributed to the development of Jämtland as the county with the most developed small-scale food production. As a result of this, Jämtland is well known as the Swedish county of gastronomy with the capital city Östersund a full member of UNESCO's Creative Cities Network. The Creative Cities Network promotes social, economic and cultural development in the developed as well as the developing world. The cities that are part of the network are supposed to create a global platform to promote cultural diversity and create knowledge on job creation within the field of creative economy and creative tourism.

The public sector is a predominant employer for almost the majority of the workforce, and the structure of business entails a large share of small-sized companies. Jämtland has the second highest number of company owners in Sweden, 8.5 per cent (average in Sweden 6.6 per cent) as against the population in corresponding regions, and it also has the highest number of enterprising women and by far, together with Dalarna, the largest share of cooperatives in Sweden. Jämtland thus has the second highest share of business owners of all the counties, with 72 per cent interested in growth, which is way above the Swedish average (Tillväxtverket, 2015a). Since 2010, the unemployment rate has been below the state average, around 7 per cent. The biggest hindrance to economic growth, lack of infrastructure, seems to be what 16 per cent of small company leaders perceive the worst, a lot higher than the Swedish average.

During 2006–12, the number of business enterprises with woman leaders in Jämtland rose from 2000 to 2800, a rise of 31.7 per cent, whereas the number of enterprises with male leadership rose from 6000 to 7000, a rise of 20 per cent. Thus, the absolute number of women leading business enterprises is almost as high as in Västernorrland, where the population is almost double that of Jämtland. The corresponding percentage is 14.3 per cent of all women 16–74 years of age, as against the national Swedish average of 11.6 per cent. Compared to all enterprises 7.9 per cent have a woman CEO, compared to the Swedish average 6.9 per cent. The division between production of commodities and services is 47.4 per cent for commodities and 52.6 per cent for service production. The Swedish average is 33 per cent and 67 per cent respectively.

Table 8.2 shows in more detail the percentages of women in different lines of business compared with the national average.

Table 8.2   Lines of business for women leaders in Jämtland (cf. national average)

Line of Business/Sector	%
Agriculture, hunting, forestry	23 (15)
Other services	18 (17)
Trade	13 (14)
Law, technology, economics	12 (14)
Hotels and restaurants	8 (4)
Nursing and care	7 (3)
Manufacturing and handicrafts	7 (7)
Culture, leisure and entertainment	5 (4)

Source: Tillväxtverket (2015a) (other sectors, together under 5% not shown).

The following description of women entrepreneurs and their networks in Jämtland is based on a recent report *Göra jämställdhet* (Doing Gender Equality) describing 30 years experience of gender-equal work in Jämtland County (Lundström, 2015). Jämtland has been known for its large number of women's networking groups since the 1980s. In the beginning it was mostly feminist groups and networks actively working to influence policy-makers and regional structures in general towards more gender-equal opportunities for women in the county. In the beginning the networks were several smaller local groups focused on local issues, but in 1989 the regional project 'Women in Jämtland' was established as a more regional initiative with the purpose to investigate women's needs, map the women's groups in the county and work as advisor for women's activities, especially in the rural parts of the county. In the beginning of the 1990s the County Administrative Board created, together with other public and private partners in the county, a women's resource centre, 'Kvinnum'. The organization had a broad aim to mobilize resources to strengthen women's position in the county mainly by giving advice to women, to coordinate activities and to generate more knowledge about the situation for women in Jämtland, and further to inspire women to stay and participate in county development. The Kvinnum initiative inspired a substantial number of local networks in the eight municipalities of Jämtland. In 1995 there were about 65 networks of different sizes in the county, some of them organized as associations and others as loose networks. Resource centres for women entrepreneurs and others were established in each of the eight municipalities. Women networks in Jämtland became very strong due to a number of factors, including local initiators, role models, public backing and expert support. Eventually the regional network Kvinnum lost public support and became a project-driven organization at the end of the 1990s. Fifteen years later there are just a few feminist groups and networks left in the county.

To summarize, women's networks in Jämtland began with a large number of networking activities in the 1980s both at regional level and local level. They were all derived from a bottom-up perspective. Eventually the County Administrative Board took over the responsibility for the networking activities by contributing money and personnel and the networks became managed by public authorities. As a consequence the county has lost the lively network activity that characterized the 1980s and 1990s and the county lacks a strong regional or local network to influence policies and structures for women entrepreneurs. In the Regional Council and County Board's (replacing the County Administrative Board since 2015) strategic plan for 2014–20 there is no explicit focus on reducing the county's unequal conditions for women entrepreneurs and women businesses.

POLITICAL ENTREPRENEURSHIP REVISITED: STATE PROJECTS ENHANCING GROWTH IN WOMEN'S BUSINESS ENTERPRISES

What do we expect of political entrepreneurs in the public sector, or alternatively women's networking, the result of which could be described as growth factors for women business companies and leadership? We are unable to identify certain effects caused by individual entrepreneurs or initiatives, apart from incentives that are easy to trace and evaluate. For the sake of comparison we have chosen a national initiative to enhance women's businesses during the period 2006–12, because national goal-setting is identical for all counties and regions, though the regional means of implementation vary, and thus also the perceived effects. This is probably the most striking effort on the state or central level to achieve a substantial growth in women's businesses. Here the state or the central level of public administration, that is, both politicians and central bureaucrats, are acting as political entrepreneurs, opening a 'window', that is, change of policies, norms and a new political agenda towards women business leaders, in order to facilitate their businesses and enhance economic growth.

On the next level – the regional – we can identify political entrepreneurs in the different counties. In this case, however, we presume that forcible national actors and/or political entrepreneurs directly influence the county administration and regional authorities and that the policy entrepreneurs are to be found mostly on the central level. On the regional level, various networks between women business leaders, or between the regional administration and women business leaders, are in fact reinforcing to some extent the bold venture by the state. This process, initiated by regional political entrepreneurs, is likely to be influenced by regional business climate, previous economic history, and the existence of previous networks and political entrepreneurs in the voluntary sector. Thus, the actors on the regional level are not likely to be the same in the Swedish counties. Our aim is to find out whether there are similarities or differences between the two Mid Sweden regions Västernorrland and Jämtland in the existence of political entrepreneurs, their methods and measures when dealing with the central task, and last but not least, in relation to the achieved effects and potential changes.

How are the incentives of the central level implemented and processed into the regions and counties in Sweden during the observation period? The Ministry for Enterprise and Innovation, in order to facilitate gender equality in their policy area, started a national programme in 2007:

'Promoting Women's Entrepreneurship'. The task was given to the Swedish Agency for Economic and Regional Growth (Tillväxtverket) to coordinate and develop a strategy aiming at enabling men and women to take part in – and likewise profit from – the publicly financed system of promoting business on equal terms (Tillväxtverket, 2011). Beside the tasks given in the programme for all the Swedish counties, extra funding was granted for seven pilot projects to enable the organizations to work with gender mainstreaming of their work, focused on promoting business in the later period of 2013–14 (Tillväxtverket, 2015a).

The results from the seven pilot projects are presented in a report analysing how they have been working with gender mainstreaming, how they have been organized, and what they have accomplished. The evaluation shows that there are large differences between the pilot projects in terms of output and results, from far-reaching changes in work procedures and routines fully or partly integrated in the regional systems for promoting business, to increased knowledge and competence in gender mainstreaming. However, the report concludes that these effects are mainly the results of short-term projects, and that the long-term effects ought to be investigated in the future (ibid).

A short comparison between the seven pilots for an analysis of the differences and similarities will then be compared to the corresponding results in Västernorrland and Jämtland, after which we will draw some conclusions about how our two case studies fit into the pilot studies as far as gender mainstreaming and concrete results are concerned, based on the reports from Västernorrland and Jämtland in the period 2006–12.

There are noticeable differences between the pilot studies, where Connect Väst seems to be most advanced, with completely new goal-setting with gender mainstreaming developed, which will result in new guidelines for steering and evaluating the work on business growth and enterprises. Education was provided during the pilot project, and will continue to a new level of gender mainstreaming. The opposite occurred with the pilot project in Kalmar County where two of the four municipalities chose to leave the project because of insufficient funding.

Region Blekinge evaluates what could be called the entrepreneurial actors. The target group was civil servants on the County Administrative Board, ALMI (support for business development), Coompanion and some other supporting actors. The result was better integration between the key actors, but note that Coompanion did not participate as much as planned. New formulas for granting business support were also important steps. Näringsliv Skåne (Skåne Business Association) managed to connect supporting financing actors to participate in the project, and all of these groups did take part in the project. New requirements on business-enhancing actions were approved because of the project. The county of Västerbotten had two pilot projects, and the results were new targets to increase the share of women enterprise applications, and likewise the granted applications for women business leaders. An investigation into previous decision-making showed much inequality in this sense, which the new guidelines are designed to overcome. New formulas have also been developed, whereby a thorough integration of equality perspectives in all documents and decision-making is foreseen. The county of Västmanland also stresses the integration of equality perspectives in all regular work with business growth, and the creation of sustainable structures for this work. A report on previous applications and results has also been done, as well as the creation of new application formulas (Von Friedrichs, 2012; Von Friedrichs and Dalborg, 2016).

Which were the effects of the national strategy in terms of means and results in Västernorrland and Jämtland? And to what extent can this be labelled political entrepreneurship by active agents and groups? In Västernorrland, the final report acknowledges a consciousness about inequality in business structures, and a lack of concrete goal-setting and concrete action in the regional strategy documents. Which are the consequences of the lack of concrete goals and actions, where there are simultaneously special actions taken for women's new business enterprises, changed attitudes towards entrepreneurship and a more flexible business structure? The results, however, show that 173 projects were accepted, and 119 completed. Fifty-seven per cent of the projects with clear equality aspirations have resulted in new business enterprises, whereas only 33 per cent without equality ambitions have done that. New strategies (Regional Growth Policy and Regional Development Strategy) have been developed where new attitudes towards equality in the business sector are underlined, but in the absence of concrete goal-setting and actions, based on how and why gender and equality actions are important, this could only be seen as a first step.

In Jämtland, the main action groups were the Association for the County of Jämtland, ALMI Företagspartner Mitt AB (ALMI Business Partners Mitt AB) and the County Administrative Board Jämtland. Two lines of action were the result of this cooperation: (1) so-called Growth Cheques that the women business leaders could apply for and (2) ALMI seminars 'Nyfiken på företag – välkommen att inspireras' (Curious About Business Enterprises – Welcome to Being Inspired). After a slow start during the first years, the project advanced most dramatically with a flood of applications and 6 200 000 SKR in Growth Cheques granted. Given the fact that the women business leaders that were granted those cheques had to double the amount, the Growth Cheques total amounted to almost 12 400 000 SKR in business developing actions. Two hundred and eighty-six women applied, and 201 were granted about 6.2 million SKR from the project. The amount of 2.25 million SKR will be paid via the regional political business support according to a published list of recipients. One of the advantages was that the County Administrative Board could combine the Growth Cheques with regular business support, which means that investment in material assets has also been possible.

In the ALMI seminars, 628 persons have participated for inspiration and advice, some of them several times. New ways of implementing Swedish legislation on regional support has led to a new project 'Innovationsdriven samhällsutveckling' (Innovation-driven Development of Society) with three lines of goal-setting: (1) smart goal-setting based on regional conditions, (2) increase the public and international image of what makes Jämtland unique and (3) efficient use of common resources (Tillväxtanalys, 2014).

Both means and accomplished results are clearly in line with political entrepreneurship in Jämtland. The total number of the Growth Cheques and the share of women business leaders that acquired this support show how many innovative public solutions have been made on a regional level. In the seminars, new ways of implementing Swedish regional support structures were discovered. Attractive, innovative and unique regional and local business images have been developed and will be continued in the next phase of national strategy 2015–20.

A comparison between the results in Tables 8.3 and 8.4 indicates that Jämtland clearly achieved the highest figures, with a remarkable growth in terms of net development, salaries and number of employees. Västernorrland on the other hand is somewhat below the Swedish average for the period in question. Compared with the final reports of public political entrepreneurial actors in Jämtland and Västernorrland, these results are hardly surprising. Whether this is the result of skilful political entrepreneurs, or their cooperation with the private business sector in Jämtland is hard to evaluate at the moment, given the comparatively short period. A continued comparative evaluation after the next phase of the national strategy after 2020 will probably provide the answer.

Table 8.3   Women's enterprises in Västernorrland County

	Number of Enterprises	Net (1000 SEK)	Number of Employees	Salaries (1000 SEK)
2006	2 759	3 554 286	5 720	847 428
2008	2 849	4 124 474	6 264	1 036 974
2010	3 030	5 131 400	6 790	1 205 844
2012	3 554	5 431 089	7 310	1 292 235
Growth 2006–12	29%	53%	28%	52%
Men's enterprises 2006–12	19%	22%	6%	24%

Source: SCB's RAMS database (2006, 2008, 2010, 2012). The numbers concern enterprises with 500 employees or fewer where the CEO is a woman. Public services and businesses are not included.

Table 8.4   Women's enterprises in Jämtland County

	Number of Enterprises	Net (1000 SEK)	Number of Employees	Salaries (1000 SEK)
2006	2 053	3 084 660	4 618	683 169
2008	2 124	3 230 865	4 863	801 235
2010	2 221	3 548 487	5 622	994 334
2012	2 704	5 417 171	6 533	127 037
Growth 2006–12	32%	76%	41%	80%
Men's enterprises 2006–12	21%	8%	4%	22%

Source: SCB's RAMS database (2006, 2008, 2010, 2012). The numbers concern enterprises with 500 employees or fewer where the CEO is a woman. Public services and businesses are not included.

Based on the results of the previous strategy, the Swedish Agency for Economic and Regional Growth in 2011 was tasked by the Swedish government with drawing up a national strategy for how women and men could avail themselves of business promotion initiatives on equal terms. The overarching goal of the strategy in this second phase (2015–20) is that women and men – regardless of ethnic background and age – should be able to avail themselves of business promotion initiatives and resources such as advice, business development assistance, cluster and business incubator activities, and financing on equal terms (see Tillväxt-verket, 2015b). As well as the seven special regional reports, the other regions have handed in rather short reports from the former period where certain funding, resources, assistance and business incubator activities are not specifically mentioned. With the new strategy light will be shed not only on women's business enterprises, but also on firms with ethnic CEOs.

Gaining access to state-funded business promotion initiatives is a step forward for women business leaders. The type and size of business support available needed to be opened up so that barriers could be abolished. Equal conditions are essential for sustainable growth. Innovation is a key for growth in both businesses and regions, fostered perhaps by creative milieus (cf. Florida, 2002) but also because of political entrepreneurs co-working with women business leaders. This means, for example, that entrepreneurs need to work more efficiently to develop new products and services in order to strengthen and maintain the competitiveness of their businesses (Tillväxtverket, 2015b).

Comparing the two regional women network initiatives, it seems rather obvious that previous paths and decisions taken, repeat themselves. As the county of Västernorrland has a tradition of business-driven development the women have organized themselves into powerful networks influencing regional policy-making to even out the differences between women and men entrepreneurs. In contrast, Jämtland, with a strong tradition of public-driven development, has made women networks develop negatively in the county with less power to influence entrepreneurship policies.

Women in Västernorrland have developed new businesses foremost in trade, service, consulting and health care. In Jämtland the creative entrepreneurship of Matlänet (Regional Food), UNESCO and other regional, international or local initiatives seems to have grown from the collaboration between public entrepreneurs on both regional and local levels, and between women's private business companies and the voluntary NGO sector. If ever, the Florida concept of creative milieu seems to foster innovative attempts to overcome low density population and infrastructure hindrances, in terms of distances and public transportation, lack of skilled labour force and the like. All in all, the conscious venture for regional development on the basis of the national strategy has been fruitful and successful in both regions, but rather differently.

CONCLUSIONS

Regional differences in terms of business structure, women's networks, business traditions and regional wealth do matter for fostering political entrepreneurship. Our study shows that even the relative level of low-density population regions on the same latitude in Sweden reveals different patterns of entrepreneurial milieus and entrepreneurial actors over time, specifically during the observed decade. Corresponding differences are, however, to be found in the other 20 regions, but according to Florida (2002) entrepreneurial geography matters perhaps more.

Forming strong networks for women's business enterprises and developing political entrepreneurship in the regions, might not, however, be mutually exclusive processes. Instead, we might think of them as mutually reinforcing and even converging processes, where benchmarking political entrepreneurship in one region leads to inter-regional public cooperation, or on a municipal level, as well. And where political entrepreneurship was needed to reinforce women's business growth initially, strong internal networks might stem from the formation of new enterprises.

National efforts to encourage the growth in number and business turnover of women's enterprises most likely will affect many, or probably a majority of regions, where the differences today are profound. New national projects and analyses will eventually level out potential cleavages. But the innovative spirit of political entrepreneurship cannot be duplicated, but has to be enhanced in the best Kirzner spirit to take advantage of specific regional assets and resources, traditions and ideas in cooperation with women business leaders. Cooperation of this kind is a perpetual process, never to be stopped, never to be repeated in the very same manner, but according to the innovative entrepreneurial behaviour of the active businesswomen.

NOTES

1. The name refers to the western part of the original Norrland (north Sweden and north Finland). Today it covers approximately the historical provinces of Ångermanland (Angermannia) and Medelpad. This county is situated on the Gulf of Bothnia, and rising from the low coastal strip is a heavily forested interior plateau, which used to supply timber for sawmilling and wood processing industries. Later on, roads and rail largely replaced the old logging routes to the coastal mills provided by the Ångerman River and other streams. Besides Härnösand, the largest city of Sundsvall, as well as Örnsköldsvik, are major shipping centres still for timber and pulp. Between 1650 and 1810 Jämtland was part of

Västernorrland, after Jämtland became part of Sweden, but because of the different ways of living and large distances, any common lines of business were never developed during that period.
2. Jämtland was originally an autonomous peasant republic with its own nation, law, currency, dialect and even parliament. However, no formal public administration was developed during that time, in this already sparsely populated region. Jämtland was conquered by Norway in 1178, and stayed Norwegian until the Treaty of Brömsebro in 1645 when it was ceded to Sweden. The province then belonged to Sweden for more than 370 years, but Swedish citizenship was only granted as late as 1699. Historically, socially and politically Jämtland has been a special territory between Sweden and Norway, and during the period of unrest of 1563–1677, it shifted alignment between the two states no less than 13 times (Länsstyrelsen Jämtland, 2015). Jämtland also started out free and remained autonomous during its time as a Norwegian dependency.

REFERENCES

Ahl, H. (2006), 'Why research on women entrepreneurs needs new directions', *Entrepreneurship Theory and Practice*, **30**(5), 595–621.

Andersson-Skog, L. (2008), 'Kvinnors företagande i ett historiskt perspektiv: mellan familj, stat och marknad' (Women entrepreneurship in a historical perspective: between family, state and market), in P. Larsson, U. Göransson and M. Lagerholm (eds), *Sesam öppna dig! Forskarperspektiv på kvinnors företagande*, Stockholm: Vinnova.

Brush, C., N.M. Carter and E.J. Gatewood et al. (eds) (2006), *Growth-Oriented Women Entrepreneurs and their Businesses: A Global Research Perspective*, Cheltenham, UK and Northampton, MA, USA: Edward Elgar Publishing.

Coffé, H. and B. Geys (2006), 'Community heterogeneity: a burden for the creation of social capital?' *Social Science Quarterly*, **87**(5), 1053–72.

Dahl, R.A. (1961), *Who Governs? Democracy and Power in an American City*, New Haven, CT: Yale University Press.

European Commission (2014), 'Statistical data on women entrepreneurs in Europe', accessed 19 May 2016 at http://ec.europa.eu/growth/tools-databases/newsroom/cf/itemdetail.cfm?item_id=7992.

Fitzgerald, M.A. and C.A. Folker (2005), 'Exploring new frontiers in women's family business leadership: the impact of women's motivations on family and business measures of success', *International Journal of Family Business*, **2**, 1–11.

Florida, R. (2002), *The Rise of the Creative Class*, New York: Basic Books.

Gurrieri, A.R. (2013), 'Networking entrepreneurs', *The Journal of Socio-Economics*, **47**(C), 193–204.

Hamilton, E. (2013), 'The discourse of entrepreneurial masculinities (and femininities)', *Entrepreneurship & Regional Development*, **24**(1–2), 90–99.

Holcombe, R.G. (2002), 'Political entrepreneurship and the democratic allocation of economic resources', *The Review of Austrian Economics*, **15**(2/3), 143–59.

Holmquist, C. and K. Wennberg (2010), *Många miljarder blir det – fakta och nyckeltal om kvinnors företag* (Many Billions it is – Facts and Key Figures on Women's Business), Stockholm: Tillväxtverket.

ITPS (2007), *Politik för att främja kvinnors företagande – beskrivning av åtgärder i Storbrittanien, Nederländerna, Danmark och USA* [Policies to Promote Women's Business – Descriptions of Measures in UK, Netherlands, Denmark and USA], accessed 25 May 2016 at https://www.tillvaxtanalys.se/download/18.527f92c214f003304d3127ba/1455009808968/politik-for-att-framja-kvinnors-foretagande-07.pdf.

Johansson, J. and M. Malmström (2008), 'Riskkapitalmarknaden – ett glastak för kvinnors företagande?' [The venture capital market – a glass ceiling for women in business?], in P. Larsson, U. Göransson and M. Lagerholm (eds), *Sesam öppna dig! Forskarperspektiv på kvinnors företagande*, Stockholm: Vinnova.

Kiewicz, K. (2007), 'Competitiveness and regions: what is the regional impact of a competitive city?' paper presented at the Regional Studies Association 'Regions in Focus' Conference, Lisbon, 2–5 April.

Kingdon, J. (1984 [2003]), *Agendas, Alternatives and Public Policies*, New York: Longman.

Kirzner, I.M. (1973), *Competition and Entrepreneurship*, Chicago, IL and London: The University of Chicago Press.

Länsstyrelsen Jämtland (2015), 'County Administrative Board', accessed 25 May 2016 at http://www.lansstyrelsen.se/jamtland.

Länsstyrelsen Västernorrland (2016), *Kvinnor och män i Västernorrland 2015* [Women and Men in Västernorrland 2015], accessed 19 May 2016 at http://www.lansstyrelsen.se/vasternorrland/SiteCollectionDocuments/Sv/publikationer/rapporter/2015/kvinnor-och-man-i-vasternorrland-2015.pdf.

Lundström, C. (2015), *Göra jämställdhet* [Doing Gender Equality], accessed 20 May 2016 at http://jamda.ub.gu.se/bitstream/1/917/1/gora_jamstalldhet.pdf.

Malecki, E. (1994), 'Entrepreneurship in regional and local development', *International Regional Science Review*, **16**(1/2), 119–53.

Malmström, M. and J. Johansson (2015), *Under ytan – hur går snacket och vem får pengarna II?* [Under the Surface – What's the Talk and Who Gets the Money II?], Stockholm: Tillväxtverket.

Marlow, S. and M. McAdam (2013), 'Gender and entrepreneurship: advancing debate and challenging myths; exploiting the mystery of the under-performing female entrepreneur', *International Journal of Entrepreneurial Behaviour & Research*, **19**(1), 114–24.

Martinez, M. and H. Aldrich (2011), 'Networking strategies for entrepreneurs: balancing cohesion and diversity', *International Journal of Entrepreneurial Behavior and Research*, **17**(1), 7–38.

McCaffrey, M. and J.T. Salerno (2011), 'A theory of political entrepreneurship', *Modern Economy*, **2**(4), 552–60.

McPherson, M., L. Smith-Lovin and J. Cook (2001), 'Birds of a feather: homophily in social networks', *Annual Review of Sociology*, **27**, 415–44.

Nyhlén, S. (2013), 'Politiska och policyentreprenörer som aktörer i en governancekontext – vilka implikationer får det?' [Political and policy entrepreneurs as actors in a governance context – what are the implications?], in P.M. Olausson and J. Nyhlén (eds), *Regioner, regionalism och entreprenörskap*, Sundsvall: Mid Sweden University.

Parker, R. (2008), 'Governance and the entrepreneurial economy: a comparative analysis of three regions', *Entrepreneurship Theory and Practice*, **32**(5), 833–54.

Petridou, E. and D. Ioannides (2013), 'Creative serendipity: when art and public entrepreneurship revitalize a downtown', in P.M. Olausson and J. Nyhlén (eds), *Regioner, regionalism och entreprenörskap*, Sundsvall: Mid Sweden University.

Petridou, E., I. Narbutaité Aflaki and L. Miles (2015), 'Unpacking the theoretical boxes of political entrepreneurship', in I. Narbutaité Aflaki, E. Petridou and L. Miles (eds), *Entrepreneurship in the Polis. Understanding Political Entrepreneurship*, Farnham, UK: Ashgate Publishing Limited.

SCB [Statistics Sweden] (2006, 2008, 2010, 2012), RAMS-database, accessed 26 May 2016 at http://www.scb.se/sv_/Hitta-statistik/Statistik-efter-amne/Arbetsmarknad/Sysselsattning-forvarvsarbete-och-arbetstider/Registerbaserad-arbetsmarknadsstatistik-RAMS/.

Schneider, M. and P. Teske (1992), 'Toward a theory of the political entrepreneur: evidence from local government', *American Political Science Review*, **86**(3), 737–47.

Schumpeter, J.A. (1934), *The Theory of Economic Development*, New Brunswick, NJ: Transaction Publishers.

Sorenson, R.L., C.A. Folker and K.H. Brigham (2008), 'The collaborative network orientation: achieving business success through collaborative relationships', *Entrepreneurship Theory and Practice*, **32**(4), 615–34.

Sundin, E. and C. Holmquist (2015), *25 år med kvinnors företagande – från osynligt till drivkraft för tillväxt* (25 Years of Women's Entrepreneurship – From Invisibility to Drivers of Growth), Stockholm: Tillväxtverket.

Sundin, E. and Y. von Friedrichs (2014), *Företagande på lika villkor? Kartläggning av företagsfrämjande aktörers attityd, strategier och operativa arbete avseende jämställt företagande i Västersnorrland län* [Business on Equal Terms? Mapping of Business Promotion Actors' Attitude, Strategy and Operational Work Relating to Equal Employment in Västernsorrland County], Härnösand: Winnet Västernorrland.

Swedberg, R. (ed.) (2008), *Schumpeter: om skapande förstörelse och entreprenörskap* [Schumpeter: The Creation and Destruction of Entrepreneurship], Stockholm: Norstedts.

Tillväxtanalys (2014), *Främja kvinnors företagande, Delrapport 1* [Promoting Women's Entrepreneurship, Report 1], accessed 25 May 2016 at https://www.tillvaxtanalys.se/download/18.201965214d8715afd16a62f/1432804266435/rapport_2014_05.pdf.

Tillväxtverket (2011), *National Strategy for Business Promotion on Equal Terms 2015–2020*, Stockholm: Tillväxtverket.

Tillväxtverket (2012), *Främja kvinnors företagande* [Promoting Women's Entrepreneurship], accessed 19 May 2016 at http://publikationer.tillvaxtverket.se/ProductView.aspx?ID=1801.

Tillväxtverket (2015a), *Utvärdering av sju pilotprojekt* [Evaluation of Seven Pilot Projects], final report, accessed 20 May 2016 at http://www.tillvaxtverket.se/download/18.7cec92bb14e05ca8aac70a05/1443039850070/Sjupilotprojekt_Info_0597_web.pdf.

148 *Political entrepreneurship*

Tillväxtverket (2015b), *Open Up! National Strategy for Business Promotion on Equal Terms 2015–2020*, accessed 20 May 2016 at http://www.tillvaxtverket. se/download/18.7cec92bb14e05ca8aac70440/1443039758198/info_0606_webb. pdf

Tillväxtverket (2016), 'Västernorrland län: Statistik om företag där de operative företagsledarna är kvinnor' [Västernorrland county: statistics on companies where the operative business leaders are women].

Von Bergmann-Winberg, M.-L. (2014), 'Social and political entrepreneurship: ways and means to develop sparsely populated regions?', in A. Lundström, C. Zhou, Y. von Friedrichs and E. Sundin (eds), *Social Entrepreneurship. Leveraging Economic, Political and Cultural Dimensions*, Cham/Heidelberg/ New York/Dordrecht: Springer.

Von Friedrichs, Y. (2012), *Den svåra styrningen mot ett jämställt företagande* [The Difficulty of Steering Towards Gender-equal Employment in Västernorrland], accessed 20 May 2016 at https://translate.google.co.uk/translate ?hl=en&sl=sv&u=http://www.vasternorrland.winnet.se/web/page.aspx%3Frefid %3D203&prev=search.

Von Friedrichs, Y. and C. Dalborg (2016), 'Gender equal entrepreneurship driver for regional renewal?' in H. Westlund and K. Kobayashi (eds), *Social Capital and Development Trends in Rural Area, Volume 11*.

9. Political entrepreneurs and immigrants' entrepreneurship

Per Strömblad

> Throughout history, Sweden owes immigrants for companies such as Findus, Handelsbanken, Gröna Lund and Securitas. By providing more support for business counselling, we increase the opportunities for even more immigrants to start and grow as entrepreneurs.[1]

Few policy-makers in contemporary democratic welfare states, no matter at what level or belonging to what specific party, would argue against the general aim of stimulating entrepreneurship. This is certainly true in the Swedish case, highlighted in this volume, where voices in more or less all spheres of the public debate seem to agree that promoting new small and medium-sized enterprises (SMEs) is an important answer to questions concerning future economic growth and prosperity. Facing not least demographic challenges, increasing the demands of people in the work force when it comes to sustaining welfare state obligations, new business opportunities need to be exploited.

The general belief in the fruitfulness of promoting entrepreneurship notwithstanding, such measures are supposed to be even more beneficial for groups that may be regarded as being in a more vulnerable position in the labour market. In Sweden, a prominent example of such a group is people with a foreign background, and this chapter focuses on conditions for entrepreneurship in this population category. Even though a detailed primary data-based review is beyond the scope here, relevant government initiatives are considered, both with respect to audits and in the light of empirical survey results.

Interestingly, when it comes to entrepreneurship, Swedish official statistics habitually reveal that, although the unemployment rate is higher among immigrants than among native Swedes, the propensity to be self-employed in small businesses is notably higher within the category of foreign born (SCB, 2013; Tillväxtverket, 2013). Generally speaking, hence, immigrants are over-represented among sole traders and this is true for men as well as for women.

Similar patterns have also been observed in other OECD countries (Andersson et al., 2013), and a not too far-fetched suspicion may be that the decision to become an entrepreneur, in reality, is less voluntary if it is primarily a strategy to avoid unemployment. At the same time, scholarly findings suggest that the degree of self-employment varies considerably among immigrants with respect to country of origin (and length of residence in the new country), and also when it comes to the diffusion of immigrant entrepreneurship over different regions of Sweden. To a large extent, these variations seem hard to explain, although several interesting hypotheses have been put forward, thus highlighting, for example, unequal access to capital from financial institutions, and geographic differences in terms of the composition of ethnic groups (cf. Edin et al., 2003; Andersson et al., 2013; Eliasson, 2014). From a policy viewpoint, an appropriate question is, of course, to what extent may political entrepreneurship, given the conceptualization of this volume, improve conditions and outcomes when it comes to immigrants' businesses activities (cf. Chapters 2 and 3)?

In the remainder of this chapter, I will utilize previous research as well as reports from government authorities, to describe and discuss conditions for entrepreneurship among immigrants in Sweden. Specifically, the question of the role of public policy initiatives in this regard will be addressed. Further, I also make use of primary data from a large-scale Swedish survey. This specific source of information (conducted by means of interviews) provides certain possibilities to investigate subjective assessments of preconditions for entrepreneurship, including variations in such assessment – not merely between people of different origin, but also across residential areas with different characteristics. As the results from this analysis will show, there may be reasons to suspect housing segregation to be an independent factor influencing the entrepreneurial level of ambition in Sweden.

IMMIGRATION, INTEGRATION AND THE SWEDISH LABOUR MARKET

In the wake of widespread global migration flows, many contemporary welfare states are characterized by increasing ethnic diversity in the population, and Sweden is no exception. In fact, Sweden has been a country of net immigration ever since the end of World War II (Ekberg, 2004). True, in the initial post-war period, only a small share of the population in Sweden was foreign born. Due to substantial immigration in the decades following, however, the population composition has repeatedly changed in a more multicultural direction. Studying official statistics after the first decade of the millennium, one finds that more than one in seven people in Sweden, or about 15 per cent, have immigrated to Sweden from other countries (SCB, 2013).[2]

During the period since 2000, yearly immigration has also tended to increase in comparison with earlier time periods.[3] This development is not least due to refugee flows that have been generated by lengthy and distressing conflicts, notably in Africa and in the Middle East. Moreover, due to the enlargement of the EU in the 2000s, an increasing internal migration in Europe has also been observed (SCB, 2013).

Obviously, demographic changes of this kind may potentially influence societal relations in countless ways. Pessimistic scenarios in this respect, such as intensified intolerance and xenophobia, are frequently in focus in social research in relevant fields (cf. Weldon, 2006; Sides and Citrin, 2007). Pure macroeconomic aspects notwithstanding, immigration may lead to increased pressures on a welfare state with a high level of ambition, with negative competition between population groups and mistrust as possible consequences.

A considerably more positive scenario may also be pictured, however, for possible outcomes of immigration. Certainly, the patterns of future migration may be very different in comparison with contemporary trends. Nevertheless, a continued substantial immigration from the developing world to a country such as Sweden may be a potential response to demographic challenges of the mature welfare state (cf. Strömblad and Malmberg, in press). Given an ageing population, preserving ambitious social policies in the future will reasonably demand an expansion of the work force. Immigration may, at least partly, be a solution to the puzzle of how to find more hands capable of assisting in future welfare state duties, as well as more taxpayers to jointly share the bill. Needless to say, such an optimistic calculation would require that new immigrants, in harmony with previous time periods in Sweden, are younger and of working age, compared to the population at large (SCB, 2013, pp. 24–7).

However, this type of optimistic scenario immediately becomes confronted with a widespread pessimism when it comes to prospects of integration into Swedish society. Indeed, the very concept of integration tends to be interpreted in many different ways, thus – seemingly usefully – lending itself to debates and suggestions from various political camps (cf. Beckman, 2011). Generously interpreted, integration is the key to unlocking a 'good version' of the multicultural society, a state of affairs where all individuals are able to realize their life projects, irrespective of ethnic or cultural background (cf. Regeringskansliet, 2008). It is obvious, however, that such a state of equality and involvement – where ethnic and cultural pluralism enrich society, rather than generating obstacles – more resembles a utopian vision than a portrait of current circumstances.

According to surveys based on registry data, the foreign born tend to be in a significantly more vulnerable position in the labour market.[4] Those who have immigrated to Sweden are to a larger extent un-employed, and the difference in the percentage of those in paid work (in the 20–64-year-old population) between Swedish born and foreign born has in recent years been approximately 25 percentage points in favour of the former (SCB, 2008, 2013). Quite expectedly, one may also note a significantly larger gap if the focus is directed towards specific groups, rather than towards aggregated levels in the entire category of foreign born. This is of course due to considerable internal differences in terms of labour market position. To exemplify, the proportion of people in paid work is particularly low among foreign born who have been residing in Sweden only for a few years; with respect to geographic origin, immigrants from countries in Africa and Asia tend to have a particularly weak position in the Swedish labour market.

Aside from labour market conditions, there are of course other potentially important indicators that may be utilized when analysing the degree of integration in society. Nevertheless, a thus more multifaceted picture rarely seems to be drawn. Focusing, for instance, on educational outcomes (SCB, 2013), bearing in mind that this may certainly have implications for future socioeconomic conditions, one notes that foreign-born pupils, in primary as well as in secondary education, tend to have lower grades compared with their schoolmates born in Sweden.[5] Further, a similar pattern is also apparent when it comes to eligibility requirements for higher education, among those who have completed upper secondary education.

Analogously, systematic differences that disfavour foreign-born inhabitants in Sweden are revealed by comparisons along other socioeconomic dimensions, such as income distribution (SCB, 2008, 2013). Moreover, net income levels tend to be lower in this population category, even taking differences in the level of employment into account. Additionally, trends in the direction of poorer health among those having a foreign background have also been observed; the differences in this respect seem to be particularly striking between foreign-born and Swedish-born women.

Further in harmony with manifested inequities, a relatively more vulnerable position seems to be associated with the motivation and willingness to exercise democratic rights. At least when it comes to voting in general elections, there is a distinct gap in participation between immigrants and native Swedes, both in local elections (in which foreign residents under certain conditions may vote) and in parliamentary elections (SCB, 2012a, 2013; cf. Adman and Strömblad, 2000; Myrberg, 2007).

The collective make-up of immigrants in Sweden is obviously heterogeneous. Two randomly chosen individuals from this population category may not have anything else in common, besides the experience of, at some point in time, having migrated to Sweden. Nevertheless, as illustrated above, official statistics clearly portray systematic biases in living conditions when immigrants are compared to native Swedes on a general level. In view of possible remedies in this regard, the remainder of this chapter is primarily concerned with the labour market, specifically with the potential of entrepreneurship.

EXPLAINING AND ENCOURAGING ENTREPRENEURSHIP AMONG IMMIGRANTS

Labour market conditions seem to be a never-ending focal point in public debates concerning integration policies in Sweden. Indeed, following discussions on this topic, one may be tempted to infer that integration, in fact, is all about how paid work (or, conversely, unemployment) is distributed across different population groups (cf. Beckman, 2011). Considering the importance attached to supporting oneself through labour and the frequently gloomy search to find a job, it is hardly surprising that self-employment appears to be particularly attractive to policy-makers to promote.

Nevertheless, it is far from self-evident how political reforms, or specific measures in this respect should be designed to give maximum effect. Evaluating potential policy influences on business conditions, or on the quality and durability of various enterprises (especially long-term influences) may generally be difficult. However, attempts to direct efforts to the heterogeneous categories of 'immigrants' or 'people with foreign background' might be particularly difficult to assess, not least because the very target group is, in practice, imprecise (cf. Riksrevisionen, 2007, 2012).

Official statistics nonetheless reveal several interesting features when it comes to entrepreneurship within the immigrant population. Data from Statistics Sweden (SCB) suggest that immigrants are over-represented in the category of self-employed in this country.[6] True, scrutinizing the entire collective of the employed, there is only a small minority who run their own business, nevertheless, there is a difference in this respect in favour of immigrants, and this pattern is similar irrespective of gender.

While 6 per cent of foreign-born women are self-employed, the corres-ponding proportion among women born in Sweden is only 4 per cent (SCB, 2013, p. 61). Among men, the difference in percentages (although not the relative difference) is even higher. Labour market statistics suggest that 9 per cent of employed men who are born abroad are working in their own businesses, while the corresponding share is 6 per cent among Swedish-born men.

Nevertheless, there are also sizable differences among immigrants, in terms of willingness and ability to run own businesses, depending on country of origin (SCB, 2008, 2013). Both among women and men, one notes a particularly high proportion of self-employed among those born in other EU countries (with other Nordic countries excepted). However, the highest proportion (12 per cent of those in paid work) is detected for men born in Asian countries. In this specific population category, by comparison, self-employment thus seems to be particularly prevalent. In contrast, it also deserves mention that the lowest rates in this regard (5 per cent among men and only 2 per cent among women) are observed for people who have migrated to Sweden from countries in Africa.

In overall comparisons between foreign- and Swedish-born entre-preneurs, one has also been able to note significant differences in terms of choice of branches of industry (SCB, 2012b). According to registry-based statistics, foreign-born entrepreneurs are markedly over-represented in the hotel and restaurant industry. Yet another observation is that companies engaged in transport and trade, to a comparatively high degree, are run by people with a migrant background.[7]

Another difference has been noticed when it comes to entrepreneurs' educational background (ibid.). In comparison with their Swedish-born counterparts, immigrant entrepreneurs tend to have a more extensive education.[8] This systematic tendency is most interesting in terms of the demands of formal qualifications and skills required to become self-employed in a given profession. It has been observed that to a higher extent immigrant entrepreneurs work in occupations that do not require a post-secondary education. At the same time in fact, they tend to be more educated than Swedish-born colleagues. In Sweden, I venture to suggest, there is a fairly widespread perception that people who have immigrated with a university diploma still have to be satisfied with unskilled jobs. Apparently, such a perception also receives some support from entre-preneurship statistics. To clarify in detail the presence of 'doctors driving taxis' would probably be a tricky assignment, nevertheless, registry data indicate that being a driver (car or taxi) is the single most common occupation among foreign-born men who are self-employed (ibid.).[9]

This kind of observation, based on official statistics, also provides some support for the suspicion that foreign-born people, more often than native Swedes, are 'forced' to earn their livelihood by means of self-employment in order to avoid unemployment. The enterprise would thus be an active response to the threat of labour market exclusion, rather than the fulfilment of a personal dream. Scholars continue to debate the possibility of examining the systematic tendency of such outcomes more rigorously (cf. Slavnic, 2010). In line with this, previous official evaluations of integration policies have concluded that it is not 'possible to provide a clear answer on whether the foreign born are forced to start their own businesses because of discrimination and exclusion from the labour market, or whether this is caused by other forces' (Integrationsverket, 2006, p. 99, author's translation).

In economic research, there have been many attempts to track and evaluate the importance of different kinds of incentives for entrepreneurship among immigrants, whereas comparisons naturally could be made both with natives and between immigrants of different origins – this being inspired not least by the above-mentioned significant variations in entrepreneurship across groups of different geographic origin (cf. Ohlsson et al., 2011, p. 38). In various statistical analyses, focus is quite naturally directed towards the propensity to, at an individual level, start and run a business. This can reasonably be operationalized through registry-based statistics of the aforementioned type. Even so, this kind of data has its limitations, which in this case may be manifested precisely in the uncertainty reflected in the quote above; that is, uncertainty in terms of how the systematic biases in the degree of entrepreneurship ought to be interpreted. What is important to bear in mind in this regard is that differences in entrepreneurship between two specific groups – remaining even when taking a series of justifiable socioeconomic variations into account – may be interpreted in a positive as well as in a negative manner.

In the first case then, the bias is primarily a manifested consequence of more developed preferences to start own businesses among members of the more entrepreneurial categories. They may have a brighter view of the actual opportunities in this respect, which in turn may be the result of entrepreneurial traditions, and thus perhaps also the right kind of stimulating social networks within the cultural community.[10] As for the other mentioned possibility, however, a more pessimistic interpretation would be that a large degree of own businesses in a given group indicates that its members habitually face obstacles in other parts of the labour market, thus their choice of self-employment is first and foremost a choice to avoid unemployment. Nevertheless, the mechanisms behind such an outcome are not self-evident. Individual experiences of labour market obstacles can arise due to a lack of skills and competences (including perhaps also perceived, rather than real, shortcomings), but they may naturally also result from discriminatory attitudes and behaviour among employers.[11] Likewise, explanations of various kinds may not be mutually exclusive; a lack of knowledge, for example concerning legal frameworks in a new country, is a state of affairs that may well worsen for a person who also becomes a victim of discrimination.

Trying to keep in mind the whole set of plausible interpretations may be a demanding task. Further adding to a complex picture of reality, however, scholarly findings suggest that origin as such has a fairly low explanatory power. According to a study by Ohlsson et al. (2011) in which they focused on individual propensity to run a business in Sweden, barely one-tenth of the variation in this regard may be explained by the individual's country of birth, controlling for, among other potentially important demographic and socioeconomic factors, length of residence in Sweden.[12] When expanding the analysis, by also taking into account local variations between labour market regions in Sweden, these scholars find that explanatory power increases only to a relatively modest extent. Hence, the results suggest that individual-level differences and regional variations the statistical model is incapable of capturing are more important for people's willingness and ability to become self-employed.

A similar study by Andersson et al. (2013) also takes into account that the length of residence among immigrants in Sweden varies, not only between but also within the various immigrant groups. Nevertheless, the results of the analyses in this study suggest that only about one-fifth of the individual variation in self-employment could be explained by the expanded statistical model. Despite the presence of interesting specific relationships – for instance, that the proportion of non-European immigrants in a given labour market region seems to have a negative influence on individual level entrepreneurship – the authors' main conclusion is that registry-based data do not contribute sufficiently in terms of explanatory power. Encouraging further research, they hence call for indicators of more intangible factors, such as degree of entrepreneurial capacity and access to capital.[13]

Indeed, in earlier reviews made by government agencies a relative lack of access to capital has been identified as a significant barrier for entrepreneurs with a foreign background (Tillväxtverket, 2013; cf. Eliasson, 2014). According to results from the survey 'Entreprenörskaps-barometern' (the Entrepreneurship Barometer), people with a foreign background 'who are not willing to become entrepreneurs' tend to have a more pessimistic view of the prospects for financing. Additionally, they also tend to regard the greater economic uncertainty that comes with self-employment as a more serious problem (Tillväxtverket, 2013, p, 13).

Subjective feelings of uncertainty, regarding the possibilities of loan financing, may naturally become a large enough obstacle for a potential entrepreneur. This is no less valid should there in fact be no objective grounds for suspecting that credit institutions, more or less unintentionally, engage in discrimination against people of foreign origin in Sweden. Efforts to monitor discriminatory acts should indeed be regarded as important in any state based on the rule of law. However, for methodological reasons it is notoriously difficult to get a clear picture of the actual prevalence of discrimination in society by means of scientific investigations (cf. Strömblad, 2014). As for the specific issue of whether banks and other lenders in Sweden tend to treat immigrant entrepreneurs worse, results from an earlier study by Tegnemo (2003) suggest that this is not the case. Tegnemo examined court decisions for a sample of companies which filed for bankruptcy in the 1990s. Judging from this material, she found no indication of poorer access to capital in companies run by immigrants, compared with the companies run by native Swedes.

A more recent study by Eliasson (2014), which is based on registry data, focuses on the potential importance of 'ethnic networks' when it comes to lending (see also Edin et al., 2003). The hypothesis tested in this study is that financially more favourable relations for immigrant entrepreneurs will be established in locations where a larger share of employees in the local banking sector are immigrants from the same country of origin as the entrepreneur. As shown by the author, data provide support for this hypothesis as the probability of being self-employed correlates positively with the 'right kind' of ethnic representation among bank employees in the local setting. Generally speaking, the relationship thus observed signifies that intangible factors such as cultural competence may be important for the evaluation of new business ideas and for the granting of loans. Hence, immigrant entrepreneurs may be at risk of being penalized in places characterized by low ethnic diversity at credit institutions.

POLITICAL ENTREPRENEURSHIP – A POTENTIAL TOOL?

As the quote introducing this chapter suggests, policy-makers in Sweden are keen to encourage entrepreneurship among the immigrant population. Establishing such an ambition increasingly since the 1990s, by governments of different political colour, this is sometimes even regarded as a contemporary part of Swedish integration policy (cf. Engstrand, 2010). Yet, what are the tools that the state more precisely may benefit from in this respect? Furthermore, in the light of our interpretation in this volume (cf. Chapter 2) of what a political entrepreneur in the public sector is expected to achieve, to what extent are the tools characterized by innovative thinking?

One response is formulated in the study by Ohlsson et al. (2011), given the remarkably low explanatory power of origin when it comes to the propensity to run a business: 'Thus our results contradict generally held opinions concerning self-employment of immigrants, according to which immigrants' entrepreneurship is discouraged by structural barriers, the effects of which could be remedied through specific policy interventions directed towards ethnic groups or administrative areas' (Ohlsson et al., 2011, p. 50, author's translation). Hence, according to this line of argument it would be futile to imagine that more targeted, seemingly more precise, policy measures would stimulate entrepreneurship within the immigrant population more efficiently. Rather, these authors advocate comprehensive interventions, which may in principle benefit all inhabitants in the country.

In the public policy toolbox, one notices efforts being made both in terms of advisory services and risk-bearing loans, by the government-owned company Almi Företagspartner AB (Almi Business Partner), a consortium that also includes IFS Rådgivning (IFS Advisory Services), whose activities are specifically directed towards entrepreneurs with a foreign background. Moreover, Tillväxtverket (the Swedish Agency for Economic and Regional Growth), as well as this agency's predecessor Nutek, has been tasked to promote counselling and development of networks in support of business establishment among the immigrant population (cf. Engstrand, 2010). Further efforts to support the creation of new businesses have also been made over the years by means of 'start-up grants', administered by Arbetsförmedlingen (the Swedish Public Employment Service).[14]

Interestingly, as the government itself examines these activities, via the National Audit Office, a number of critical issues are identified. The envisioned prioritization of immigrants (along with women, as a population category) seems to have had only a highly limited impact in empirical practice, at least in comparison with declarations in political rhetoric. Nutek, the forerunner of Tillväxtverket, as well as Almi, have both been criticized by the National Audit Office (Riksrevisionen, 2007) on the grounds that outcomes of efforts have failed to live up to the priorities of public policy. Put in the words of this examiner: 'Only to a very limited extent, Nutek manages to reach out to the groups given priority' (Riksrevisionen, 2007, p. 7, author's translation). An important factor in this respect, one argues, is that few Nutek programmes have been designed inclusive enough to, in actual fact, have the capacity to support people with a foreign background, not least due to a focus on manufacturing industry. In addition, facing a rather diffuse set of complex goals, focus tends to be directed towards the overarching aim to support entrepreneurs in general – at the expense of the realization of public policy intentions to increase entrepreneurship among people with a foreign background.

Although loans provided by Almi seem to have reached people with a foreign background on a proportional basis, they argue for an increase in the level of ambition (Riksrevisionen, 2007). Put somewhat bluntly, Almi should be able to use its resources in order to help finance a larger share of businesses run by members of this population category. Furthermore, auditors argue that the specific Almi activities directed towards business development could have been utilized more energetically to the benefit of the target groups.

An overarching problem also seems to be shortcomings in terms of agencies' own monitoring systems. In a more recent report (Riksrevisionen, 2012), Almi as well as Arbetsförmedlingen are criticized on grounds of significant shortcomings when it comes to the internal evaluation of the efficiency of programmes directed towards people with a foreign background. For instance, one points towards insufficient documentation in terms of action plans for participants, contributing to an overall lack of knowledge concerning the potential impact of efforts. Moreover, there is a lack of internally designed statistics and measurements, obstructing, for example, a systematic evaluation of loan applications. Hence, although a cautiously formulated conclusion is that measures taken are likely to 'allow more foreign born people to start and run a business' (Riksrevisionen, 2012, p. 9, author's translation), a significant knowledge deficit seems to persist when it comes to efficiency.

In practice, the power of government officials in their potential roles of political entrepreneurs – presumably, not least, through opportunities linked to 'priority' and 'implementation' previously discussed in this volume – seems to be highly limited. The outcome does not correspond to government targets; to an even lesser extent, moreover, the outcome suggests that principal public sector actors in this field may fulfil the role of real catalysts of change when it comes to immigrant entrepreneurship. Indeed, high hopes for creativity and innovativeness, in the design of support for new entrepreneurs, may easily become unrealistic. Seemingly, though, a rather loosely formulated 'more of the same' policy has led to a restricted scope of action, rather than to inspiration, among the potential political entrepreneurs.

DOES SEGREGATION MATTER FOR THE APPRAISAL OF ENTREPRENEURSHIP?

In the light of previously mentioned scholarly results, suggesting that demographic features of the environment may affect immigrant entrepreneurship, this chapter will close with an attempt to also provide an empirical contribution. For this purpose, I make use of a previously conducted large-scale survey, 'Medborgarundersökningen 2003' (the Swedish Citizen Survey 2003), in which respondents with a foreign background intentionally constituted a disproportionally large share of the sample.[15] This particular data set may provide an interesting complement, while, in contrast to economic studies discussed above, it contains measures of subjective opinions and attitudes. Indeed, this has also been explicitly requested (Andersson et al., 2013, p. 901). Furthermore, the available data set also permits geocoding. Specifically, I have matched registry-based statistics for residential areas to all participants in the Swedish Citizen Survey 2003. For each respondent the geocoded data set includes aggregate information concerning the neighbourhood composition of the population. This, in turn, provides some possibilities to examine whether prevailing differences between residential areas, in terms of origin and ethnicity (cf. Fritzell and Strömblad, 2011), may affect attitudes concerning entrepreneurship irrespective of individual-level differences in origin.

For the purpose of empirical analysis, a measure of 'subjective entrepreneurial potential' (SEP) was defined on the basis of responses to a survey question on evaluation of opportunities to start up a business. Respondents were requested to answer according to a 0–10 scale, ranging from 'no possibilities at all' to 'very large possibilities', the overall mean being close to the mid-point on this scale (or 4.8 to be precise).[16] At the same time, though, there are significant differences between population groups. While native Swedes seem to be fairly optimistic in this respect (with a mean SEP value of 5.4), different categories of immigrants generally reveal a much more negative view of the possibilities to start businesses (with mean values of SEP varying between 2.2 and 2.8 in the categories examined).

Utilizing a series of regression analyses, the aim was to investigate whether the residential area proportion of immigrants may affect individual-level assessments of the possibilities to become entrepreneurs.

As shown below, a number of other variables (apart from the obvious control of individual-level origin) are also included in the analyses; the purpose of which being to account for the uneven distribution of population categories across neighbourhoods in Swedish cities.[17]

Table 9.1 *Predicting subjective entrepreneurial potential (SEP) by residential area proportion of immigrants and individual-level demographic and socioeconomic factors*

	Model 1	Model 2	Model 3
Proportion of immigrants	–0.030*	–0.037***	–0.037***
Origin			
Swedish born (ref.)	0.000	0.000	0.000
Foreign born 'west'	–1.82***	–0.474	–0.481
Foreign born 'east'	–1.90***	–0.503	–0.511
Foreign born 'south'	–2.74***	–1.49*	–1.54*
Education	0.159***	0.088*	0.087*
Income	0.000	0.000	0.000
Age	0.199**	0.079	0.080
Age squared	–0.003***	–0.002**	–0.002**
Male (vs. Female)	1.09***	–0.151	–0.152
Discrimination			0.203
No. of observations (*N*)	1062	651	651
Coefficient of determination (R^2)	0.18	0.20	0.20

Note: Statistical significance: *** $p < 0.001$, ** $p < 0.01$, * $p < 0.05$. Entries are ordinary least-squares (OLS) estimates, adjusted for cluster correlation based on residential areas, as defined for the purpose of the analysis. The dependent variable SEP is measured on a 0–10 scale, running from 'no possibilities at all' to 'very large possibilities', referring to subjective evaluations of the possibilities to start up a business. See Appendix for details, including coding on the independent variables.

The results from the empirical analyses are summarized in Table 9.1. As the table shows, three models were estimated. The first two models are identical, yet estimated with different selections of observations from the total sample (as revealed by the *N*). Specifically, the Model 1 estimation is based on the entire sample, whereas for Models 2 and 3 only respondents with a foreign background are considered, that is, they are either foreign born, or born in Sweden but with at least one foreign-born parent. By this procedure, the potential importance of experiences of discrimination may be examined as well, as the survey questions in this regard were only asked of respondents having a foreign background in one way or the other.

The division of the sample notwithstanding, one may note that the results from the estimations are substantially similar. Hence, the general tendencies for the relationships between the selected explanatory factors and SEP appear to be the same, regardless of whether one focuses on the whole population or on people with a foreign background. Before studying the estimated effect of the segregation-related measure (the proportion of immigrants in the residential area), we may note that the demographically related differences mentioned above remain in the more multifaceted analysis. People born in Sweden (including those who have foreign-born parents) tend to judge their entrepreneurial potential more optimistically in comparison with immigrants. In particular, immigrants from the 'south' – that is, non-European immigrants from countries in Africa, Asia and Latin America – are significantly less likely to regard self-employment as a realistic option, in comparison with native Swedes. Further, a higher level of education seems to encourage entrepreneurial ability, whereas income (accounting for other socioeconomic differences) apparently does not matter in this respect. We may also note a somewhat curvilinear effect of age in this regard (older people tending to be more optimistic up to a certain age, after which one tends to be more pessimistic). As for gender differences, men seemingly assess their entrepreneurial potential more positively than women; interestingly, though, such a gender gap is not traceable among respondents with a foreign background (as reflected in the insignificant coefficients for the variable 'Male' in Models 2 and 3).

Considering then the estimated relationship between SEP and the population composition of the neighbourhood, we note an interesting negative coefficient (which is fairly consistent in size and statistical significance throughout the three model estimations). Substantially, this result suggests that a given person's assessment of entrepreneurial capacity tends to be more negative in residential areas with a large proportion of foreign-born inhabitants. Importantly, such a possible contextual effect is thus observed even accounting for the origin of each respondent, and all other individual-level demographic and socio-economic differences mentioned.[18] In view of this, residential segregation – even in traditionally egalitarian Sweden (cf. Eger, 2010) – seemingly affects subjective evaluations of the possibilities to start up a business. In areas where most neighbours are foreign born, the prospects in this respect tend to appear less promising than in areas predominantly populated by native Swedes. Such an entrepreneurial pessimism, generated in immigrant-dense neighbourhoods, is reasonably detrimental to the efficiency of public policy efforts in order to stimulate new businesses.

As already noted, results from the empirical analyses are largely similar when respondents with a foreign background are considered separately. As an additional inquiry, given this category, Model 3 (in comparison with Model 2) was expanded with a measure of experiences of discrimination on the basis of origin (built, in turn, on a series of questions asked only of respondents having a foreign background). The idea was to test if perceptions of negative treatment, for instance in contacts with authorities, are more common in immigrant-dense residential areas and also negatively related to evaluations of entrepreneurial capability, whereby the negative contextual effect may be explained (among people having a foreign background, that is). As the result from the Model 3 estimation reveals, however, experiences of discrimination do not seem to affect SEP evaluations. Thus, poor entrepreneurial self-confidence in the most multicultural parts of Swedish cities may perhaps instead be due to a more general feeling of social marginalization developed in these urban areas.

CONCLUSIONS

For several decades Sweden has been a country of immigration, a process by which multicultural diversity has increased. Nevertheless, equal opportunity despite ethnic or national origin seems to be a distant goal, rather than something indisputably safeguarded in a democratic welfare society of the globalization era. In light of unequal preconditions, not least in the labour market, there has for a long time been a political ambition to cultivate entrepreneurship in the immigrant population. An increasing level of self-employment – preferably in groups that otherwise struggle hard to compete in the labour market – is expected to stimulate employment, both to the benefit of the actual entrepreneur, who can thus make a living, and in terms of the possibility for small businesses to expand and contribute to the creation of new jobs in the economy. The attractiveness of such a win-win plan notwithstanding, its reality seems hard to attain and influence.

Evaluators of public policy activities in this area tend to criticize what they perceive as imprecise objectives and an overall ambiguity. In various ways, potential political entrepreneurs in the public sector have been commissioned to facilitate entrepreneurship. Seemingly, however, such endeavours are filled with challenges, and available tools tend to be few and blunt. Triggering political entrepreneurship in order to stimulate new businesses is probably easier formulated than attained – there is a gap to bridge between the ideological vision and the desired checklist of innovative as well as efficient measures. In addition, economic research has hardly been able to provide a clear trail map to facilitate the fine-tuning of actions. Differences in the degree of self-employment, between as well as within various categories of immigrants, remain unexplained to a large extent. Consequently, it is not an easy task to determine where and when 'targeted' measures in actual fact should be implemented.

However, it may be fruitful to direct the spotlight not only on differences between population groups but also on spatial differences. In comparison, Sweden represents without doubt a highly egalitarian society, but even so prevailing patterns of housing segregation might provoke a spatial stigmatization of multicultural residential areas (cf. Fritzell and Strömblad, 2011). In view of the results from the empirical contribution in this chapter, this may perhaps then also trigger more gloomy prospects in terms of assessments of opportunities to become an entrepreneur. If this should be the case, such a consequence obviously stands in stark contrast to highly cherished policy objectives of intensified entrepreneurship in Sweden.

NOTES

1. Official comment by then Minister for Enterprise, Annie Lööf, regarding a scheduled government effort of SEK80 million to, primarily through advisory activities, increase self-employment among people with a foreign background in Sweden (Näringsdepartementet, 2014).
2. Reviewing post-war immigration in Sweden, the economist and migration scholar Jan Ekberg (2004) notes that the proportion of foreign born in the population amounted to a mere 1 per cent at the beginning of World War II, and as late as 1970 the corresponding proportion did not exceed 7 per cent. Around 40 years later, one may thus note that this share has more than doubled.
3. In absolute figures, approximately 60 000 people migrated to Sweden on a yearly basis until 2006. In more recent years, the number has been around 100 000. Also taking emigration into account, however, the net immigration figure tends to be half that. Still, it is worth mentioning that a considerable escalation of immigration has also been witnessed in previous time periods, for example in the wake of the large flow of refugees from the Balkan War in the beginning of the 1990s.
4. The category labels 'foreign born' and 'Swedish born' are to be found in the terminology of official population statistics; moreover, they correspond to what in this chapter I refer to as immigrants and native Swedes. That is, the term 'immigrant' should merely signify the experience of, at a given point in time, having migrated to Sweden, thus not implying ethnically or culturally grounded characteristics (for an empirical contribution, and a critical discussion, regarding connotations of the term 'immigrant' in Sweden, see Myrberg, 2010).

5. Furthermore, previously mentioned patterns, in the significance of length of residence in Sweden and geographic origin, seem to be reproduced when it comes to educational accomplishments.

6. In statistical compilations of this kind, the category 'self-employed' typically refers to people who run businesses in the forms of sole proprietorships (*enskild firma*) or partnership (*handelsbolag* or *kommanditbolag*), hence activities in a limited liability corporation (*aktiebolag*) are excluded in the delimitation of self-employment.

7. According to registry data from Statistics Sweden, 18 per cent, or scarcely one-fifth, of all self-employed are foreign born (SCB, 2012b). However, for businesses in the hotel and restaurant sector, the corresponding share is 70 per cent, while in comparison only a small fraction of self-employed farmers are foreign born.

8. In contrast, the tendency among the Swedish born seems to be that the qualification requirements of the occupations of the self-employed largely correspond to their level of education (SCB, 2012b).

9. Arguably, the understanding that a gap exists between level of education and labour market position has been nourished by popular culture. In the Swedish motion picture *Se upp för dårarna* (2007) [released as *Mind the Gap* for the English-speaking market] one of the characters, who has migrated to Sweden, makes a living as an underground train driver but simultaneously misses his former job in his country of origin as a cardio-thoracic surgeon.

10. For the potential importance of social networks in the China towns of the United States (the 'classic ethnic enclaves', one may assert) see Wong (1998).

11. When it comes to the self-employed, there is also a possibility that one is discriminated against by potential customers (cf. Andersson et al., 2013, p. 900) something that, in turn, might lead to a greater risk for bankruptcy.

12. The analyses of this (registry-based data) study also included the Swedish-born population. Further, it may be noted that the explanatory power of country of origin was somewhat higher for women than for men.

13. Arguably, the influence of the first-mentioned factor – yet almost certainly powerful in terms of pure explanatory power – would be less interesting while, in that case, the distance between the explanation and what is to be explained is small. It would hardly be surprising if 'entrepreneurial capacity' tends to be greater among entrepreneurs than among non-entrepreneurs.

14. See also the discussion on policies to support entrepreneurship among women in Chapters 7 and 8.

15. Though this particular survey was conducted more than ten years ago, it is highly valuable due to the unique considerable oversampling of respondents with a foreign background, together with the possibility of utilizing geocoded information (described below), For a detailed description of sampling and other technical procedures of the Swedish Citizens Survey 2003, see Myrberg (2007, pp. 24–5).

16. The question was asked to gainfully employed respondents who at the time of the survey did not report that they were self-employed. See Appendix at the end of this chapter for further details for this and other variables included in the analysis.

17. In order to restrict the scope of the empirical contextual analyses to proper residential areas, only respondents living in smaller or larger cities, and in SAMS areas (see Appendix) with a minimum population of 500 people, are included.

18. An additional control for length of residence in Sweden (among the foreign born) did not influence the result; interestingly, no relationship (controlling for the other variables in the table) between this time factor and SEP could be observed. Further, studying potential interaction effects, results suggest that there are no significant differences between Swedish born and foreign born in terms of the actual strength of the contextual effect.

REFERENCES

Adman, P. and P. Strömblad (2000), *Resurser för politisk integration* [Resources for Political Integration], Norrköping: Integrationsverket.

Andersson, L., M. Hammarstedt, S. Hussain and G. Shukur (2013), 'Ethnic origin, local labour markets and self-employment in Sweden. A multilevel approach', *The Annals of Regional Science*, **50**(3), 885–910.

Beckman, L. (2011), *Den rimliga integrationen* [Reasonable Integration], Stockholm: Dialogos.

Edin, P.-A., P. Fredriksson and O. Åslund (2003), 'Ethnic enclaves and the economic success of immigrants. Evidence from a natural experiment', *Quarterly Journal of Economics*, **118**(1), 329–57.

Eger, M.A. (2010), 'Even in Sweden: the effect of immigration on support for welfare state spending', *European Sociological Review*, **26**(2), 203–17.

Ekberg. J. (2004), 'Inledning' [Introduction], in J. Ekberg (ed.), *Egenförsörjning eller bidragsförsörjning? Invandrarna, arbetsmarknaden och välfärdsstaten. Rapport från Integrationspolitiska maktutredningen, SOU 2004:21* [Income through Work or Benefits? The Immigrants, the Labour Market and the Welfare State. Report from the Government Commission of Inquiry on the Political Integration of Immigrants in Sweden], Stockholm: Fritzes.

Eliasson, T. (2014), 'Essay 2: Immigrant entrepreneurship and the origin of bankers', in *Empirical Essays on Wage Setting and Immigrant Labor Market Opportunities*, Uppsala: Uppsala University.

Engstrand, Å.-K. (2010), 'Inledning' [Introduction], in Å.-K. Engstrand (ed.), *Möjligheternas marknad – en antologi om företagare med utländsk bakgrund* [Market of Opportunities – An Anthology of Entrepreneurs with Foreign Backgrounds], Stockholm: Tillväxtverket.

Fritzell, J. and P. Strömblad (2011), 'Segregation och social tillit' [Segregation and social trust], in S. Alm, O. Bäckman, A. Gavanas and A. Nilsson (eds), *Utanförskap*, Stockholm: Dialogos.

Integrationsverket (2006), *Rapport integration 2005* [Integration Report 2005], Norrköping: Integrationsverket.

Myrberg, G. (2007), *Medlemmar och medborgare. Föreningsdeltagande och politiskt engagemang i det etnifierade samhället* [Members and Citizens. Society Participation and Political Involvement in the Ethnic Community], Uppsala: Acta Universitatis Upsaliensis.

Myrberg, G. (2010), 'Who is an immigrant?', in B. Bengtsson, P. Strömblad and A.-H. Bay (eds), *Diversity, Inclusion and Citizenship in Scandinavia*, Newcastle upon Tyne, UK: Cambridge Scholars Publishing.

Näringsdepartementet (2014), '80 miljoner kronor för att stärka invandrares företagande' [SEK80 million to strengthen immigrants' entrepreneurship], press release, 14 August, Stockholm: Regeringskansliet.

Ohlsson, H., P. Broomé and P. Bevelander (2011), 'Egenföretagande bland invandrare och svenskfödda i Sverige – en flernivåanalys' [Self-employment among immigrants and Swedish born in Sweden – a multilevel analysis], *Ekonomisk debatt*, **2011**(8).

Regeringskansliet (2008), *Skr. 2008/09:24: Egenmakt mot utanförskap – regeringens strategi för integration* [Empowerment Against Exclusion – the Government's Strategy for Integration], accessed 20 May 2016 at http://www.regeringen.se/rattsdokument/skrivelse/2008/09/skr.-20080924-/.

Riksrevisionen (2007), *Statens företagsfrämjande insatser. Når de kvinnor och personer med utländsk bakgrund?* [National Business Support Operations. After the Women and People of Foreign Origin?], RiR 2007:11, Stockholm: Riksrevisionen.

Riksrevisionen (2012), *Etablering genom företagande – är statens stöd till företagare effektiva för utrikes födda?* [Establishment Through Entrepreneurship – Is Government Support for Entrepreneurs Effective for the Foreign Born?], RiR 2012:26, Stockholm: Riksrevisionen.

SCB [Statistics Sweden] (2008), *Integration – en beskrivning av läget i Sverige. Integration, rapport 1* [Integration: A Description of the Situation in Sweden. Integration Report No. 1], Stockholm: Statistiska centralbyrån.

SCB [Statistics Sweden] (2012a), *Svenskt valdeltagande under 100 år. Demokratistatistik, rapport 13* [Swedish Turnout in 100 Years. Democracy Statistics, Report No. 13], Stockholm: Statistiska centralbyrån.

SCB [Statistics Sweden] (2012b), 'Utrikesfödda egenföretagare är mer välutbildade än inrikesfödda' [Foreign-born self-employed are more educated that native-born], Article No. 2012:91, Stockholm: Statistiska centralbyrån.

SCB [Statistics Sweden] (2013), *Integration – en beskrivning av läget i Sverige* [Integration – A Description of the Situation in Sweden], Integration Report No. 6, Stockholm: Statistiska centralbyrån.

Sides, J. and J. Citrin (2007), 'European opinion about immigration. The role of identities, interests and information', *British Journal of Political Science*, **37**(3), 477–504.

Slavnic, Z. (2010), 'Invandrares småföretagande i Sverige – en kritisk skildring av forskningsfältets utveckling' [Immigrant small business in Sweden – a critical portrayal of the research field's development], in Å.-K. Engstrand (ed.), *Möjligheternas marknad – en antologi om företagare med utländsk bakgrund*, Stockholm: Tillväxtverket.

Strömblad, P. (2014), 'Att acceptera eller inte acceptera diskriminering' [To accept or not accept discrimination], *Surveyjournalen*, **1**(1), 3–14.

Strömblad, P. and B. Malmberg (in press), 'Ethnic segregation and xenophobic party preference: exploring the influence of the presence of visible minorities on local electoral support for the Sweden Democrats', *Journal of Urban Affairs*.

Tegnemo, A. (2003), *Diskrimineras invandrarföretagare i Sverige? En empirisk studie av småföretagskonkurser under 1990-talet* [Are Immigrant Entrepreneurs in Sweden Discriminated Against? An Empirical Study of Small Business Bankruptcies in the 1990s], Rapport från Integrationspolitiska maktutredningen, SOU 2003:17. Stockholm: Fritzes.

Tillväxtverket [Swedish Agency for Economic and Regional Growth] (2013), *Företagare med utländsk bakgrund. Entreprenörskapsbarometern* [Business People with a Foreign Background. Entrepreneurship Barometer], Stockholm: Tillväxtverket.

Weldon, S.A. (2006), 'The institutional context of tolerance for ethnic minorities. A comparative, multilevel analysis of Western Europe', *American Journal of Political Science*, **50**(2), 331–49.

Wong, B. (1998), *Ethnicity and Entrepreneurship: The New Chinese Immigrants in the San Francisco Bay Area*, Boston, MA: Allyn and Bacon.

APPENDIX

The following variables, based on information from the Swedish Citizen Survey 2003, are utilized in the empirical analyses:

Subjective entrepreneurial potential (SEP)   SEP is the dependent variable in the analyses, based on the survey question 'What possibilities do you think you have to start your own business if you want?' The variable ranges from 0 to 10, reproducing the response scale, anchored in 0 = 'no possibilities at all' and 10 = 'very large possibilities'.

Proportion of immigrants   A contextual variable, defined as the percentage of foreign-born residents in each respondent's neighbourhood. The spatial division is based upon so-called SAMS (Small Areas for Market Statistics) areas, constructed by Statistics Sweden in order to approximate actual residential areas, and thus facilitate small-scale geographic description in terms of demographic and socioeconomic characteristics.

Origin   A series of dummy variables based on the survey question 'Are you born in Sweden?', after which those who answered no were asked to specify their country of birth. Four categories were constructed, and utilized for the dummy variables: Swedish born, Foreign-born 'west' (immigrants from other part of Western Europe or the Western World), Foreign-born 'east' (immigrants from Eastern Europe), and Foreign-born 'south' (immigrants from other parts of the world). See Myrberg (2007, pp. 174–6), for a more detailed description and empirically based motivation of this categorization.

Education   A continuous variable, based on the survey question 'How many years of full-time education do you have?'

Income   A continuous variable, based on registry data on yearly family disposable income (SEK × 1000).

Age   A continuous variable, based on registry data on the respondent's year of birth.

Male (vs Female)   A dichotomous variable based on registry data, coded 1 for male respondents and 0 for female.

Discrimination   A dichotomous variable that takes on the value of 1 for respondents who reported that they ('during the past 12 months') themselves had been badly treated because of their foreign background, and 0 for those who did not report any such experiences of discrimination. The survey question (directed, naturally, only to respondents with a foreign background) was further specified by explicit reference to a number of contexts and situations. Specifically, the variable takes into account (1) housing-related contacts, for example with a landlord or neighbours; (2) contacts with public authorities, for example with the tax office, the social security office, or the police; (3) visits to a restaurant, dancehall or a sports event; (4) purchases or hire of something as a private customer; (5) encounters in the street or in public transport; and (6) contacts within a context other than those mentioned.

10. Political entrepreneurs, higher education and young entrepreneurship

Martin Nilsson and Tobias Bromander

In the international research community, there is an ongoing discussion about whether university education in entrepreneurship[1] actually increases entrepreneurship, that is, if young students will bring new entrepreneurial skills and innovations to the working field. From the political side, particularly in countries where the universities are mostly state universities, as in most European countries, there is also an expectation that universities will contribute to entrepreneurship and economic growth in the surrounding region. Meanwhile, it appears that the model of how universities and industry collaborate to stimulate entrepreneurship is based on an ideal situation, such as the conditions that exist in Silicon Valley, with prestigious universities and multinational companies offering very good political, economic and educational opportunities to achieve synergistic effects.

In the case of Sweden, the assumption has been that universities/colleges[2] are supposed to be regional driving forces for entrepreneurship. One of the aims behind the expansion of the number of universities across the country in the 1990s was to strengthen regional competitiveness, including the ambition to stimulate economic growth. Since then, the role of universities, as contributing to entrepreneurship and regional growth, has been problematized. So far, no empirical studies have indicated the role of the university as an exclusively successful regional driving force and no one has really concluded that universities have been successful in bringing together innovation and the ability of young students to become entrepreneurial after graduation.

This chapter explores the idea of the entrepreneurial university. The first part begins with defining the entrepreneurial university and provides examples of various models of entrepreneurial universities. The first part ends with a discussion on what the research has concluded regarding whether or not universities have been successful in promoting young entrepreneurship, particularly as part of students' education. In the second part, we discuss how state-led universities in Sweden, as potential political entrepreneurs, are trying to achieve the policy objective of establishing entrepreneurial university. The final part of the chapter explores challenges that Swedish universities are facing in the promotion of entrepreneurship in higher education.

THE MEANING OF AN ENTREPRENEURIAL UNIVERSITY

At the centre of the discussion on the entrepreneurial university is the issue of established or emerging geographical regions, where universities can remain at the forefront of science while working in close cooperation with industries. One such region is the Bay Area's Silicon Valley, where Stanford University and other universities (e.g., the University of California at Berkeley) and IT companies, together with engaged students, create new ideas, technologies and products for the world market. Besides Silicon Valley, MIT in Boston is another example of a university that specializes in both research and education linked to entrepreneurship.

In Europe, major universities have also acted as growth engines, aiming to promote entrepreneurship in research and student training, in cooperation with businesses and civil society organizations. The role of the university, as a driving force for entrepreneurship, has been reinforced in Europe by the European Union (EU), which has stressed the importance of entrepreneurship as part of higher education (Commission of the European Communities, 2006). In Sweden, this has been further strengthened by the Swedish higher education policy goal that entrepreneurship should be a natural part of university and college operations (Regeringskansliet, 2009).

Although entrepreneurship education can primarily be traced back to the 1930s – in particular, to Japan and Kobe University – most courses and programmes can be found in US business schools (see Keat et al., 2011). In the 1960s and 1970s, only a handful of universities offered training in entrepreneurship; in the 1980s, over 300 universities offered this training, and today over 3000 universities are involved in issues of entrepreneurship (Morris et al., 2013, pp. 3–10). However, universities approach issues of entrepreneurship in different ways by offering single courses, academic programmes, research centres, research profiles and/or teaching methods. Often, entrepreneurship education has been used to refer 'to the pedagogical process involved in the encouragement of entrepreneurial activities, behaviours and mind set' (Binks, 2005, p. 2), which has institutionalized a culture of entrepreneurship amongst teachers, researchers, administrators and students (see Florida, 1999; Baldieri, 2014).

So, what is the entrepreneurial university all about? First, the entrepreneurial university aims to create an entrepreneurial culture within education, the main feature of which is to train students in entrepreneurship skills. This is achieved through special student projects and education programmes, the outcome of which is often measured by the formation of new ideas leading to new types of businesses and social and cultural projects (see Wang and Wong, 2004; Hannon, 2005; Kuratko, 2005; Keat et al., 2011). Second, the nature of the entrepreneurial university relates to how the university is organized and the constant changes and innovations that characterize higher education (Roffe, 1999; Binks, 2005). This can range from purposefully differentiated student recruitment and the development of research to alternative sources of funding and participation in community projects. An entrepreneurial university is characterized by an organization that constantly adapts to the changing reality and constantly renews itself in order to be as successful as possible. Third, the entrepreneurial university makes use of 'entrepreneurial management' (governance), which means it is a market-oriented university, open to innovation and commercialization and prepared to lead purposeful work for excellence in research and education. The term 'entrepreneurial management' is often associated with academic entrepreneurship and technological innovation (see Clark, 1998; Etzkowitz, 2004; Phan and Siegel, 2006). By means of entrepreneurial management, the entrepreneurial university promotes research in business innovation, supports high-quality training programmes and develops scientific minds, resulting in new patents, advanced course offerings and an increase in regional economic growth.

An entrepreneurial university pursues all these elements in order to be successful. It is therefore about more than just training students in entrepreneurship (see Morris et al., 2013, p. 239). In an entrepreneurial university, faculties, administrative staff and students are encouraged to take risks and to be innovative in order to develop creative ideas in an environment where students and teachers can learn from their mistakes, move forward with new innovative ideas and empower the university; this requires energy, an entrepreneurial mentality and innovative approaches. Within academia, this means that entrepreneurship is about the following (cf. Nählinder, 2011):

- teaching entrepreneurship, including the knowledge of how new innovations are created and the skills to put them into practice;
- teaching entrepreneurship to encourage entrepreneurship and economic growth;
- teaching and research on entrepreneurship or the scientific study of the subject; and
- organizing the university to stimulate greater entrepreneurship.

Morris et al. (2013) argue that there are at least four models of creating entrepreneurial universities (cf. Baldieri, 2014; Hampden-Turner, 2009). In all these four models, there are similar challenges:

1. *Entrepreneurship through an independent foundation.* In this model, different universities can apply for financial resources from a private foundation. The foundation is added to a central department and falls directly under the authority of the rector of each university. This department will have the resources that are necessary for the faculty to stimulate entrepreneurship using a holistic approach across various campuses. In the USA a number of universities, such as Syracuse University, University of Wisconsin-Madison and Florida International University, have chosen this model.
2. *Centre for entrepreneurship.* In this model, a special centre is established as a result of research in the field, often linked to technical innovation or different business school ventures. Stanford University in Silicon Valley is one such example, in which the university's business school, along with faculty, has created the Stanford Entrepreneurship Centre. This centre works with Stanford researchers, students and departments and with companies and organizations outside the university. Even MIT in Boston belongs to this category.
3. *Entrepreneurship beyond the business schools.* This is considered to be the most common form of organization. It means that entrepreneurial activities are essentially centred around each university's business school, but with the addition of certain arrangements and activities involving other faculties and departments. Oklahoma State University and Indiana University are examples of this form of organization.
4. *Entrepreneurship through a diffusion process.* This model of entrepreneurship develops from below in each faculty and department across the university. Cornell University is one example where the

deans control financial resources and can stimulate various activities to promote entrepreneurship across the university's departments.

PREVIOUS RESEARCH ON HIGHER EDUCATION AND ENTREPRENEURSHIP

Whatever kind of entrepreneurial approach or model is chosen, the question remains as to whether the approach is successful or not. There is limited research on the level of success of entrepreneurial universities (see Kuratko, 2005; Duval-Couetil, 2013). Furthermore, there is an absence of major studies on the entrepreneurial university and limited studies have pointed in different directions in terms of the positive effects of training entrepreneurship within academia. Some studies (Vaneven-hoven, 2013, p. 466) argue that entrepreneurship training programmes have aimed at teaching the character traits of entrepreneurs, including motivation and determination. These studies have identified both positive and negative outcomes of such programmes with no clear-cut evidence of the actual outcomes. It has been argued that there is no identified successful method for teaching entrepreneurship and that no explanation has been given on how entrepreneurial training is related to students' different backgrounds, skills, innate talents and possibilities to establish strategic networks for entrepreneurship. These tentative results have raised the question of whether it is really possible to teach entrepreneurship or if successful entrepreneurship has to do with innate characteristics that can't be taught. Other studies (Sánchez, 2013) have argued that teaching and research on entrepreneurship actually increase the number of entrepreneurs. This is due to increased knowledge among students of how to translate theory into practice, how to become an entrepreneur and how to develop the motivation and confidence to be successful. However, these studies also state that there is a need for improved comparative studies into students' actual acquired skills after graduation and the priorities and objectives of their education. There is also the need for research into the challenges or problems that newly graduated students in entrepreneurship face. Finally, what aspects of academic training in entrepreneurship actually have a positive impact on graduated students' ability to become entrepreneurial need to be identified.

Duval-Couetil (2013, p. 397) argues that a review of the research shows that there is some positive correlation between entrepreneurial education and entrepreneurship in later working life; however, there are a number of problems with these studies. Examples of such problems include the fact that they often do not take into account the extent to which students already have entrepreneurial abilities before the training begins and often the studies need to take a longer period of time before and after graduation into consideration. Duval-Couetil's (2013) conclusion therefore agrees with the conclusion made by other scholars, such as Rideout and Gray (2013), that academia still knows too little about how entrepreneurship education works and how it actually affects entrepreneurship in practice.

Regardless of the model used or how to organize entrepreneurship in the university, Morris et al. (2013, p. 254) argue that a number of aspects are important for success. First, it requires an academic leader with a firm foundation in the field of research. Second, there is the need for a definition of entrepreneurship that is known throughout the university, a clear organizational structure, infrastructure and financial resources. Third, it requires a communicated motive or reason as to why the university should focus on entrepreneurship. Fourth, it also requires clear, focused content in all programmes, courses, research and collaborations with companies and other partners. Fifth and finally, within the university, there must be an entrepreneurial culture, entrepreneurial beliefs and the ambition to train students to become entrepreneurial, to start businesses and, thereby, eventually contribute to regional growth.

ENTREPRENEURSHIP IN SWEDISH HIGHER EDUCATION

Valeiro et al. (2014), among others, argue that governments can play a proactive role in stimulating entrepreneurship in higher education. A government might have a national plan or a specific agenda for entrepreneurship, account for financial resources, construct an education system or simply make statements at or follow up on universities, all of which can encourage universities to advance entrepreneurship. Since the late 1990s, the Swedish higher education system, which is essentially organized around state colleges and universities, has publicly expressed the ambition that entrepreneurship should permeate the entire organization of the university, including education and research. The triggering factor for such an approach arose from research in the field, international trends in the world (USA, China, the rest of Asia and the OECD), the European Commission (Commission of the European Communities, 2006) and the Swedish government (Regeringskansliet, 2009), which, in terms of political decisions, has had particular impetus in this area. From a political perspective, entrepreneurship is a fundamentally important way for a state to become competitive and prosperous. In Swedish universities, numerous political entrepreneurship initiatives have been started with the focus that entrepreneurial knowledge and skills should be learned, even though this does not mean that all students will become successful entrepreneurs (see Sánchez, 2013).

In practice, this means that most Swedish universities, in one way or another, have a mission to act as political entrepreneurs, with the aim of stimulating and enabling the higher education sector to contribute to entrepreneurship through research and university education (see Sánchez, 2013, pp. 447–8). The Swedish political agenda follows the approach of the European Commission since the 1990s when it began to spread the message that higher education should develop entrepreneurship (Commission of the European Communities, 2006; European Union, 2012). In 2009, the Swedish government adopted 'a strategy for entrepreneurship in the education sector' stating:

> Entrepreneurship education may involve specific skills required to start and run a business, such as business administration and business planning. Entrepreneurship education can also include more general skills that are useful even outside the business world, such as project management and risk management. To educate entrepreneurs also means to inspire creativity and willingness to take responsibility for achieving a goal. (Regeringskansliet, 2009, p. 6)

From a Swedish government perspective, it is argued that Swedish universities should initiate entrepreneurship training and how such education should consist of specific skills required to start a business as well as general skills of fostering creativity and innovation. In addition, entrepreneurship training should also highlight the economic, cultural and social context and allow representatives of the education sector to cooperate with entrepreneurs in the business sector. As stated:

> A university entrepreneurship education can involve both theoretical and practical studies of the process of assessing the commercial viability of an idea to establish a company in the market. Higher education in entrepreneurship can also, more generally, prepare students for work with change processes in large and small organizations, in both the private and public sectors. (Regeringskansliet, 2009, p. 9)

To implement the Swedish strategy for entrepreneurship in the education sector, the government identified 11 actions, three of which would more specifically affect the Swedish higher education sector. This included (1) a survey of the programmes that encourage entrepreneurship, (2) support for colleges and universities to stimulate entrepreneurship and (3) a special focus on the type of education in the field of entrepreneurship. These actions aimed to promote entrepreneurship in universities as a tool to provide greater competitiveness, growth and increased employment in Swedish society. This political push for entrepreneurial training in higher education was a result of decades of decreased numbers of Swedish industrial jobs and growing global competition. At an appearance at the World Economic Forum in Davos in 2013, the former prime minister, Fredrik Reinfeldt, described the Swedish trajectory: 'We used to have people in the industry, but they are basically gone' (Reinfeldt, 2013).

The creation of new small businesses has been stated by politicians in Sweden to be the cornerstone of meeting global economic competition and the transformation of the industrial manufacturing sector in Sweden. In order to secure tomorrow's prosperity, there is a need for more entrepreneurial innovations and businesses. From a Swedish political perspective, there are high hopes that entrepreneurship training in higher education can contribute to a growing number of small businesses and in the long run to regional growth and employment. There are very few politicians and business representatives in Sweden who do not speak warmly of the development of entrepreneurship training, emphasizing higher education as a potential trigger for entrepreneurship and growth.

In recent years, and in line with the government's strategy, some Swedish universities have begun to focus on entrepreneurship education. By 2015, Swedish universities offered a wide range of courses, under-graduate and graduate programmes on entrepreneurship. As a part of the 2009 Swedish political strategy, the Swedish state agency for higher education identified four universities with potential to provide for the highest international class of entrepreneurship and innovation (Högs-koleverket, 2009). One of the four universities selected by the Swedish government in 2009 was Linnaeus University (LNU, previously Växjö University and Kalmar University) with particular focus on the Inter-national Master's Programme in Entrepreneurship and Innovation. LNU also initiated the project 'The Entrepreneurial University' from 2012 to 2014. The goal of the project was to embed in all university programmes an entrepreneurial approach with the long-term goal to provide for the highest number of entrepreneurs among Swedish students (Nilsson, 2010; Linnéuniversitetet, 2012). LNU's initiative for entrepreneurship should be viewed in light of the Swedish government's ambition that universities should be regional engines of growth and to live in symbiosis with their surrounding communities.

CHALLENGES TO ENTREPRENEURSHIP TRAINING IN SWEDISH HIGHER EDUCATION

The idea of higher education contributing to the establishment of new entrepreneurs, companies and regional growth is far from new. Nevertheless, many colleges and universities have a long way to go before they can be seriously recognized as 'entrepreneurial universities'. Previous efforts in entrepreneurship education have provided several valuable lessons. As noted earlier in this chapter, this form of education requires that the university organizes itself internally and that the entire university understands the mode and purpose of this form of organization; it also requires a clear leadership that can create excitement about the vision of the entrepreneurial university (Morris et al., 2013). Thus, there are a number of organizational challenges that concern every university internally; there are also a number of external challenges that, to some extent, are out of the control of the universities. These are now to be discussed by answering the questions of whether it is possible to train people to entrepreneurship, whether trained entrepreneurship results in regional growth and whether higher education provides for more businesses in Sweden.

Is it Possible to Train Entrepreneurs?

The most fundamental question is whether anyone can become an entrepreneur. The issue has been debated for a long time. Reasonably, it can be assumed that not all people have the opportunity to become entrepreneurs. However, if it is impossible to acquire the necessary skills to become an entrepreneur, the educational initiatives aimed at finding tomorrow's young entrepreneurs seem to be rather fruitless. This is regardless of the university organization, training content or teaching methods. The question of whether entrepreneurship is essentially an innate gift or a talent that can be refined through practice is not new. On the contrary, it has been the subject of discussion, both in research and in society, for a long time. Answering the question of whether it is possible to train entrepreneurs depends in part on how entrepreneurship is defined and what properties are attributed to the concept.

A first attempt to define the concept is to distinguish between an entrepreneur and a business owner. A common misconception is that a business owner is synonymous with an entrepreneur (Bjuggren et al., 2012). Entrepreneurs are often business owners, but far from all business owners are entrepreneurs. According to Joseph Schumpeter (1934

[2008]), an entrepreneur possesses special characteristics that distinguish him or her from other business owners. As with all concepts, the concept of entrepreneurship can be given a narrow or a broad meaning. Cantillon (1931) defines entrepreneurship as person X being able 'to identify and exploit business opportunities'. This is a broad definition, which means that almost all business owners are included in the category of the entrepreneur. Cantillon's approach to entrepreneurship is, to a certain extent, in line with the Swedish government's approach to growth and increased employment. The Swedish government often describes entrepreneurship as the medicine that will make Sweden more competitive in the future in terms of knowledge-intensive industries and activities. In this case, entrepreneurship is defined as the creation of economic activities that contribute to the growth of society. The government's strategy for entrepreneurship in education (Regeringskansliet, 2009) has clearly stated the long-term objective that entrepreneurship must become an essential part of how unemployment is avoided. Therefore, various Swedish governments have, on several occasions, stressed the importance of entrepreneurship as a common thread in Swedish education.

However, the question remains: why is there the need for entrepreneurship education? It is important to distinguish between two different purposes of entrepreneurship in higher education. The first aim of entrepreneurship is to provide tools for new companies to be established in Sweden. Several companies also provide a basis for increased growth. With this aim, entrepreneurship and growth seem to be closely linked (Ahl, 2006; Potter, 2008). This is also a very clear and tangible aim. An advantage of this type of objective is that the increasing number of enterprises is also relatively easy to measure.

A second aspect of entrepreneurship is to help people develop the ability to discover and explore existing opportunities. Being able to see opportunities where others see problems and finding solutions to those problems is an ability that characterizes the entrepreneur. This aim of entrepreneurship training also relies on several definitions of the term. Among other things, the former Swedish Agency for Businesses (today, the Swedish Agency for Economic and Regional Growth) defined entrepreneurship as follows: 'Entrepreneurship is a dynamic and social process where individuals, alone or in collaboration, identify opportunities and make something with them to transform ideas into practical and targeted activities in a social, cultural or economic context' (Nutek, 2008). This social process, which the Swedish Agency for Businesses describes, requires individuals to have the ability or skill to implement entrepreneurial actions. It is this ability or skill that universities' entrepreneurship education aims to provide. For a university, this means one has to decide what one means by entrepreneurship, because each definition raises somewhat different expectations of the outcome of any form of education involving entrepreneurship.

Does Entrepreneurship in Higher Education Affect Regional Development in Sweden?

In Sweden, regional development and higher education have long been considered as existing symbiotically (Nilsson and Weibull, 2007). In times of recession in particular, politicians have emphasized the need for training and have spoken warmly about universities and colleges' roles in increasing regional growth. Swedish universities are often described as engines of growth. Higher education is expected to provide highly skilled workers for regions' labour markets and thereby enhance growth, employment and entrepreneurship (Olofsson, 2012). Especially in weaker regions, there is a hope that higher education can provide greater economic power (Danilda and Granat Thorslund, 2010). However, there are no simple conclusions about the relationship between universities and regional success (Olsson and Wiberg, 2003). According to Nabi and Holden (2008), the level of entrepreneurship among university graduates has increased and has, therefore, to a greater extent than before, been recognized as a source of competitiveness and as a motor of growth and development (Wetter and Wennberg, 2007). In light of this background, there should be many good possibilities for the entrepreneurial university to contribute to regional development, but only if one defines entrepreneurship as the starting up of businesses.

The Swedish National Board of Housing has also emphasized the importance of the relationship between higher education and growth. The government mandated the Board to develop a vision for Sweden called 'Vision 2025'. One of the areas identified in this vision was the role of universities as engines of regional growth. The Board notes that: '[v]iable university towns have enabled a wider range of skills available in the country. University campuses have become local cores for development in major regions. Hinterland around university towns has been expanded and more municipalities have greater professional breadth' (Boverket, 2013).

While opportunities for entrepreneurial universities seem to be fairly good, there are also challenges. Perhaps the biggest challenge involves getting students to settle in the nearby region after completing their studies. This mainly depends on the ability to get a job, but it also depends on other aspects that influence people's decisions about where to live and work, among other things, the availability of housing. Although the labour market for graduates is relatively good in, for example, Stockholm, the housing market is a major obstacle for the region's ability to secure its competence in the future. A further requirement is that there must be a relatively good business environment in the region (Nilsson, 2010).

Does Entrepreneurship Education Lead to More Businesses?

Who starts businesses after university? Before we tackle this question, it is appropriate to examine the extent to which young people actually want to become entrepreneurs and business owners. There is a plurality of increments thereof. Although the results are not entirely consistent, there is no doubt that a lot of people have the opportunity to become entrepreneurs. The Swedish Growth Board makes periodic surveys of young people's attitudes towards enterprise and uses the data to design initiatives in the area. This agency is one of many that perform recurring measurements. The 2012 Entrepreneurship Survey (Tillväxtverket, 2013) showed, among other things, that 49 per cent of the Swedish population aged 18–70 years would consider becoming entrepreneurs. Asked whether they would be willing to become entrepreneurs, 68 per cent of the age group from 18–30 years stated that it was an alternative to traditional employment. Young people, in particular, think positively of entrepreneurship.

A recent study also highlights young people's positive attitude towards entrepreneurship (Drivhuset, 2013). Although this study shows that a low percentage of students have started businesses, it also shows that a high proportion of respondents would be willing to start a business. Altogether, 70 per cent were positive about the notion of starting a business. American studies have also confirmed that entrepreneurship courses are relevant for students' ability to start businesses. A survey by the University of Arizona shows that students who attended entrepreneurship programmes were more likely to start businesses than other students in university business administration programmes (Charney and Libecap, 2000). These studies are more positive and more in favour of the idea of educating students in entrepreneurship and starting new businesses. However, since the idea of entrepreneurship and education is a relatively new phenomenon in Sweden, the development of this form of education should be followed in the coming years before definitive judgements can be made.

CONCLUSIONS

The concept of the entrepreneurial university or entrepreneurship in higher education can mean different things. Regardless of this, there is a clear trend across the world of more and more universities of different types working to stimulate entrepreneurship. There is the hope that this will stimulate more young people to become entrepreneurs, that more innovation and companies will be created and that, above all, this will lead to regional growth. However, the research community has not yet provided clear evidence that entrepreneurship within universities actually leads to these consequences. In Europe and in Sweden, there is a political mission on increased entrepreneurship from both the EU and the Swedish government, which have developed strategies for how schools and universities should develop entrepreneurship further. Therefore, this can be seen as a political initiative among Swedish state universities as potential political entrepreneurs, which now also have the task of stimulating entrepreneurship in its various forms. The future challenge for Swedish universities is to live up to this requirement, not least because there is really no clear answer as to whether such a strategy can be successful. The challenge for the entrepreneurial university is whether it can really lead more students to be trained in entrepreneurship and subsequently become young entrepreneurs and whether this will lead to regional growth. However, the fundamental questions remain intact: is it possible to train young entrepreneurs, does it lead to regional develop-ment, and does entrepreneurship training actually lead to an increase in successful businesses? In the research community, these questions have not yet received clear answers.

NOTES

1. The concepts of academic entrepreneurship, entrepreneurship training or the entrepreneurial university are used to illuminate this research discourse. The concepts have some common traits, but the major difference is that entrepreneurship education is only focused on training, while others also include research and to some extent the university's activities as a whole.
2. A few colleges in Sweden are managed by sponsored foundations, such as Chalmers University of Technology, Stockholm School of Economics and Jönköping University, but they are still financially dependent on support from the government.

REFERENCES

Ahl, H. (2006), 'Why research on women entrepreneurs needs new directions', *Entrepreneurship Theory and Practice*, **30**(5), 595–621.

Baldieri, C. (2014), *University Entrepreneurship in Italy*, Pisa: Universitá de Pisa.

Binks, M. (2005), *Entrepreneurship Education and Integrative Learning*, Birmingham, UK: National Council for Graduate Entrepreneurship.

Bjuggren, C.M., D. Johansson and M. Stenkula (2012), 'Using self-employment as proxy for entrepreneurship: some empirical caveats', *International Journal of Entrepreneurship and Small Business*, **17**(3), 290–303.

Boverket (2013), *Vision för Sverige 2025* [Vision for Sweden 2012], Karlskrona: Boverket.

Cantillon, R. (1931), *Essai sur la nature du commerce* [Essay on the Nature of Trade], London: Macmillan.

Charney, A. and G.D. Libecap (2000), 'The impact of entrepreneurship education: an evaluation of the Berger Entrepreneurship Program at the University of Arizona, 1985–1999', *Working Paper Series*, Eller College of Business and Public Administration, University of Arizona, Tucson, Arizona, accessed 21 May 2016 at http://papers.ssrn.com/sol3/papers.cfm?abstract_id=1262343.

Clark, B.R. (1998), *Creating Entrepreneurial Universities: Organizational Pathways of Transformation*, New York: Pergamon Press.

Commission of the European Communities (2006), *Implementing the Community Lisbon Programme: Fostering entrepreneurial mindsets through education and learning, Brussels, 13.2.2006 COM (2006) 33 final*, accessed 21 May 2016 at http://eur-lex.europa.eu/legal-content/EN/TXT/?uri=CELEX%3A52006DC0033.

Danilda, I. and J. Granat Thorslund (2010), *Innovation and Gender*, Stockholm: VINNOVA, Tillväxtverket and Innovation Norway.

Drivhuset (2013), *Attityd 12/13. Studenter är framtidens företagare* [Attitude 12/13. Students are the Future Entrepreneurs], Drivhuset.

Duval-Couetil, N. (2013), 'Assessing the impact of entrepreneurship education programs: challenges and approaches', *Journal of Small Business Management*, **51**(3), 394–409.

Etzkowitz, H. (2004), 'The evolution of the entrepreneurial university', *International Journal of Technology and Globalization*, **1**(1), 64–77.

European Union (2012), *Effects and Impact on Entrepreneurship Programmes in Higher Education, Brussels, 2012*, Entrepreneurship Unit, Directorate-General for Enterprise and Industry, European Commission, accessed 21 May 2016 at http://ec.europa.eu/growth/tools-databases/newsroom/cf/itemdetail.cfm?item_id=5894&lang=en&title=Effects-and-impact-of-entrepreneurship-programmes-in-higher-education.

Florida, R. (1999), 'The role of the university: leveraging talent, not technology', *Issues in Science and Technology*, **15**(4).

Hampden-Turner, C. (2009), *Teaching Innovation and Entrepreneurship: Building on the Singapore Experiment*, Cambridge, UK: Cambridge University Press.

Hannon, P.D. (2005), *The Journey from Student to Entrepreneur: A Review of the Existing Research into Graduate Entrepreneurship*, Birmingham, UK: National Council for Graduate Entrepreneurship.

Högskoleverket (2009), *Granskning av intresseanmälningar gällande spetsutbildningar inom entreprenörskap och innovation* [Examination of Interest Regarding Cutting-edge Programmes in Entrepreneurship and Innovation], Diarienummer U2008/7251/UH, Stockholm: Swedish National Agency for Higher Education.

Keat, O.Y., C. Selvaraja and D. Meyer (2011), 'Inclination towards entrepreneurship among university students: an empirical study of Malaysian university students', *International Journal of Business and Social Science*, 2(4), 206–20.

Kuratko, D.F. (2005), 'The emergence of entrepreneurship education: development, trends, and challenges', *Entrepreneurship Theory and Practice*, 29(5), 577–98.

Linnéuniversitetet (2012), 'Det entreprenöriella universitetet. Kunskap i arbete' [The entrepreneurial university. Knowledge of work], accessed 21 May 2016 at https://lnu.se/globalassets/det-entreprenoriella-universitetet-folder.pdf.

Morris, M.H., D.F. Kuratko and J.R. Cornwall (2013), *Entrepreneurship Programs and the Modern University*, Cheltenham, UK and Northampton, MA, USA: Edward Elgar Publishing.

Nabi, G. and R. Holden (2008), 'Graduate entrepreneurship: intentions, education and training', *Education and Training*, 50(7), 545–61.

Nählinder, J. (2011), 'Entreprenörskap – mer än "bara" entreprenören' [Entrepreneurship – more than 'just' the entrepreneur], in M. Bergmann-Winberg (ed.), *Politikens entreprenörskap – kreativ problemlösning och förändring*, Malmö: Liber.

Nilsson, L. and L. Weibull (2007), 'Universitet, högskolor och regional utveckling' [Universities, colleges and regional development], in L. Nilsson (ed.), *Det våras för regionen: Västsverige 1998–2005*, Göteborg: SOM-institutet.

Nilsson, N. (2010), 'Linnéuniversitetet. Det entreprenöriella universitetet' [Linnaeus University. The entrepreneurial university], Växjö/Kalmar: Linnéuniversitetet.

Nutek (2008), *Entreprenörskap i stort och smått* [Entrepreneurship Large and Small], Stockholm: Nutek.

Olofsson, A. (2012), 'Konflikten mellan kontroll och förändring – exemplet entreprenörskapsutbildning i det svenska utbildningssystemet' [The conflict between control and change – the example of entrepreneurship education in Swedish education], in M. Stigmar and T. Sandstedt (eds), *Kvalitet och Kollegialitet – Vänbok till Leif Lindberg*, Växjö.

Olsson, B. and U. Wiberg (2003), *Universitetet och den regionala utmaningen* [The University and the Regional Challenge], Stockholm: Institutet för studier av utbildning och forskning.

Phan, P. and D. Siegel (2006), *The Effectiveness of University Technology Transfer. Foundations and Trends in Entrepreneurship*, Delft: Now Publishers.

Potter, J. (ed.) (2008), *Entrepreneurship and Higher Education*, Paris: OECD.

Regeringskansliet [Swedish Government] (2009), *Strategin för entreprenörskap inom utbildningsområdet* [Strategy for Entrepreneurship in Education], Stockholm: Svenska regeringen, utbildningsdepartementet/näringslivsdepartementet, accessed 21 May 2016 at https://www.orebro.se/download/18.61e77c7c133 d55aabdf80001961/1392723834211/Strategi+f%C3%B6r+entrepren%C3%B6 rskap+inom+utbildningsomr%C3%A5det.pdf.

Reinfeldt, F. (2013), 'Achieving inclusive growth in the new European context', speech at the World Economic Forum in Davos, 23 January.

Rideout, E.C. and D.O. Gray (2013), 'Does entrepreneurship education really work? A review and methodological critique of the empirical literature on the effects of university-based entrepreneurship education', *Journal of Small Business Management*, **51**(3), 329–51.

Roffe, I. (1999), 'Transforming graduates, transforming firms', *Education + Training*, **41**(4).

Sánchez, J.S. (2013), 'The impact of an entrepreneurship education program on entrepreneurial competencies and intention', *Journal of Small Business Management*, **51**(3), 447–65.

Schumpeter, J. (1934 [2008]), *Schumpeter – om skapande förstörelse och entreprenörskap* [Schumpeter – Of Creative Destruction and Entrepreneurship], Stockholm: Norstedts akademiska förlag.

Tillväxtverket (2013), *Entreprenörskapsbarometern 2012* [Entrepreneurship Barometer 2012], accessed 22 May 2016 at https://translate.googleuser content.com/translate_c?depth=1&hl=en&prev=search&rurl=translate.google. co.uk&sl=sv&u=http://publikationer.tillvaxtverket.se/ProductView.aspx%3FID %3D1881&usg=ALkJrhhnl-p_ZYwe2WBPK8azyKDEJ7hAgg.

Valeiro, A., B. Parton and A. Robb (2014), *Entrepreneurship Education and Training Programs around the World – Dimensions for Success*, Washington, DC: The World Bank.

Vanevenhoven, J. (2013), 'Advances and challenges in entrepreneurship education', *Journal of Small Business Management*, **51**(3), 466–70.

Wang, C.K. and P.K. Wong (2004), 'Entrepreneurial interest of university students in Singapore', *Technovation*, **24**(2), 163–72.

Wetter, E. and K. Wennberg (2007), *Utbildningsbakgrund och nyföretagande: en översikt av akademikers entreprenörskap i Sverige 1990–2002* [Educational Background and Business Creation: A Survey of Academics' Entrepreneurship in Sweden 1990–2002], Stockholm: Civilekonomerna.

PART IV

Conclusions

11. Political entrepreneurship: final remarks

Daniel Silander and Charlotte Silander

This book has explored the role of political entrepreneurship in promoting growth, entrepreneurship and entrepreneurial diversity in Sweden. The co-authors defined a political entrepreneur as a 'politician/ bureaucrat/officer/department within the publicly funded sector who with innovative approaches encourages entrepreneurship/business and where the goals are growth, employment and the common good'. The aim of the study was twofold: (1) to explore how political entrepreneurs may act to promote formal and informal institutions favourable to regional growth and welfare, and (2) to investigate how political entrepreneurs may act to promote entrepreneurial diversity that promotes entrepreneurship and private enterprise among traditionally less entrepreneurial societal groups in Sweden.

The almost decade-long global economic recession had a severe negative impact on Europe. Most European societies, including the Swedish, have had numerous political and public debates on how to transform the economy into one featuring growth and employment. In times of recession, political steps that could boost the economy are not only wanted but also desperately called for. In such times of economic and social stress, the political entrepreneur becomes a cornerstone for societal development.

The different chapters have contributed to a greater understanding of one or more themes of the book: (1) political entrepreneurship and entrepreneurship; (2) political entrepreneurship and regional growth; and (3) political entrepreneurship and entrepreneurial diversity. Although several chapters referred to Nordic, European and European Union (EU) conditions, the analytical focus has been on Sweden, with the book providing several case studies and comparative illustrations on Swedish political entrepreneurship in regional and local settings. By exploring political entrepreneurship in Sweden, we believe that this book has contributed to broader insights on favourable and unfavourable conditions for entrepreneurship that transcends Swedish borders. Although the brief summary of each chapter below far from captures the extended discussions and analysis presented by the authors, a few words are provided simply to highlight some of the messages presented.

The first part of the book focused on the notions of political entrepreneurship and entrepreneurship. It was argued in Chapter 1, 'Introduction: the political entrepreneur for regional growth and entrepreneurial diversity', that there is limited research on political entrepreneurship. It was also argued that, despite public debates on the importance of political–economic collaboration in seeking national, regional and local growth, employment and sustained welfare, there are limited empirical studies on what politicians and public servants can and should do to better promote conditions for entrepreneurship and entrepreneurial diversity. This book therefore focused on Sweden; however, with years of economic crisis in Europe, and in times of growing global competition, the call for political innovative measurements has echoed far beyond Swedish borders.

The limited research on political entrepreneurship required at first a clear-cut definition of what political entrepreneurship is all about and who the political entrepreneur is. Such a discussion was presented in Chapter 2, 'The political entrepreneur' (although it was also touched upon in other chapters). It was stated that there exists a bulk of economic studies on entrepreneurship, but a limited number of studies on political entrepreneurship. It was further acknowledged that the social sciences have had a growing interest in societal entrepreneurship and how such an approach has led to deeper insights into how entrepreneurship may develop beyond the business sector. It was further argued that one type of societal entrepreneurship, that involving the political entrepreneur, needed particular attention. It was argued that the role of the political entrepreneur is to act innovatively, to find new windows of opportunity, to be creative minded, to be a go-getter and to question established norms and values regarding what entrepreneurship is about and who the entrepreneur might be. The political entrepreneur challenges existing rules, regulations and routines by initiating new ideas on how to better promote entrepreneurship and entrepreneurial diversity for growth, employment and the common good. The political entrepreneurship is all about thinking and acting beyond the traditional way of doing things. It happens when the political entrepreneur initiates ideas about new formal and informal norms on entrepreneurship and is successful in spreading such norms to make them 'the new game in town' for the public promotion of entrepreneurship. On an aggregated level, norms become institutions. Political entrepreneurship is therefore about establishing new formal and informal institutions for entrepreneurship. It requires fostering both favourable organizational as well as cultural conditions for entrepreneurship.

This study also shed light on how such political entrepreneurship must engage norm change within the democratic framework and the rule of law. Chapter 3, 'Legitimate and legal boundaries for political entre-preneurship', acknowledged how political entrepreneurship is vital for dynamic and innovative developments, but also how certain obstacles have to be overcome and avoided. For example, this chapter discussed in particular political entrepreneurship in relation to conflicts of interest, nepotism and corruption. These potential challenges may lead to both illegitimate and illegal political entrepreneurship and is specifically important to address (1) in times of economic recession and desperate societal needs for growth and employment for sustained welfare and (2) in times of networking and the mushrooming of a network society. The integration of the public and the market has embedded collaboration in networks between potential political entrepreneurs and entrepreneurs in the business sector. It was stated how the network society has led to deeper relations within the entrepreneurial networks of both public and economic actors. Research has pointed to the importance of networks for successful entrepreneurship. It is within these networks that political entrepreneurs should be engaged. However, the network society comes with challenges to democracy and to the legitimacy and legality of political entrepreneurship.

The second part of the book focused on political entrepreneurship and regional growth. Chapter 4, 'Political entrepreneurship, industrial policy and regional growth', addressed the growing interest, in the context of financial and economic crisis, in how to conduct industrial policy for regional growth. There has been great pressure on politicians to find successful approaches to industrial policy – in other words, to become political entrepreneurs by acting innovatively to identify the right indus-trial policy. This chapter discusses vertical and horizontal industrial policy. The industrial policy may be vertical, targeting specific industries and companies, or horizontal, focusing on creating favourable conditions for all. In addition, this chapter addresses the challenge to the political entrepreneur of finding the best-suited spatial scale for political influ-ence. It is argued that the political entrepreneur must decide if the industrial policy is designed to prioritize existing industrial clusters and certain spatial areas or to be neutral regarding regions and local settings. These questions are more interesting than ever when taking into account the EU industrial and regional policy that focuses on smart specialization as industrial policy and the limited empirical studies that actually exist on how to create and implement spatial industrial policies.

Chapter 5, 'Political entrepreneurship, infrastructure and regional development', focused on the importance of a developed infrastructure system for regional growth. Infrastructure was discussed in terms of material and non-material public capital. While material public capital may consist of roads, railways, harbours, airports and utility networks and so on, non-material public capital in this chapter was discussed in terms of regional accessibility to knowledge and markets. A historical discussion is presented on the role of infrastructure in the transformation of Sweden from an industrial society to a knowledge society and how public policies have changed from previously being national to regional in perspective with private-sector influences on how to improve regional infrastructure capacities. Four illustrative case studies were presented, two material and non-material infrastructure initiatives, symbolizing improved long-lasting economic results. These infrastructure investments were proposed by visionaries that could foresee positive outcomes in regional development despite reluctant or sceptical public opinions. In recent times, regional lobbying from the private sector has become an important triggering factor for new infrastructure projects, but with expressed reluctance to new regional infrastructure investments mostly from the government.

Chapter 6, 'Political entrepreneurship and sustainable growth in rural areas', discussed opportunities and challenges to local growth and how local political entrepreneurs strive to find new innovative paths for local sustainable development. Small communities, low densities, limited resources, a poor infrastructure and traditional norms and values on how things should work are altogether challenges to political entrepreneurship that seeks new, innovative ways of promoting rural growth, employment and welfare. First, this chapter elaborated on the conceptualization of the political entrepreneur and presented two types: the policy and issue entrepreneur. Second, based on a time-spatial perspective, the authors explored the role of political entrepreneurs in three Swedish rural settings to seek local growth and how local development can be achieved both by policy entrepreneurs through structural changes and by issue entrepreneurs focusing on single issues. Third, using a time-spatial perspective, this chapter shed light on how, why, where and when political entrepreneurship may be conducted in settings of possibilities and problems. Political entrepreneurship is all about challenging and changing traditional norms and in this analysis, rural development was a result of local political entrepreneurs' being successful in understanding the local order. From there, networks can be built, resources can be found and windows of opportunity can be identified.

The third part of the book focused on political entrepreneurship and entrepreneurial diversity. In Chapter 7, 'Political entrepreneurs and women's entrepreneurship', discussed the scope and conditions for women's entrepreneurship in Sweden. It was argued that women as entrepreneurs are on the European and Swedish political agendas and are especially targeted with the goal of increasing the level of self-employment. Both the EU and Sweden have policies on entrepreneurial diversity that include women's entrepreneurship. This chapter, however, identified how many Swedish public programmes designed to promote women's entrepreneurship primarily embrace an economic growth perspective, leading to the wrong conclusions that women entrepreneurs are lacking the will or the knowledge needed to achieve successful entrepreneurship. It was also argued that most programmes have approached the individual entrepreneur, leaving structural barriers for women's entrepreneurship as a forgotten perspective. One strategy for promoting women's entrepreneurship has been to make use of higher education. Over the past decade, there has been an increase in the number of entrepreneurship education programmes at universities. The main objective has been to teach entrepreneurship and to provide theoretical and empirical tools for young women (and men) to be used for self-employment. Despite such a strategy, the proportion of self-employed Swedish women has remained low. In fact, self-employment through entrepreneurship and starting up businesses seems to be a career path only when it is required to get a job. Swedish women with obtained university degrees are more likely to pursue better salaries as employed than as self-employed individuals.

Chapter 8, 'Political entrepreneurs, networking women entrepreneurs and business growth', acknowledged a growing bulk of studies on women's entrepreneurship, but there are limited sources on regional analysis in Nordic states, including Sweden. Thus, the chapter explored the impact on women's entrepreneurship from regional structures and business traditions, but also the function of regional and local networking, including political entrepreneurs. By exploring, from a comparative perspective, two Swedish counties, the authors set out to analyse the role of political entrepreneurship for women's business entrepreneurship. What are the favourable conditions for political entrepreneurship; what are the needed relations, counter-relations or complementary relations, to business networks for political entrepreneurship to exist; and finally, in what ways do local and regional structures and business traditions impact the above issues? Overall, it was argued that all of these factors of regional structures, business traditions and existing networks are essential for political entrepreneurship. It was also argued that regional networking and regional political entrepreneurship should be considered as reinforcing and converging processes rather than as being contradictory.

In Chapter 9, 'Political entrepreneurs and immigrants' entrepreneurship', the importance of entrepreneurship for growth and welfare was stated, especially to tackle demographic challenges in order to uphold the Swedish democratic welfare state. This chapter explored entrepreneurial diversity in Sweden by focusing on citizens with foreign backgrounds. Citizens with foreign backgrounds are regarded as a societal group that meet many challenges in the Swedish labour market. Sweden is also a state with multicultural diversity based on decades of labour migration to Sweden as well as refugees. This chapter discussed the importance of Swedish political entrepreneurship for promoting entrepreneurial diversity to provide for increased growth, new jobs, employment, welfare and integration. Based on official statistics, it was stated that a higher unemployment rate exists among immigrants than among native Swedes, but it was also stated how foreign-born individuals have a higher rate of self-employment in small businesses. It was also argued, however, that the level of entrepreneurship among immigrants seems to differ by country of origin, length of stay in Sweden and residential areas. One tentative finding is how housing segregation may be an important explanatory factor for entrepreneurial activities. However, the reasons behind the variation in the level of self-employment need more research. This is vital for political entrepreneurs to gain insight on what measures to implement, where and when.

Chapter 10, 'Political entrepreneurs, higher education and young entrepreneurship', addressed a third marginalized group – young entrepreneurs. As was also discussed in the chapter on women's entrepreneurship, this chapter explored the Swedish debate on universities as potential regional engines for growth. There has been an outspoken vision in Swedish politics to see universities as entrepreneurial universities for regional development – ones that act as political entrepreneurs to encourage young people to go into self-employment by starting up businesses. Since the 1990s, Swedish universities have increased in number with the expectations of promoting regional growth and employment. By educating students in entrepreneurship, universities have been expected to provide new skills and innovations to the labour market. However, there are very limited studies on the role of Swedish universities to promote regional growth. There are also questions about whether universities have become entrepreneurial universities by providing students with necessary skills and tools to become self-employed or to become entrepreneurial after graduation or if the increase in the number of programmes on entrepreneurship has, in fact, led to more companies being created and regional growth. There is a great need for further studies on the nature and role of the entrepreneurial university in Sweden and, if so, under what conditions universities can become regional engines for growth and entrepreneurship.

Based on this book, what then are the lessons learned to serve as guidance for future research? Beyond the specific gains of new knowledge about the political entrepreneur and political entrepreneurship in Sweden, we have identified three missions for future research. First, although both politics and media stress the importance of political entrepreneurs in a healthy and wealthy economy, there are still limited studies in this area. This book is one attempt to begin a long journey of collecting more empirical insights on how we can study and understand political entrepreneurship. Research in the social sciences and economics has emphasized how entrepreneurship, growth, employment and welfare are promoted based on the collaboration among different types of entrepreneurs. At the same time, as research on economics has stressed the importance of knowing more about what institutional conditions foster entrepreneurship and growth, the field of social sciences has identified the network society and the integration of the public and economic sectors and how politicians and public servants must engage these networks to develop successful policies.

Second, although there is no single-handed successful entrepreneurship policy, and there are different regional and local settings for growth and employment, political entrepreneurship is about understanding regional and local settings and exploring the windows of opportunities in such contexts. This book has provided several case studies on political entrepreneurship in Sweden, but this research area is in great need of further explorative studies on the nature of successful political entrepreneurship. Although we have discussed formal and informal institutional frameworks for entrepreneurship, there is limited knowledge about what institutional factors should be promoted or not in different specific regional and local contexts. As was stated in this book, the political entrepreneur should act innovatively and as a go-getter to promote entrepreneurship, but what this actually means in specific regional and local settings with different structural conditions and historical economic legacies is vaguely explored. There is a great need for economic and social science research on what (measures) the political entrepreneur should take, where (settings) to do so and when (time). This book has contributed to a greater understanding of political entrepreneurship, measures, settings and timetables, but we need to engage the area more systematically with comparative perspectives on successful and failed examples.

Third, this book has explored political entrepreneurship for entrepreneurial diversity by focusing on groups of citizens who have traditionally been excluded by traditional existing norms and values on entrepreneurship and has also focused on who the entrepreneur is. In several chapters, women's, immigrants' and youngsters' entrepreneurship was discussed. Although these groups are far from homogeneous, existing research shows how existing norms and values with regard to entrepreneurship have too often excluded the notion of entrepreneurial diversity: the importance and justice of supporting entrepreneurship from societal groups other than white, middle-aged men. Future research needs to address not only what the political entrepreneur should do in specific regional and local settings to promote entrepreneurship and growth, but also how to make use of all of the societal groups' ideas and creativity to promote growth, employment and welfare. Gaining more knowledge about how to promote entrepreneurial diversity is not only about gaining insight on how to achieve increased growth and employment, but also about fostering an improved society of justice, equality and integration – that is, landmarks of a consolidated democracy, a prosperous economy and a healthy welfare society.

Index